23 Days: The Final Collapse of Nazi Germany

23 Days

The Final Collapse of Nazi Germany

MARLIS G. STEINERT

Translated from the German
by RICHARD BARRY

Walker and Company / New York

First published in the United States of America in 1969 by the Walker Publishing Company, Inc.

Library of Congress Catalog Card Number: 72-86411

Printed in the United States of America from type set in the United Kingdom.

Originally published in German in 1967 under the title *Die 23 Tage der Regierung Dönitz* by Econ-Verlag G.M.B.H., Düsseldorf and Wien

Copyright © 1967 by Econ-Verlag GmbH, Düsseldorf und Wien

This translation published simultaneously in the United Kingdom in 1969 under the title *Capitulation 1945 The story of the Dönitz régime*

This translation Copyright © 1969 by Constable and Company Limited

Frontispiece: a portrait of Admiral Karl Dönitz reproduced from *Die Deutschen Generalfeldmarschaelle 1935-45* by Otto E. Moll (Erich Pabel Verlag, 755 Rastatt/Baden) by kind permission of Ullstein G.M.B.H., Berlin.

Contents

Preface

HISTORIANS, writers and journalists have recently shown much interest in the short period of German history between the disappearance of Hitler and the assumption by the Allies of supreme governmental authority in Germany. The twentieth anniversary of unconditional surrender produced a spate of treatises, reports and comments. Hitherto the 'Dönitz Government', as the last official Reich government is usually called, has been dealt with only in eyewitness accounts or as a side issue when considering subjects of greater historical importance. Now, however, that documents confiscated by the Allies after the war are returning to German archives from London and Washington in increasing quantity, it is possible to treat more exhaustively the civil and military responsibilities which fell to Karl Dönitz, to the Acting Reich Government appointed by him and to the Oberkommando der Wehrmacht [OKW – the High Command of the Armed Forces] in May 1945.

To understand the actual historical occurrences, some knowledge is required of the nature, character and views of the actors who participated in those occurrences. Before dealing with actual events, therefore, it seemed necessary to give a short biographical sketch of each of the main personalities in this 'drama', particularly seeing that there are no comprehensive accounts of the careers of the three most important figures of the period, Karl Dönitz, Alfred Jodl and Schwerin von Krosigk. This, therefore, has governed the layout of this book.

The book opens with a Prologue describing the internal and external collapse of the Third Reich, the ideas and plans of the previous rulers, the dispersion of the centre of power and the formation of a new, much reduced, governmental machine. This is followed by Part I which deals with the careers of the new Head of State and his associates.

Part II of the book describes the activities of the new ruling élite. Dönitz having a dual function, both military and civil tasks are dealt with, before and after the central and decisive event of unconditional surrender. A whole series of hitherto unknown details, primarily concerning the demobilisation of the Wehrmacht, the final acts of okw and the formation and activities of the Acting German Government, are here brought to light.

Part III examines the political ideas developed during this short period.

Part IV is concerned primarily with events centred round the arrest of Dönitz, of okw and of the last official German government. Not enough is said here about the Allied attitude, firstly because the book is concerned almost exclusively with events on the German side, secondly because, so far, no satisfactory accounts of this complex problem are available.

I attempted by correspondence to clarify certain outstanding problems – but results were unsatisfactory. No really adequate information concerning differences within the wartime coalition about treatment of the Dönitz Government will be to hand until the Anglo-Saxon records have become public property.

This book makes no claim to the discovery of new basic knowledge. Its purpose is to make some small contribution to an understanding of German history and to describe the acts, hopes and thoughts of the government leaders of the time. The persons who emerge are neither heroes nor scoundrels, but men who served a regime, which history has unequivocally condemned, partly from false idealistic motives, partly from ambition. There can be no excuse for participation in the measures of the Third Reich. To understand them, however – and we can only surmount that which we understand – we must put ourselves in the position of those involved. Anyone who reads into this an apologia for National-Socialism fails to understand the true purpose of the writing of history. Its aim must be to present things 'as they actually were'.

For the idea of writing this book I am indebted to Professor Jacques Freymond, with whom I have worked for years and who is a personal friend. It could not have been written without his support and the help of the *Institut Universitaire de Hautes Etudes Internationales* in Geneva, which he directs. At this point, therefore, I would like to thank Professor Freymond most sincerely and warmly for his unselfish and invariably encouraging advice, his support and his suggestions.

My thanks go also to all the research establishments which have allowed me to use their records. I am particularly indebted to: Dr. Vogel, Dr. Kahlenberg and Herr Porten of the Bundesarchiv, Coblenz; to the Head of the Document Centre in the Military History Research Establishment, Freiburg im Breisgau, Dr. Wilhelm Arenz, and to Drs. Maierhöfer and Brausch; to Dr. Hoch of the *Institut für Zeitgeschichte,* Munich; to Dr. Puchner and Herr Hans Kreutzer of the State Archives, Nuremberg; to Mrs. Petterson, Head of the US Document Centre, Berlin; to M. Pierre Pagneux, head librarian of the *Institut Universitaire de Hautes Etudes Internationales,* Geneva; to Dr. Michels, Head of the Municipal Library in Essen, and his staff; finally, and most important, to Fräulein Dieckmann of the Library of Science and Dr. Schröter, Head of the State Archives in Essen.

I am particularly grateful for the discussions and interviews which I have had with personalities who played an important role in events between the death of Hitler and the institution of Four-Power control in Germany. I would mention especially Grand Admiral Dönitz, Count Lutz Schwerin von Krosigk, Frau Luise Jodl and Messrs. Günter Hessler, Walter Lüdde-Neurath and Hans-Joachim Riecke.

My thanks go to my friend Hermann Kammenhuber of Saarbrücken, who read the manuscript in detail. It was also read by Dr. Saul Friedländer of Geneva and Peter Becker of the Department of History, University of South Carolina. Both made valuable suggestions and earned my warmest thanks.

MARLIS G. STEINERT

Prologue: Collapse

FROM the first days of 1945 Allied forces had been ploughing remorselessly into Germany both from east and west. The Ardennes offensive, launched on 16 December 1944, had ground to a halt after a few days and had had to be finally abandoned on 28 January. General Eisenhower's forces had gone over to the counter-offensive and seized the initiative. In March Americans, British and French reached the west bank of the Rhine on a broad front; on 6 March Cologne was captured; on 7 March the Americans crossed the Rhine at Remagen by the only bridge still intact; on 8 March they captured Bonn and Bad Godesberg; on 15 March the US Third Army crossed the Moselle at Coblence; on 24 March Montgomery's 21st Army Group forced the Rhine at Wesel; on 27 March General Eisenhower declared that the German armies in the West had been 'whipped'.

On 12 January the First White Russian Front had opened offensive operations in the East with a break-through at Baranov directed on Berlin. Further north the First Baltic Front drove into Courland and the Second and Third White Russian Fronts into East Prussia, cutting it off completely on 4 March. In the south the four Ukrainian Fronts moved forward simultaneously into Silesia, Czechoslovakia, Hungary and Austria. The core of the famous Great German Reich, which was to stretch from the Atlantic to the Volga, from North Africa to the North Cape, was under assault.

Within the Reich the situation was catastrophic. Communications had collapsed almost totally. Expresses and through-trains ceased running at the end of January; canals were out of action; goods traffic was down to a minimum. With the front now on the Rhine, rich brown coal resources and valuable brown coal power stations were lost. In February the Ruhr was still producing 8,100 wagons of coal a day; by mid-March the figure had dropped to 2,000–3,000. This shortfall could no longer be made good from Upper Silesian production, since the main mines there were already in enemy hands. Three-quarters of the Ruhr steel capacity had been destroyed and more than 50% of the power supply; fuel production was down to 5% of normal. On 15 March 1945 Speer, the Minister for Armaments and War Production, noted: 'A final collapse of the German economy in four to eight weeks' time must therefore be anticipated with certainty. No output of armaments can then be guaranteed, nor will the railways or shipping be able to meet demands – with the possible exception of operational movements. *After this collapse the war cannot be carried on militarily. . . .*'[1]

This view was re-emphasised on 28 March by Dönitz, the Naval Commander-in-Chief. At the Führer's conference he stated that the daily coal deliveries of 900 tons enabled supply to be maintained only to Army Groups Courland and North; no coal-burning ships were available for any other purpose. This implied a 50% reduction in transport for troops, wounded and refugees. On 12 April he reported that, owing to the fuel position, no submarine sorties would be possible after 20 April and during the month all supply, and indeed all movement, by sea would cease.

The Reich's financial position was equally desperate. On 8 February Schwerin von Krosigk, the Finance Minister, forwarded a Finance Ministry memorandum dated 10 January to Göring, Goebbels, Funk, Lammers the Head of the Reich Chancellery, Bormann the Head of the Party Chancellery, and Dr. Fischböck, the Prices Commissioner. It showed that Reich expenditure had risen from 63 billion marks in the first year of war to 160 billion in the fifth year. Against this rising expenditure receipts were continually falling; they now provided only 44% cover. Half the military outgoings could only be covered by the issue of paper money; the national debt, which in the first year of war had risen by two and a half billion a month, was now rising by seven billion a month; already it totalled about 350 billion and the situation was aggravated by the conversion of long-term indebtedness into short-term. For the sixth year of war the Finance Minister calculated that expenditure would reach 160–180 billion against re-

ceipts of 50 60 billion, resulting in a credit requirement of
110–120 billion and an increase of the national debt to some
420 billion.

An additional factor was the increased note circulation; this had
quintupled during the war, the most disturbing feature being the
rate of increase: in the first year of war it had risen by 2·1 billion,
in the fifth year by 9·6 billion and in the first four months of the
sixth year by no less than 11·5 billion, more than all the first three
years combined.

The result of these inflationary developments, the Finance
Minister emphasised, was growing loss of confidence in the
currency. Goods were taking its place, 'primarily the cigarette'.

The Reich's bankruptcy in face of final military defeat was
clearly reflected in the faces of the refugees flooding westwards
from the East – and in the fate which awaited them. A report of
6 March showed that their number had already risen to ten
million.

Nearly one and a half million died as they fled. Houses and
public buildings were being reduced to rubble and ashes by the
Allied bombing. Civilian casualties rose to 600,000.[2] Discourage-
ment and despair were widespread because of this situation and
the Allied demand for unconditional surrender, on which
Roosevelt was still bent despite its numerous disadvantages. By
their uncompromising insistence on *delenda est Germania* the
Allies had presented Goebbels' propaganda with a further
pretext to proclaim total war; they had emasculated the German
resistance movement and reinforced the military leaders in their
view that, the loophole of a compromise peace being closed,
there remained no alternative but to continue the fight, hopeless
though it was recognised to be[3] – 'to sell our skins as dearly as
possible, that is to fight on as long and as stubbornly as we could
in the hope of wearing the enemy down and so perhaps making
him more willing to negotiate'.[4]

The population's mood and its miseries were clearly set out in
a long report by the Internal Intelligence Service of the RSHA
[Reichssicherheitshauptamt – Central Security Department]:[5]

'Since the Soviet break-through every member of the community
knows that we are facing the greatest national catastrophe and

that it will have the most serious repercussions on every family and every individual. . . . The population is suffering severely from the bombing terror. Human ties are being largely severed. Tens of thousands of men at the front do not now know whether their relatives, their wives and children, are still alive or where they are. . . .

'For the first time in this war the food position is making a noticeable impact. The available rations leave people hungry. The potato and bread supply is no longer adequate. . . .

'Since the Soviet offensive defeatism, in the superficial sense in which that word is now used, has become general. No one can conceive how we can still win, or even wish to win, this war. . . .

'All planning is becoming an impossibility. . . .

'In recent years the German people has accepted every sacrifice. Now for the first time it is becoming weary and exhausted. Everyone is still trying to avoid admitting that this is the end. Until very recently there remained a vestige of that confidence in a miracle which adroit propaganda about new weapons has kept alive since mid-1944. In their hearts of hearts people still hoped that, if the fronts could somehow hold, we might arrive at some political solution to the war. Now no one believes that with our present resources and possibilities catastrophe can be avoided. The last spark of hope lies in some salvation from without, in some quite extraordinary development, some secret weapon of enormous potency. Even this spark of hope is dying. . . .

'Many are coming round to the idea of doing away with themselves. The demand for poison, for a pistol or some other method of putting an end to one's life, is high everywhere. Suicide in sheer despair at the certainty of approaching catastrophe is the order of the day. . . .

'Confidence in the leadership has recently plummeted. Criticism of the Party, of specific leaders and of our propaganda is generally prevalent.

'There can be no question of genuine hatred of the enemy. There is pronounced fear of the Soviets. The people's attitude to the British and Americans is one of critical appraisal. . . .'

This report mirrors the entire gamut of reactions to the hopelessness of the situation, from wild wishful thinking to black despair.

The proposals and actions of leading political and military circles in these last months and weeks preceding the ultimate collapse produced a similarly variegated pattern of emotions, hopes and intentions. They ranged from plans for internal political re-organisation, partially motivated by their authors' lust for power, through open or undercover peace feelers and daydreamings based on improbable developments, to fanatical calls for a fight to the end, leading only to self-destruction.

Outstanding among internal political measures aiming at concentration of power in the hands of the Party was a note initiated by Bormann in March 1945 and entitled 'For the Preservation of NSDAP Leadership'; its ultimate object was to reinforce the position of the Head of the Party Chancellery.

A similar interpretation must be placed on the plan for a Cabinet reshuffle proposed by Goebbels in mid-February. Hitler was to remain Head of State, Goebbels to assume the functions of Chancellor and Foreign Minister, Himmler those of War Minister and Commander-in-Chief of the Wehrmacht and Bormann those of Party Minister.[6] Basically the object was increased power for the Propaganda Minister and concentration of military authority in the hands of the Reichsführer-SS.

Even within the SS ambitious plans took shape. A draft of 3 April 1945, for instance, probably written by SS-Standarten-führer [Colonel] Franke-Grieksch, Head of the Personnel Section in the RSHA, was entitled 'The German Freedom Movement (Popular Movement)'. Ostensibly its primary objects were an internal purge of the Party and new external political contacts, but it was clearly an expression of opposition from within the system. The proposed purge was to free the Party 'from a degenerate Party bureaucracy and the ubiquitous corrupt Party bosses, from a ruling caste in State, Party and Party organisations which has deceived itself and others for years', also however from 'a biased, un-German Führer cult within the country and an empty arrogance of power in foreign policy'. The German people was to be preserved 'from reversion to the obsolete concept of capitalism, politically active clergy, the divisive party wrangling of parliamentary democracy, narrow Austrian, Bavarian, Rhineland or other particularism and communist class warfare which divides a people'.

The real object of the proposed internal political changes was to instal Himmler as Chancellor alongside Hitler as Führer.

The 'will of the people' was to be expressed through two chambers: first, a German 'Volksthing' [Popular 'Thing' – the assembly of the old Germanic tribes] consisting of district representatives elected by universal secret suffrage; secondly, the 'Ordensrat' [Council of Estates] to be selected according to 'the strictest standards of proven political, soldierly and personal qualities'. The government was to be responsible to both Chambers, to guarantee freedom of speech but also to suppress subversive political agitation.

The foreign policy programme included a twelve-point 'European peace settlement', the salient feature of which was the formation of a 'Sworn European Community' comprising all European peoples; they would nevertheless retain their 'individual existence' and the right 'freely to form their own political organisation'. In addition a 'European arbitration system' was proposed; the long-term aim was voluntary adherence to a 'Germanic Reich'.

Externally therefore the concept was of a Europe based on the 'call of the blood', such as Hitler had always foreshadowed, tempered, however, by the introduction of a federal system and excluding any claim to sole leadership by Germany. Internally there was clearly a trend towards abandonment of the dictatorship principle and some indication of a return to the principle of separation of powers, although traces of totalitarianism still remained in the way in which the Second Chamber was to be constituted and the call to suppression of political 'agitation'. This emerged even more clearly in the rejection of political parties and parliamentary democracy and the polemics against 'politically active clergy' and capitalism. Equally, strict centralisation was the order of the day and the division of Germany into small states was rejected.

As regards internal political changes Franz Seldte, the Reich Minister and ex-leader of the Stahlhelm, went even further in his thinking. Talking to Himmler and Schellenberg, the Head of the Foreign Intelligence Service (Amt [Branch] VI) in the RSHA and in charge of military intelligence since the arrest of Admiral Canaris,[7] Seldte expressed the view that the dictatorial character of the system must be abolished. At the Nuremberg trial Seldte presented himself as a long-standing protagonist of the two-chamber system and he now apparently insisted on the separation of legislature and executive demanding the abolition of the People's Court* and the holding of elections in order to break the one-party system and permit the formation of other parties. Talking to Schellenberg on the evening before Hitler's 56th birthday, Seldte proposed that next day Hitler be forced to issue a proclamation transferring power to Himmler and introducing all these measures.[8]

Seldte was not the only one to discuss internal political change with prominent members of the SS. For anyone who wished to engineer a change at the top, no matter whether his motives were moral, patriotic or selfish, only two possibilities were open: he must assure himself of the support either of the Wehrmacht or the SS. Since the failure of the coup of 20 July 1944, however, the Wehrmacht was of no further account for such purposes. All subsequent attempts to do away with Hitler and his immediate advisers required SS assistance and, therefore, inevitably carried the stamp of opposition from within the system. They all foundered on the hesitancy of Himmler, who, like all the other plotters of *coups d'état* and assassinations, could not bring himself to break the oath of allegiance which he had sworn to Hitler. This loyalty, impervious to reason, has given rise to much discussion and criticism, but in the German scale of values of the time it was an overriding, absolute factor, only to be eradicated by total defeat and a prolonged process of revaluation. This much is clear from a remark made by Colonel-General Jodl while in prison: 'In these days disloyalty has become a moral virtue – what a reversal of all values.'

Such were the efforts to influence the outcome of the war and avert the threatened collapse of the Reich by internal changes. The foreign policy plans and initiatives of the final few months are also worth examining.

* The notorious Court under Freisler which had dealt with 'defeatists' and the 20 July 1944 conspirators.

All plans and proposals sprang from the belated realisation that Germany had lost the war militarily and that her future existence depended upon attachment either to the West or to the East. Their basis was the hope that the enemy coalition would fall apart and lead to a reversal of alliances. For numerous reasons supporters of a Western orientation were vastly in the majority. The widespread centuries-old fear of the East played its part, as did a sense of the values common to Western civilisation and the conviction stemming from the Imperial period that a mortal struggle between German and Slav was inevitable. Hitler had used the fear of the East to good purpose and had concealed his expansionist plans behind the theory of the inevitable German/Slav conflict.

Among the pro-Westerners was the Reichsführer-SS, Heinrich Himmler. As early as 1941 he had been considering the possibility of an understanding with England.[9] He attempted to use not only his own intelligence channels and the services of neutral intermediaries, but even hoped to exploit the contacts of the German resistance movement. His efforts met with an icy reception from the British and never advanced beyond the exploratory stage. Schellenberg, who was quickly alive to the real potential of the Allies, was working on other lines of approach as early as the summer of 1942; in his efforts to galvanise the Reichsführer into an offer to negotiate with the West he was supported by Felix Kersten, Himmler's Finnish masseur. On Schellenberg's initiative and using material assembled in his office the so-called 'Egmont Reports' were drafted, painting a highly-coloured picture of Allied strength and the deteriorating position of Germany; Karl Wolff, the Waffen-SS General, sent Himmler a private letter. But none of this moved the still hesitant Himmler to make a serious peace offer. Not until he heard of Hitler's collapse on 22 April 1945 and had also received alarming reports of his state of health, giving the Dictator only two days to live, did Himmler decide to act. During the night 23/24 April he discussed the situation with the Swede, Count Folke Bernadotte, who had come to Germany to arrange the move to Sweden of Norwegian and Danish concentration camp prisoners, and authorised him to transmit to the Western Powers a peace offer in his (Himmler's) name.[10]

After a long telephone conversation between Truman and

Churchill the offer was rejected, with an indication that the British and Americans were only prepared to negotiate if parallel proposals were made to the Soviet Union.[11]

De Gaulle did not even deign to answer a peace offer made to him. In it Himmler had described an alliance with Germany as France's only method of recapturing her grandeur. The Anglo-Saxons, he said, would continue to regard France as a satellite, while the Soviet Union would try to overthrow and destroy her.[12]

Further soundings on the possibility of talks with the Western Powers were made by von Ribbentrop, the Foreign Minister. In January 1945 he and Fritz Hesse, a senior Foreign Service officer [Legationsrat] had drafted an *aide-mémoire*, despatched to all German diplomatic missions for communication to the Western Powers via neutral intermediaries. It was entirely unsuccessful, as were advances made in Madrid and special missions by Hesse and von Schmieden, another Foreign Service officer.[13]

Ribbentrop's *aide-mémoire*[14] made much of Stalin's plans for world conquest and emphasised that the Morgenthau Plan policy was playing into the hands of the Soviets. It continued that 'on the day of Germany's defeat' England must 'in her own basic interests oppose the Soviet Union in Germany with all her available resources'. Any idea that the German people would support 'certain emigrés or members of the former bourgeois parties in a coalition government or some such' was mere wishful thinking. For Ribbentrop National-Socialism still represented the only force for law and order in Germany; should it disappear, the people would inevitably fall victim to communist propaganda. 'In England's own interests', therefore, further reduction of the power of Germany was lunacy: 'Today the old English concept of the balance of power in Europe would work against England and for the Soviet Union'. A new balance must therefore be sought – Germany-Europe-England against the Soviet Union. If, however, England refused to realise that her war policy 'was supporting the greatest enemy of America's future', then 'events must take their course . . . and victory in Europe will go to the strongest. . . . In no case, however, would this be England or America, but only the Soviet Union.'

When all these attempts to convince the Western Powers of the necessity for an alliance with Germany produced nothing,

Ribbentrop seems to have hatched plans for co-operation with Russia, in other words the precise opposite of his original *aide-mémoire* – Germany/Russia versus England. After reading it, however, Hitler forbade any negotiations with foreign countries.[15]

That pro-Soviet tendencies existed is proved by a proposal dated 5 April 1945 entitled 'Avoidance of Catastrophe', the source of which is obscure.[16] Disintegration in the West and the – temporary – stabilisation of the eastern front had given the author the fantastic idea that 'quite extraordinary opportunities exist, not merely to avoid collapse, but holding out immense possibilities for the future'. In view of present circumstances the time had passed when a 'separate peace' with the British and Americans or 'armistice negotiations with the East to make the West ready to negotiate' were feasible. In the author's view, therefore, a peace offer to the Soviet Union was now the only chance. Co-operation with Germany, he argued, would establish Soviet influence throughout Europe and give her free passage into the Persian Gulf, the Kirkuk oilfields and the Mediterranean. To form this new power grouping the USSR and Germany should combine in a 'socialist Union'; paralleling the 1943 recognition of the sixteen Soviet republics as independent states, the European peoples would form 'national self-governing states'.[17] Germany would recognise 'the Soviet republics of Poland, Lithuania, Esthonia, Latvia, Finland, Bulgaria, Rumania, Macedonia, Greece and possibly Turkey'; 'Western Upper Silesia,' on the other hand, 'together with the pre-1918 Prussian areas of the Warthegau and West Prussia' would remain German. Moreover Germany was to be allowed 'a free hand in western and northern Europe, particularly against Great Britain'.

Schwerin von Krosigk, on the other hand, continued to urge contact with the Western Powers. As a specialist Minister he was only a fringe figure in the National-Socialist system and was hardly in touch with Hitler's circle. If he wished to bring influence to bear in favour of some person or thing, he was generally reduced to writing in order to obtain a hearing. As his anxiety for the fate of his country increased, he was driven to do more than propose 'draconian anti-inflationary measures' such as raising indirect taxes on cigarettes and increasing charges for postal services, railways, public transport, cinemas, radio, newspapers and hotels. Between February and April 1945 he wrote no fewer than six letters to Goebbels urging that 'all possible lines should be pursued'. In particular he found it irresponsible that the posts of Ambassador or Minister to neutral countries such as Spain and Portugal should be left vacant. Valuable opportunities for contacts were being lost, he said, 'merely because proposals on these questions did not originate from the only office drawer which is looked upon with favour'. Though not a Catholic himself, he regarded intervention by the Pope as offering the most hopeful possibilities: 'The Pope must weep bitter tears every day when he sees that Poland threatens to be lost to him, that France is following suit and that chaos already reigns in Italy to the accompaniment of ever louder Bolshevist noises.' Ought not this situation of the Pope to be exploited, von Krosigk asked. 'Any move towards more lenient treatment of his flock would increase his hostility to Bolshevism and perhaps bring him out into the open. The Pope is held in such high regard by large sections of the British and American public that a pronouncement by him might be a decisive contribution to the result we desire. . . .'

Although the Pope had apparently already rejected any proposal on these lines, von Krosigk returned to the charge in a subsequent letter: 'It is not generally realised what influence the Pope has in America. Although the evangelicals are in the majority, they are split into innumerable sects, whereas the Catholics form a solid bloc, in which the Pope's voice carries much weight. In the long run no American government could pursue a policy contrary to the views of this united bloc.' In addition to the Pope, von Krosigk considered that the economic argument should be used against the Americans; if it was pointed out to them, he said, what a competitor the Soviet Union would be if supported by Germany, this could not fail to have its effect.

Von Krosigk suggested other intermediaries such as Burckhardt, the Swiss historian and former League of Nations Commissioner in Danzig, and Salazar, the Portuguese Prime Minister. On the German side, he said, contact men must be prominent personalities of international repute. He suggested von Neurath, the ex-Foreign Minister, von Papen or Karl Lindemann, the President of the Chamber of Industry and Commerce. Neither he nor the majority of Germans realised at the time that these people were equally unacceptable to the Allies, who regarded them either as Nazi stooges or as racketeers.

Von Krosigk's insistence on the necessity for peace feelers sprang both from a realisation that there was no time to lose and from 'a conviction that the political situation will force a break-up of our enemies' artificial coalition'. He did not, however, believe that this would occur automatically and therefore urged an active policy 'in order to bring about the break at a time when we are still on our feet'. For this purpose 'an atmosphere must be created enabling the British to break away at the right moment. For the British a change of front carries with it very great difficulties; these are not only of an internal nature – the prevailing hatred of Germany in the Labour Party; they stem also from the character of the leading personalities, perhaps not so much Churchill as Roosevelt. Unless we play an active part, these difficulties may prove stronger than all the inducements to break away from the alliance.'

During a discussion on 9 April Goebbels and von Krosigk found themselves largely in agreement. Goebbels stressed the growing differences between the Anglo-Americans and the Russians. The point, he said, was to keep on one's feet until the inevitable break occurred. He thought that this might come in three to four months.[18] When von Krosigk reiterated his proposal for unofficial contacts, Goebbels agreed and told him in confidence 'that certain steps in this direction had already been taken, that the first tentative reports had given the impression that a blank refusal need not be anticipated from the Americans, nor, surprisingly, from the Soviets; England, on the other hand, being clearly the most threatened by American and Russian superiority, was adopting a totally negative attitude. . . .' Goebbels laid the blame for all the difficulties on the Foreign Minister, whom both loathed. Unfortunately he could not openly criticise Ribbentrop in front of Hitler, since the latter would then be convinced that he, Goebbels, coveted the post of Foreign Minister. Goebbels suggested that von Krosigk might like to speak to the Führer. This von Krosigk had no wish to do. He had not had an interview with Hitler since 1938 and the Führer's aversion to financial problems was well known. Since, moreover, he insisted that everyone must keep to his own domain, it was useless to ask for an interview to discuss general political problems. In this connection von Krosigk bemoaned the lack of a Chancellor or Deputy to the Führer to relieve him of the less important decisions. This, he said, showed the weakness of an absolute dictatorship. In spite of his objections Goebbels volunteered to arrange an interview with Hitler, saying that the Führer appreciated von Krosigk's honesty and frankness.

During this conversation Goebbels related the well-known incident when he had read to Hitler Carlyle's account of the Seven Years' War. When he mentioned the death of the Czarina, the effect of which was a sudden change of fortune, the 'Miracle of the House of Brandenburg', tears had suddenly come to Hitler's eyes.[19]

Further suggestions by von Krosigk show the extent to which he and many others were still prone to illusion. He believed that Germany still had both the means and opportunity to influence the members of the enemy alliance.

Regarding Russia von Krosigk considered the volunteer divisions under the Russian General Vlassov [captured and used by the Germans to form anti-Russian units] as 'one of the strongest trumps which we still have in our deck, not so much because of the military help which the volunteer divisions can give us, but because of the propaganda impact it may perhaps have on the Russian soldier, particularly in the event of Bolshevist military set-backs. They are already war-weary; if a rapid victorious end to the war and the continuation of unhampered looting and rape can no longer be guaranteed, dropping at the appropriate moment the magic slogan of "Peace" among the Russian mass may well be the trumpet under whose blasts the Soviet Jericho will collapse. . . .'

If such a development was to occur, he continued, Germany must decide, as he had been urging for years, to differentiate between Bolshevism and the Russians, to abolish the discriminatory 'Eastern badge' and state clearly her attitude to a future non-Bolshevist Russia. As far back as 1942, for instance, he had proposed in a letter to Göring a flexible policy towards the various ethnic groups in Soviet Russia; in a letter to Ribbentrop of 9 December 1943 he had demanded that a distinction be drawn between Bolshevism and Russia and that this policy be pursued to its ultimate conclusion. But his urgings, like the efforts of certain circles in the Foreign Ministry and the Wehrmacht, had remained fruitless, stifled by the brutal methods of men like Erich Koch and by the Ministry for the East. Although his previous proposals had been answered either not at all or by meaningless verbiage, since none of the Party dignitaries had ever taken them seriously, nevertheless in the spring of 1945 von Krosigk was found insisting upon a clearer definition of German foreign policy and upon the pursuit of every opening, however small:

'Yalta having shown us the form of Europe which Britain, America and Russia intend to impose, we must counter-attack. It is not enough to remain on the political defensive and merely fulminate about the chaos into which Europe will be plunged – that must be done too but it is not enough; we must show the world in far clearer outline than has been done so far, a picture of the future Europe as *we* see it. As regards our relationship with a nationalist Russia, we must not be obsessed by fear lest a man like Vlassov become over-powerful and so a danger to us. By such fears we have frittered away the potentialities of the best Frenchmen and the assistance they could give us – Doriot's life has been thrown away, for instance; we are therefore ourselves partially responsible for the tragedy in the West. . . .' As regards the US and Britain von Krosigk urged that officer prisoners 'who have behaved impeccably towards us' should be released. 'They have lost confidence in their own statesmen's political line and have realised the fearful danger to their own countries represented by Bolshevist chaos in Europe'; he would therefore 'despatch them into the enemy camp as Trojan horses full of dangerous *ideas*. . . .'[20]

This was not the end of von Krosigk's sudden spurt of activity. He next drafted a study on Germany's relationship to England and England's guilt;[21] this led to a discussion with Schellenberg and Himmler, with whom he had been at loggerheads for years over the question of the Frontier Protection Service. He found both of them in agreement with his demand for a more active policy. The ambitious young Schellenberg, however (he was only 35), foresaw few possibilities in this direction, 'not because they did not exist, but because the unintelligent Ribbentrop sabotaged any initiative which did not originate from him – and those that did were useless; moreover we have clearly not yet brought home to the highest quarters that they too will have to make sacrifices'.

Schellenberg then proceeded to attack the Reich's Jewish policy, saying that 'one could only treat a people as we have treated the Jews if that people is completely under one's thumb;

since only one-third of the Jews were in our power and the
remainder lived outside our sphere of influence, our treatment of
the Jews was worse than a crime; it was folly'. Finally all negotiations were bedevilled by personalities; the regime's leaders were
anathema abroad. In order to clear the Reichsführer-SS in the
eyes of the world, therefore, he had organised a campaign in the
foreign press on the theme that many of the crimes of which
Himmler was accused might have been done in his name but
were not of his making.[22]

During the discussion Himmler added the King of Sweden to
the list of personalities through whom contacts might be sought.
He too made derogatory remarks about Ribbentrop and considered it unlikely that the enemy alliance would break up on its
own; finally, however, he took refuge in his belief in miracles.
Referring to the possibilities of an understanding with England –
of the difficulties of which he was fully aware – von Krosigk
stated that Germany must accept not only territorial sacrifices
but also certain internal changes. He referred to re-establishment
of the Reich Presidency[23] and abolition of the single-party
system. In this his thinking ran parallel to that of Seldte with
whom he was already in touch.

In the highest Party and governmental circles, therefore,
intrigue was rife, the most ludicrous hopes were being nourished
and impractical plans being formed. Meanwhile, however, another
enterprise succeeded – and it did so because its end result was
action, not on the political, but on the military level. For months
the SS General, Karl Friedrich Wolff, had been trying to establish
contact with the Western Allies. In March 1945 a meeting with
Allen Dulles took place in Zürich and after one or two further
talks the capitulation of the Italian front was signed on 29 April
at Field Marshal Alexander's headquarters in Naples; it took
effect at midday on 2 May.[24]

In the light of this whole spectrum of reactions, ranging from
suggestions, hopes and probings to the last-minute unilateral
efforts to surrender, what was Hitler's attitude? He must long
since have realised the inevitability of the situation. Letters from
Field Marshals Rommel and von Kluge,[25] memoranda from
Speer,[26] and the daily situation reports left no room for doubt
that both militarily and economically the war was lost. Nevertheless Hitler had forbidden any reference to its termination. He

remained immured in his bunker under the Reich Chancellery, emerging but seldom and in touch with the outer world only through the radio, telephone and a carefully controlled visitors' list;[27] any 'defeatist' he threatened with death. Behind any factual dispassionate information he suspected a 'Generals'' conspiracy. At the end of January Colonel-General Guderian, the last Army Chief of Staff but one,[28] visited Ribbentrop and asked him to take immediate steps to bring the war to an end either in the East or the West. Ribbentrop refused to tell the Führer and was taken a-back when Guderian asked him what he would say if the Russians appeared in Berlin in four weeks' time. At the military briefing conference shortly afterwards Hitler said: 'If the Chief of the General Staff gives information to the Foreign Minister, he is guilty of treason.'

He expressed himself similarly to Speer.[29] His authorisation to Ribbentrop and Wolff[30] to put out feelers to the West cannot therefore be taken as indicating any desire to end the war. It was based on the hope of an early collapse of the enemy coalition and in any case was only given half-heartedly and without conviction. Early in the year he had said to Ribbentrop: 'Nothing will come of it, but if you insist you can try.' When his Foreign Minister asked on 23 April what he should do in the event of capitulation, Hitler was even vaguer; all he said was: 'Try to remain on good terms with Britain.'[31]

On the same day Hitler told Field Marshal Keitel that he had for some time been conducting negotiations with England via Italy and that he had summoned Ribbentrop to discuss the next steps. In fact, however, the only action in the foreign policy field taken on 23 April was that of Speer; he urged Hitler to fly certain Czech industrialists out to France, 'in order that, using their American connections, they may conduct negotiations to save Czechoslovakia from the Bolshevists'. The initiative for this came from Frank, who was planning to hand over power to a national anti-communist government in Prague and himself move west or north-west with all German authorities, troops and members of the German minority. All these plans came to nothing, however, owing to the rapidity of the Russian advance and the fact that on Eisenhower's orders the Americans halted on the line Budweis–Pilsen–Karlsbad.[32]

During these closing months of the war, therefore, Hitler's

primary object was to utilise contacts with the enemy and keep channels of communication open until the moment arrived when the ill-assorted Allied coalition fell apart. Foredoomed to failure though it was, the Ardennes offensive had been the last attempt to break the strategic encirclement of Germany and recover the initiative lost since 1942. Thereafter the Dictator simply clung to the hope of a miracle. Germany must hold on at any cost. The last man and the last round must be expended, the sinking morale whipped up and any weakening of the will to resist countered by measures of increasing savagery. With his characteristic, 'uncanny' will-power Hitler forced his views upon his minions, even at the end when he was physically no better than a wreck, compelling them to issue ever more drastic orders and utter ever more unyielding battle-cries.

In the event of surprise occupation of certain areas by the enemy, Party leaders were to don Wehrmacht uniform, so that they might escape arrest by the Allies and so continue to exert their influence. As a counter to that of the enemy, German propaganda concentrated on Allied war crimes. A list was to be compiled of 'all enemy war criminals responsible for crimes against German and allied members of the Wehrmacht, against German and allied members of the Wehrmacht in enemy captivity and against German and allied civilians'.

This propaganda plan does not seem to have had the desired effect. Apart from a few infractions of international law in French prisoner of war camps, for instance, the Navy could report few instances of criminal action by the enemy. A naval report of 18 February 1945 stated: 'This entire propaganda plan has been thought up by OKW as a counter to the enemy's atrocity propaganda. All these accusations refer, not to maritime incidents, but to incidents in the land theatres of war. Apart from a few attacks on hospital ships, some alleged instances of firing on men in the water and hitherto unconfirmed cases of misuse of enemy aircraft markings, the opposing navies have far less of which to accuse each other than is the case on land.'

Early in February Keitel decreed drastic measures against deserters and members of the Wehrmacht 'guilty of treason while in enemy captivity'. They were to be punished by Reich courts martial which were to report death sentences to the Reichsführer-SS. If a man could not be found or the crime had been committed after 15 December 1944, the accused's family was held responsible.

On 15 February Dr. Thierack, the Reich Minister of Justice, issued a decree constituting summary courts in 'Reich Defence Districts threatened by the enemy'; in the closing days of the war special summary courts were set up in Salzburg, Bad Reichenhall, Traunstein, Rosenheim, Munich and Murnau; they were manned by one military judge and if possible two officers, and were to be ready at all times to deal with 'malingerers and any form of subversive or treasonable activity.' If the senior member of the court could not be contacted and for urgent military reasons execution could not be postponed, these courts were empowered 'to pronounce sentence of death on the opinion of one member only, if the facts and legal position are clear'. Every officer was enjoined 'to hand malingerers and traitors over to the nearest summary court'. In the northern area plans provided for a 'summary court on circuit' under the chairmanship of General Eugen Müller.

Further to raise resistance potential, on Hitler's instructions 'Führer reserves' were formed under General Ritter von Hengl, Head of the Army 'National-Socialist Leadership Staff'. All non-essential Wehrmacht offices were disbanded and the officers thus released re-employed as necessary. Some of them were issued with fresh papers to enable them to act as partisans behind the front.

Cities were declared fortresses;[33] 'all military transport and communication facilities, industrial establishments and supply depots, as well as anything of value within Reich territory which could in any way be used by the enemy immediately or in the foreseeable future for the prosecution of the war'[34] was to be destroyed; Germany was to be turned into a communications desert and the population moved into the interior of the Reich.[35]

In a 'Special Abbreviated Situation Report' of 27 March 1945 the Commander-in-Chief of the Navy said: 'We know that the life of our people is at stake. For us the coming year will be decisive. We have no time to lose. . . . Let us fly at anyone prepared to give up, to subscribe to the fatuous phrase: "It's no use any more. . . ."

'Let us prove to our enemies that the destruction of Germany will demand a greater price in blood and toil and take longer than they are prepared to afford. Then they will have to abandon this aim. We shall keep our place in Europe and we shall have won the war. . . .

'Let us fly at anyone who, even in the smallest degree, falters in his loyalty to the National-Socialist state and to the Führer. Such people can be swayed only by fear, cowardice and weakness. We are the strong and the faithful.'

To his staff Admiral Dönitz declared that for military men in their position there was only one course open – to do their duty as soldiers. He cited historical examples – Gneisenau at Kolberg, Lettow-Vorbeck in German East Africa and von Graudenz, the fortress commandant of 1806. When the latter was summoned to surrender by French negotiators who argued that further resistance was useless since the Kingdom of Prussia no longer existed, von Graudenz replied: 'Then I am King von Graudenz, for I know no other duty than to defend this fortress.'

The more desperate the situation, the more pressing were Dönitz' exhortations: 'I need not explain to you that in our situation capitulation is equivalent to suicide, is certain death, that capitulation implies the death, the annihilation sooner or later of millions of German people and that, compared with this, the toll of blood exacted by even the sternest battles is trifling. . . .'

Strong words followed in Nazi propaganda style – pride and honour which would never bow to the enemy, the necessity for fanaticism among the troops and for trust in Adolf Hitler. 'However the situation may develop, the Navy must stand as an unshakeable fighting entity. It will never bow to the enemy yoke!'

On April 1 Martin Bormann, the Head of the Party Chancellery, issued an equally stirring call to Party officials: 'Everywhere the battle against the enemy invading the Reich must be conducted relentlessly and stubbornly. Gauleiters, District Leaders, other political leaders and commanders of formations will fight in their Gau or district, will conquer or die. Anyone who, without an express order from the Führer, leaves his area when under attack by the enemy or fails to fight to the last gasp, is a cur . . . he will be branded and treated as a deserter. Let hearts be high and all weaknesses be overcome. Our only motto now is: conquer or die. . . .'

Roosevelt's death revived the hopes of Hitler and his entourage. Even more rational circles such as Naval Headquarters admitted to a cautious optimism. The Navy War Diary of 13 April reads:

'Although in the present stage of the war immediate repercussions upon the *military* situation can hardly be expected, the *political* results are not yet foreseeable and might be far-reaching. . . .'

Schwerin von Krosigk referred to the event not only as a 'judgement of God' but as a 'gift of God' which must be earned if its full benefits were to be reaped; he re-emphasised that 'the path now being open, we must tread it *actively* and *immediately*'.

In a proclamation of 15 April Hitler announced that Bolshevism would meet the ancient fate of Asia and bleed to death before the Reich capital. 'Berlin remains German, Vienna will be German again, and Europe will never be Russian. . . . At this moment when Fate has removed from the earth the greatest war criminal of all time, the turning-point of this war will be decided.'[36]

The truth was very different. On the very next day the Russians launched a major offensive and the 'powerful artillery' which, according to Hitler, would receive them, was found to exist only in his imagination. After a pause for reorganisation the Army Groups of Marshals Zhukov and Koniev forming the First White Russian and Ukrainian Fronts moved forward on Berlin in a relentless pincer movement. During a briefing conference lasting from 3.0 to 8.0 p.m. on 22 April Hitler for the first time admitted the possibility of defeat. He decided to remain in Berlin and share the fate of the capital. On this same day the German forces in the west under Field Marshal Kesselring[37] were driven back into Inner Thuringia and those in the north-west to the area south of Hamburg and the Elbe. South of Berlin the leading Soviet troops had reached the line Treuenbrietzen–Zossen, directly threatening the central Army ammunition depot; north of the city they were in contact with the outer defences.

On the previous day Hitler had ordered SS-Obergruppen-führer [General] Felix Steiner to launch a large-scale counter-attack against the Russians in the Berlin suburbs and he now waited in vain for news of him. But, like all Hitler's other orders in these closing weeks and months, the plan was based upon imaginary non-existent reserves. In addition, command channels were in complete confusion so that it was impossible to know precisely what forces were actually available. General Heinrici describes the situation thus: 'Astounding though it may seem, it was in fact almost impossible to discover what forces were located in the Berlin area and in Brandenburg-Mecklenburg. The primary reason was the overlapping of command channels. There was the SS, responsible only to Himmler; there was Göring and his Luftwaffe over which the Army had no authority; there were innumerable reserve units under command, not of the front, but of Jüttner, the Commander of the Replacement Army, and therefore also indirectly under Himmler; near the coast were numerous naval units, partially incorporated in the defence system but mostly still under the Navy; there was a mass of shattered units from East and West Prussia arriving daily by sea at Swinemünde for accommodation and reorganisation in the interior. It was difficult to keep a tally since neither the SS nor the Luftwaffe gave accurate figures. Everyone was trying to keep an undercover reserve which he could one day use for his own purposes. . . .'

Hitler's decision to defend Berlin in person merely increased the confusion and contributed to a further dispersal of authority.

When the danger began to loom that Anglo-American and Russian forces might meet in central Germany and so split the Reich in two, the original plan was to conduct the defence from a northern redoubt comprising Mecklenburg, Schleswig-Holstein, Denmark and Norway, and a southern redoubt in Bohemia and Bavaria. Accordingly on 11 April an order was issued[38] for the formation of two separate command posts preparatory to the establishment of Headquarters North and South; since Hitler still refused to acknowledge facts or speak of northern and southern zones, these headquarters were entitled A and B.[39] On 12 April Hitler had agreed that, should the evacuation of Berlin prove necessary, the Commander-in-Chief of the Navy (Dönitz) should move to the northern area.[40] On 15 April a further more detailed order laid down that, should Hitler be in the southern area, Grand Admiral Dönitz with a small army staff under Lieutenant-General Kinzel should take command in the north; should Hitler be in the north Field Marshal Kesselring would command the south. The High Command of the Luftwaffe and the Reichsführer-SS were to be 'kept informed of decisions as quickly as the technical possibilities of communications allow'.[41] This order, however, was only to come into force on issue of a special decree. On 20 April, his fifty-sixth birthday, the Führer decided that, should the Reich be split, he would go to the southern area. Dönitz was charged with 'immediate preparations for the fullest use of all possible sources of man-power and material' in his area and empowered 'to issue the orders necessary for this purpose to all authorities of State, Party and Wehrmacht'.[42]

The operational echelon of Headquarters South drawn from OKW [Oberkommando der Wehrmacht – High Command of the Armed Forces] and OKH [Oberkommando des Heeres – High Command of the Army] under Lieutenant-General August Winter, the Head of the OKW Operations Staff,[43] had already left for Berchtesgaden and on 21 April Dönitz took leave of Hitler and moved to his new command post in Plön. Remaining in Berlin was only a small OKW nucleus of Headquarters North, which was temporarily to retain overall command. Field Marshal Keitel and Colonel-General Jodl were both quite clear that exercise of military command from the bunker would shortly become impossible, but Hitler was determined to conduct the defence of Berlin himself and, if it failed, to shoot himself; neither the protests of Keitel and Jodl nor telephone calls from Himmler and Dönitz could make him change his mind. He told Jodl that he ought to have taken this decision, which he described as the most important of his life, in November 1944. He ought never to have left East Prussia, he said. He still believed that his presence in Berlin would rouse the troops to fresh efforts in its defence.

During his breakdown on 22 April[44] Hitler made a remark which was to have far-reaching consequences. He said that physically he was in no state to fight. The risk of falling, wounded, into enemy hands was too great. Moreover he was not the right man to conduct negotiations with the Allies. Göring was more suitable.[45] The fact that he should mention Göring in connection with negotiations was proof of Hitler's contempt for the C-in-C of the Luftwaffe, since in his eyes only 'a cur' would capitulate. Göring's star had been on the wane for years. His ostentation, his profligate mode of life, but even more the failure of his Luftwaffe, had increasingly discredited him with his Führer. In Nuremberg Göring admitted that his real influence had lasted until the end of 1941 or early in 1942 and that it had fallen sharply in 1943.[46] From this time on Hitler frequently criticised him, their long private conversations becoming rarer and finally ceasing altogether. He was no longer summoned to important conferences.[47] When they took leave of each other on 21 April on Göring's departure for Berchtesgaden, the atmosphere was frosty.

Hitler's depression did not last long. The same day he was discussing with Keitel the possibilities of relieving Berlin. Keitel was ordered to 'turn the western front round in order to prevent the complete encirclement of Berlin and to take command of the counter-attack himself'.[48] The Twelfth Army under General Wenck was to disengage from the West, fight its way through to Berlin and join hands with the Ninth Army south of the city. Keitel, who had had no contact with troops throughout the war, proposed to take this message to General Wenck in person. General Krebs, who had relieved Guderian as Army Chief of Staff at the end of March and was responsible for the Eastern Front,[49] remained with Hitler as his sole military adviser. Jodl, who had advised strongly against remaining in the Berlin 'mousetrap', moved to Krampnitz to assemble the operational staff of Headquarters North.

On 23 April Hitler, full of optimism, opined that during the day two battalions of the 'Grossdeutschland' division and perhaps one or two other battalions might arrive. Quite in the old snappy style he spoke of the 'piggery' threatening on the River Havel (eastern Germany) and said people must look out that none of Seydlitz's men of the 'Free Germany National Committee' wormed their way in.

Meanwhile, via Koller his Chief of Staff, Göring had heard of Hitler's remark about his suitability as a negotiator. Clearly he thought that the Führer had resigned and was leaving to him responsibility for initiating surrender negotiations. Being an experienced intriguer, however, he first discussed the whole matter with Lammers, the Head of the Reich Chancellery who was also in the southern area, and then sent a very carefully worded telegram to Hitler. Referring to the 29 June 1941 decree nominating him Führer's deputy, Göring enquired whether Hitler agreed that he should now assume full freedom of action both internally and externally. Should he receive no reply by 10.0 p.m. (23 April) he would assume that the Führer was no longer a free agent. The telegram closed with the words 'May God protect you and I hope that you will still be able to come here from Berlin'. Sometime after 5.0 p.m. Göring sent a further radio message to Ribbentrop urging him to come south by air if he had heard nothing further from him or Hitler by midnight. Explanatory telegrams were also sent to Colonel Below, the Luftwaffe representative at the Führer's Headquarters, and to Colonel-General Jodl for Field Marshal Keitel.

Hitler was incensed. He had either forgotten the remarks made in his excitement or, more probably, they had merely been meant to indicate an alternative in the event of his death. Göring's enquiry seemed to him treachery; possibly he had been told of Göring's intention to fly to Eisenhower next day and negotiate. Bormann, the ambitious and unscrupulous Head of the Party Chancellery, no doubt helped to foster his suspicions. It even seems possible that Bormann suppressed Göring's telegram and showed Hitler only the one to Ribbentrop.[50]

Göring was forbidden to take any action on the lines proposed. Speer who had flown to Berlin to place himself once more at Hitler's disposal sent a letter to General Galland urging him to do all in his power 'to prevent Göring flying off as he proposed'. At this point Speer must have suggested to Hitler that Dönitz be nominated as his successor. Dönitz had been told of Göring's telegram by Bormann at 10.25; twenty minutes later he telephoned Colonel-General Stumpff ordering him to close all airfields in the Northern Zone to prevent any ministers present flying south in accordance with Göring's order. Göring was dismissed from all his offices including that of Nazi Crown Prince. He was succeeded as C-in-C of the Luftwaffe by General Ritter von Greim, whom Hitler ordered to Berlin by telegram on 24 April.[51] Bormann despatched a further telegram to Göring informing him that his action was a betrayal of the Führer and National-Socialism but in view of his previous services the extreme penalty would not be exacted. He then ordered the SS commanders in the Obersalzberg to arrest Göring, Koller and Lammers.[52] A further telegram on 30 April ordering the SS guards to execute all the 23 April traitors was not carried out since the SS officer on duty refused to recognise Bormann's authority.[53]

During the eight days between this decision of 22 April and his suicide Hitler still hesitated and recoiled from the inevitable. By 24/25 April he had clearly recovered from his breakdown and refused to abandon the battle for Berlin as lost. He concentrated all command authority in his own hands. During the night 24/25 April Jodl signed an order laying down that overall operational responsibility rested with OKW. It was to receive its directives from Hitler himself and, moreover, to do so via

General Krebs, the Army Chief of Staff and a bosom friend of Bormann's. In the Southern Zone Headquarters Staff B under General Winter was to issue operation orders for Army Groups South and Centre and Commanders-in-Chief South-West and West; in the north, however, Commanders-in-Chief Norway, Denmark and North-West, Twelfth Army, Army Group Vistula, Ninth Army and the forces in East Prussia and Courland were to be under direct command of OKW. Headquarters Staff A under Dönitz was therefore still non-operational. OKW's primary task was laid down as follows: 'By attacking with all forces and resources and with the greatest possible speed, to re-establish contact with Berlin on a broad front and so bring the battle of Berlin to a victorious conclusion.' Hitler's frenzied optimism following his breakdown of 22 April was unaffected even by the report of first contact between Soviet and American troops. There were said to have been small differences of opinion when they met and Hitler saw in this 'striking proof of our enemies' disunity'. His hopes rose so high that he exclaimed: 'Any day, indeed any hour, war may break out between the Bolshevists and Anglo-Saxons over their German loot'.

President Truman's declaration on this occasion reads as if designed to answer and demolish Hitler's hopes: 'The union of our armies in the heart of Germany means first, that the last faint desperate hope of Hitler and his gangster government has been extinguished. The common front and the common cause of the powers allied in this war against tyranny and inhumanity have been demonstrated in fact, as they have long been demonstrated in determination.'[54]

Hitler now made his final effort to save Berlin and himself.[55] He ordered Dönitz to abandon all naval operations and move all naval troops to Berlin by air to reinforce the front.[56]

Hitler was lavish with expressions of gratitude for the men provided by Dönitz. They were the bravest the Admiral possessed, he said, and Dönitz was determined to get them to Berlin.

As late as 26 April General Helmut Weidling commanding LVI Panzer Corps, who had been appointed 'Commandant of the Berlin Defence Area' by Hitler, was still talking of 'a day of hope'. A telegram to Dönitz on the same day from Voss, the Naval representative in the Führer's Headquarters, also painted a hopeful picture of the situation. Voss reported successes by Wenck's army in the south-west and by Ninth Army in the south-east and progress by Steiner's Group in the north. In the inner city the situation had deteriorated however, he said; the government quarter was under continuous very heavy artillery fire and a hail of bombs. In Voss' view all possible assistance must be provided from outside, since the next forty-eight hours would be decisive. [57]

After violent artillery preparation and with powerful air support the Russians launched a further attack at 5.0 a.m. on 27 April. Gatow and Tempelhof airfields were lost, making further air supply impossible. During the second briefing conference of the day in the Führer's bunker General Krebs reported that he had told Jodl that no more than twenty-four to twenty-six hours were still available to effect a junction with Wenck's and Busse's armies. Otherwise an attempt at a rapid break-through from all sides must be reckoned with.

While the Chief of Staff was recounting this gloomy news, Dr. Werner Naumann, Permanent Secretary in the Ministry of Propaganda, arrived with the information that according to reports from Radio Stockholm the Reichsführer-SS had started negotiations with the Western Allies. [58] The news must have hit Hitler harder even than Göring's 'treachery'. Relations with 'the faithful Heinrich' had indeed cooled somewhat of late. Bormann and Kaltenbrunner, Himmler's greatest rivals, had missed no opportunity of rousing Hitler's ever-ready suspicion. Himmler's failure as an Army Commander [59] had also affected his influence. Nevertheless Hitler apparently thought clarification of these rumours necessary before taking action. The last loyal servant he still had was Admiral Dönitz and so he was asked whether anything was known in his area about this report. On 28 April speech with Berlin was impossible between 5.0 a.m. and 4.30 p.m. and so the question was not put until 4.50 p.m. The answer ran: 'Nothing known here. Will clarify and if necessary issue denial.'

In Berlin meanwhile the tragedy was nearing its climax and its end. During the day the inner defence ring was breached. A radio message despatched to the 'Führerbau' Munich by Bormann at 10.0 p.m. testified to the increasingly gloomy atmosphere in Hitler's entourage and their growing suspicion of the military leaders: 'Instead of spurring on the relieving troops with orders

and exhortations, authoritative quarters are silent. Loyalty seems
to be giving way to disloyalty. We remain here. Reich Chancellery
already in ruins.'[60]

For Hitler's evening briefing conference General Weidling
assembled all conceivable evidence – including a letter from Prof.
Sauerbruch describing the ghastly fate of the wounded – to
prove to the Führer the hopelessness of continuing the fight.
He had ordered his sector commanders to the Reich Chancellery
at 10.30 p.m. since he was counting on important new directives.
Graphically he described the hopelessness of the situation –
break-through after break-through by the Russians, loss of
ammunition, food and medical depots, cessation of air supply.
As a last resort he proposed a break-out from the 'Berlin pocket'.
The proposal was supported by General Krebs and violently
criticised by Goebbels. After prolonged thought Hitler admitted
that the situation was hopeless. Even should the break-out
succeed, however, he said, they would only be going from one
pocket into another. Then it might be that he would have to
await the end either in the open or in some farmhouse. Better
therefore that he remain in the Reich Chancellery.

That Hitler's decision was governed by sheer egoism is shown
by a remark he made during the briefing conference of 25 April:
'If fate decided otherwise, then I should vanish from the stage of
world history as an inglorious fugitive' – and he repeated the
words 'inglorious fugitive' twice. He gave as a further reason the
necessity for him to set an example to 'all those whom I now
reproach for their defection'. If he won this battle, he would be
able to 'eliminate a number of Generals and other commanders
who had failed at the decisive moment'.

So Hitler stayed in Berlin to 'break the might of the great
Asiatic Khan'.

At five minutes past midnight on 28 April Admiral Voss
telegraphed from the Führer's Headquarters: 'We hold on to the
end.' At about this time Hitler visited Field Marshal Greim, lying
wounded in his room and still unable to depart owing to shortage
of aircraft, and gave him final instructions. The Russians were
preparing to storm the Reich Chancellery, he said, the Luftwaffe
was to support Wenck's break-through to Berlin and carry out
attacks against their positions. Greim was also charged to
ensure that Himmler was arrested.[61] At 4.05 a.m. Bormann sent a

similar instruction to Dönitz: 'Foreign press reports fresh treachery. The Führer expects you to act with extreme rapidity and severity against all traitors in the Northern Zone. There will be no exceptions. Schörner, Wenck and others must now prove their loyalty to the Führer by relieving him as soon as possible.'

At 1.35 p.m. the last conversation with the Military Commandant of Berlin took place. Then the captive balloon by which radio telephone speech was relayed to the radio station was hit by Russian artillery. During the afternoon OKW moved to Dobbin in Mecklenburg, Himmler's old command post. At 11.0 p.m. it received a curtly worded radio message from the Führer's bunker which sounded like an SOS: 'Report at once: 1. Where are Wenck's leading troops? 2. When will they attack again? 3. Where is Ninth Army? 4. What is direction of Ninth Army's break-through? 5. Where are Holste's leading troops?' Two hours later Keitel replied that Wenck's advanced guard was held up south of Lake Schwielow and that Twelfth Army could not therefore proceed with its attack towards Berlin; Ninth Army was encircled and Holste's Corps had been forced on to the defensive. The end was now foreseeable; there could now be no question of the relief of Berlin. But Hitler's morbid suspicion still smelt treachery. Bormann was instructed to send the following telegram to Dönitz:

> Dönitz,
> Our impression grows stronger daily that the divisions in the Berlin theatre have been standing idle for several days. All the reports we receive are controlled, suppressed or distorted by Keitel. In general we can only communicate through Keitel. The Führer orders you to proceed at once and mercilessly against all traitors. [There followed a postscript]: The Führer is alive and is conducting the defence of Berlin.[62]

During the previous night, 28/29 April, Hitler had made all the essential arrangements preparatory to his death. He had married his long-standing mistress, Eva Braun, and dictated his personal and political testament. Karl Dönitz was nominated Reich President, Supreme Commander of the Wehrmacht, Minister of War and Commander-in-Chief of the Navy; Goebbels was nominated Reich Chancellor, Bormann Party Minister, Seyss-Inquart Foreign Minister, Gauleiter Giesler Minister of the Interior, Field Marshal Schörner Commander-in-Chief of the

Army, Ritter von Greim Commander-in-Chief of the Luftwaffe, Gauleiter Hanke, the defender of Breslau, Reichsführer-SS and Chief of the German Police. Other appointments were: Justice – Thierack; Culture – Scheel; Propaganda – Dr. Naumann; Finance – Schwerin von Krosigk; Economics – Funk; Agriculture – Backe; Labour – Dr. Hupfauer; Armaments – Dr. Saur. As Leader of the German Labour Front Ley was also nominated a member of the Cabinet. Göring and Himmler were expelled from the Party and deprived of all rights and offices. No mention was made of Speer, Ribbentrop and Seldte or of Hitler's long-standing military assistants, Keitel and Jodl.

Various factors contributed to the nomination of Dönitz as Head of State. Speer had suggested it when he took leave of Hitler on 23 April;[63] Goebbels and Bormann too must have exerted some influence. Hitler's confidence in the Admiral was obviously also important and in the last few days this confidence had been increased by Dönitz' readiness to provide troops. Ultimately, however, force of circumstances must have decided the issue. After Himmler's defection hardly anyone else was in the field. The C-in-C of the Luftwaffe had only just been appointed and was not enough of a public figure; Schörner, whom Hitler made C-in-C of the Army, was widely disliked in the Wehrmacht and Keitel was regarded merely as Hitler's tool or a 'technical General'. Dönitz was therefore the only Service Commander-in-Chief left. Moreover his nomination lent credibility to Hitler's call to continue the struggle.

In his testament Hitler declared that he preferred death to 'cowardly abdication or indeed capitulation'. This he regarded as the great shame. His views on suicide had changed, for originally he had called it an act of cowardice. Nevertheless when Field Marshal Paulus had surrendered at Stalingrad he had said that he would have done better to shoot himself or bury himself alive. A commander should fall on his sword, he had said, when he saw that the battle was lost.[64]

Now that his own battle was lost he wished to die 'an honourable death' in Berlin – Goebbels had persuaded him that in a maximum of five years' time he would have become a legendary figure and National-Socialism a mythology. So he left to Dönitz the doubtful glory of going down fighting on the ruins of the Reich like a captain with his ship.

Three copies of the political testament were made. SS-Standartenführer Wilhelm Zandler, Bormann's personal assistant, was to deliver one copy, together with Hitler's marriage certificate, to Dönitz, and Major Johannmeier, Hitler's Army aide, another to Field Marshal Schörner. The third copy was destined for the archives and entrusted to Heinz Lorenz of the Propaganda Ministry.[65] Keitel and Dönitz were informed by radio that couriers with important documents were on their way.[66] The testament, incidentally, never reached them.[67]

Hitler committed suicide about 3.30 p.m. on 30 April.[68]

At 6.07 p.m. Bormann despatched the following radio message:

> Grand Admiral Dönitz: In place of the former Reich-Marshal Göring the Führer appoints you, Herr Grand Admiral, as his successor. Written authority is on its way. You will immediately take all such measures as the situation requires.

Why, at this point, the somewhat misleading announcement of Dönitz' nomination to the succession but no information on Hitler's death? Bormann and Goebbels were clearly trying one last manœuvre to save their skins and their power. Escape from Berlin was more or less out of the question. If they were to take over the offices allotted to them by Hitler, the fighting round Berlin must be stopped and contact established with Dönitz. Moreover Himmler, who was located close to Dönitz, had to be eliminated. If Dönitz could be led to believe that he was Hitler's sole successor, he would hardly be willing to share his power with the Reichsführer-SS. Goebbels and Bormann therefore despatched a negotiator to Russian headquarters. He was to inform them of Hitler's death and of Goebbels' and Bormann's official positions and at the same time ask for an armistice. They entrusted this task to General Krebs, the Chief of the General Staff, who was a Russian speaker. Accompanied by Colonel Dufving, Chief of Staff to the Commandant of Berlin, Krebs crossed the enemy lines at 3.30 a.m. on 1 May and was conducted to Colonel-General Chuikov, commanding 8 Guards Army. He produced three documents: plenary powers to negotiate, a list of the new government and a letter from Goebbels and Bormann proposing a temporary cessation of hostilities in Berlin 'to create a basis for peace negotiations between Germany and the Soviet Union'. After an interminable discussion between Chuikov and Krebs, in

which Army General Sokolovsky commanding the First Byelo–
Russian Front later participated, the Soviets gave their answer.
It comprised four points:

1. A demand for the unconditional surrender of Berlin.

2. A guarantee of the lives of members of the armed forces in Berlin
   together with retention of their decorations and personal
   possessions; officers to retain their swords; wounded to receive
   medical treatment.

3. A promise that, if the Soviet proposals were accepted, members
   of the new government and their staff would not be treated as
   prisoners of war.

4. An opportunity for members of the new government to gain
   touch with Dönitz in order that they might put forward a peace
   proposal to the three Allies.

No guarantee was given that the three Allied governments
would enter into negotiations with the German government.

General Krebs left the Soviet lines shortly after 1.0 p.m. and
returned to the bunker. Bormann had meanwhile sent a second
telegram to Dönitz telling him that Hitler's testament was in
force and that he (Bormann) would join him as soon as possible.
Until he did so, no public announcement should, in his view, be
made. Possibly an interim report by Colonel Dufving, who had
returned to the bunker earlier, had convinced Bormann of the
hopelessness of their efforts.

When Krebs returned, the news he brought destroyed the last
hopes of a separate agreement with the Russians. Goebbels
rejected the demand for the unconditional surrender of Berlin
and so informed General Chuikov in writing under an SS flag of
truce which crossed the Soviet lines at 6.0 p.m.

Shortly thereafter the Russian Colonel Antonov was ordered to
capture the Reich Chancellery. Fighting restarted with renewed
vigour, until about 5.0 p.m. on 2 May General Weidling, the last
Commandant of Berlin, crossed the Landwehr canal and summoned all German troops still resisting to lay down their arms.
Goebbels with his family had meanwhile committed suicide, as
had Generals Krebs and Burgdorf. The remaining inmates of the
bunker, including Bormann, attempted to save themselves by
flight. Bormann's fate is still unknown.

After Krebs' return Goebbels and Bormann had at last told

Dönitz of Hitler's death and the more important arrangements for the succession:

> The Führer died yesterday at 15.30 hours. Testament of 29 April appoints you as Reich President, Reich Minister Goebbels as Reich Chancellor, Reichsleiter Bormann as Party Minister, Reich Minister Seyss-Inquart as Foreign Minister. By order of the Führer the testament has been sent from Berlin to you, to Field Marshal Schörner and for preservation and publication. Reichsleiter Bormann intends to go to you today and to inform you of the situation. Time and form of announcement to the Press and to the troops is left to you. Acknowledge receipt.[69]

Part One

THE PERSONALITIES

Hitler's will put an end to all speculation about the succession. The tyrant himself had provided for some form of continuity. He must have realised that not all his nominated office-holders would survive but he had not calculated upon his last testament being transmitted piecemeal. Hitler certainly had no doubt of Dönitz' willingness to assume the task assigned to him. His loyalty and devotion as C-in-C of the Navy, his readiness to obey the Supreme Commander of the Wehrmacht and Führer of the Third Reich, and Germany's desperate situation made any refusal unthinkable. Like a new edition of the 'King of Graudenz', the fortress commandant of 1806 (see p. 19), Hitler must have thought, Dönitz would never 'bow to the enemy yoke', would fight to the end and would go down with the remnants of the Reich.

As we know, Karl Dönitz is still alive today, as are several of the men who declared themselves ready to guide the destinies of Germany in May 1945. Some of them had already been nominated by Adolf Hitler to the offices which they assumed under the new Head of State; others had fallen into disfavour; the majority were appointed by Dönitz himself. In view of the clearly approaching catastrophe, it is legitimate to wonder what motives actuated these people to undertake a task with so little prospect of success or recognition.

A period of transition from war to peace invariably makes exceptional demands on all official, military and civilian authorities; it produces numerous reorientation problems. To direct so fundamental a readjustment, professional experts and experienced politicians are required to prepare for the morrow. In Germany's case, however, this transition coincided, not only with the collapse of the State, the economy and the finances, but with the demand of the victors for dissolution of the previous political regime, and this gave rise to difficulties of unimaginable dimensions. Where to find the experts who did not bear the mark of yesterday – and that in a country where all communications were at a standstill? One had to do the best one could with the 'know-how' men immediately available even if their political record was not as immaculate as one might have wished. Where to find uncontaminated politicians in a state which had systematically hounded into emigration, locked up or liquidated all non-conformers? At the end of a total war and a totalitarian state must not the men in power during the transition period inevitably be adherents of, or at least sympathisers with, the previous political regime?

Alternatively perhaps these men were motivated by something different – a higher standard of sense of duty and genuine love of their country. For what other reasons would they be likely, at this juncture, to undertake so thankless a task offering so few prospects?

These considerations are highlighted by the following more or less detailed portraits of the leading German political and military figures of May 1945. None of the members of the new government or the new military leaders had been an opponent of Hitler Germany – at best they had been 'fellow-travellers'. Almost all, however, were men with a strong sense of duty and devoted patriots, qualities which in most cases had led them to tolerate, if not actually to participate in, the practices of the criminal National-Socialist State. In many cases personal ambition and careerism were additional factors. Hitler had shown a masterly ability to exploit their strengths and weaknesses in various ways. All were trying to evade the consequences of a policy in which, in Joachim Fest's words, they had 'collaborated with their eyes shut'.

CHAPTER ONE

Karl Dönitz

HISTORY provides many instances of military leaders or experts to whom in moments of supreme danger the fate of their country has been entrusted or who have assumed this responsibility on their own initiative. Few, however, can have faced so difficult a situation or been so totally unprepared for political office as Karl Dönitz.

When Hitler committed suicide Dönitz was 54 years old and had reached the height of his ambition in his profession: for two years he had been C-in-C of his Service, the Navy. In addition he had recently been placed in charge of parts of the civil and military administration in so far as they were responsible for defence preparations in the North German area. The real instruments of power, however, the Army, the Luftwaffe, the Waffen-SS and the political machine were outside his authority.

Nothing in his previous existence had indicated that he had any ambition apart from his military career. On the contrary his attention had been almost over-concentrated on his profession.

Karl Dönitz was the son of an engineer in the Zeiss works, born in Berlin-Grunau on 16 September 1891. It may seem surprising that he should have chosen to become a naval officer and devoted his life entirely to the requirements and demands of the Navy. Knowledge of his background and educational environment, however, makes his choice understandable.

For centuries Dönitz' ancestors had been squires and magistrates in the Elbe area near the mouth of the Saale. Permanent conflict with the Slavs had been their daily bread and they had always been ready to spring to arms at any sign of danger from the East. Later generations had been equally ready to defend themselves; their sons became officers or evangelical pastors, the latter frequently as defiant in their attitude as the soldiers. Their education instilled into them a sense of duty and a rugged asceticism. Their cardinal principle was a strict social order, authority and leadership from above being matched by respect and unquestioning obedience from below. Karl Dönitz, like the rest, was brought up on these ancient Prussian and Frederician principles. His father would have 'let himself be cut into little pieces' for 'his' Kaiser, William I.[1] Dönitz' character was permanently stamped by these impressions from his home and the generations-old tradition of readiness to defend oneself against anything coming from the East.

On matriculating in Weimar in 1910 he had already made up his mind to enter the Imperial Navy. His thirst for adventure had been whetted by reading Nansen's and Sven Hedin's books; annual holidays on the Baltic had stirred his love of the sea; the experiences of some of his relatives in China and Egypt had given him an urge to travel. As a naval officer, young Dönitz hoped to see the world and give 'his' Kaiser, William II, proof of his loyalty. Moreover his choice of a career was fashionable at the time. As the Service became more technical, an increasing number of young men from the educated classes were choosing a naval career, although they might not strictly originate from the 'waterfront'.

Karl Dönitz completed his initial sea training in the *Hertha*, followed by a special course at the Naval School in Flensburg-Mürwik. As Sub-Lieutenant he served in the *Breslau* in the Mediterranean. There he was overtaken by the outbreak of war. Shortly thereafter the two cruisers, *Goeben* and *Breslau*, were ostensibly sold to the Turks and their crews employed to train the Turkish Navy.

Action by the *Goeben* in the Bosphorus in 1915 soon triggered off Turkish entry into the war. Both ships, *Goeben* and *Breslau*, then sailed under the Turkish flag and gunfire from the *Breslau*, in which Dönitz was still serving, set fourteen Russian ships on fire outside Novorossisk. When the cruiser had to be laid up for overhaul, Dönitz was posted to a Naval Air detachment in Gallipoli, where he remained until 1916. He did not return to Germany until after his promotion to Lieutenant and was then posted to the arm, the development and promotion of which was to be his primary object in life for many years – submarines.

Here he found what was dearest to his heart, the 'unique spirit of comradeship engendered by destiny and hardship shared in the community of a U-boat's crew, where every man's well-being was in the hands of all and where every single man was an indispensable part of the whole'.[2]

Between 1916 and 1918 Dönitz learnt the trade of war first as Watch Officer and then Commander of an attack submarine. In the early hours of 4 October 1918 he had personal experience of the deficiencies of the current offensive tactics. South-east of Sicily he attacked a heavily laden convoy; after torpedoing a merchant ship he was forced to dive since an enemy destroyer was heading straight for him; he and his crew were expecting a depth charge at any minute but this did not materialise. Cautiously UB 68 rose once more and followed the convoy. The sudden arrival of dawn, however, necessitated another dive and this nearly resulted in catastrophe. Owing to a fault in the longitudinal stabiliser gear the boat stood on its head and sank rapidly. Soon it reached a depth of 200 ft at which the water pressure was the maximum it could stand. Dönitz ordered the compressed air tanks to be filled immediately. After a few agonising minutes the submarine, now far too light, shot to the surface and appeared in the middle of the enemy convoy. Sirens screeched, guns fired and the enemy destroyers attacked. UB 68 could not dive again as her compressed air was exhausted and she had been holed in several places.[3] There was no alternative but to give the order 'Abandon ship'. Dönitz was rescued by one of the escorting destroyers and so his time as a submariner ended. He was now a prisoner of the British. Nevertheless he had learnt a basic lesson: a lone U-boat could not make a successful attack; the material and psychological odds were too great. To cope with a large number of escorts, a large number of submarines must be employed. His experience led later to the group and 'Wolf-pack' tactics so successfully employed in World War II.

To Dönitz' military mind nothing could be more distasteful than captivity. He mulled continuously over the problem of escape from this, to him, dishonourable existence. Finally he and two of his companions lit upon a typical, though foolish, idea; they pretended to be mad and mimicked the manœuvres of a U-boat, running around with their heads down, going 'bzz, bzz, bzz'. Naturally British psychiatrists did not fall for this child's play. The 'madmen' were placed in solitary confinement and soon recovered.[4] Consumption of tobacco juice, however, proved more effective, producing symptoms similar to those of blackwater fever and resulting in early release.[5]

Returning from captivity in July 1919, Dönitz reported to the headquarters of the new Reich Navy. The Personnel Desk officer asked him whether he wished to continue to serve. For Dönitz the naval profession was attractive only if there was some hope of going to sea in a U-boat again. When the Personnel officer expressed the opinion that Germany would have submarines again in the foreseeable future, Dönitz decided to remain a regular. He had to contain his love for submarines for years, however, since Germany was allowed none under the Versailles Treaty. During the next few years Dönitz mastered surface- and torpedo-boat tactics. On promotion to Lieutenant-Commander he was given command of 4 Torpedo Boat Flotilla and there at last had the opportunity to develop the principles of 'his' pack tactics.

During a tour of duty in Naval Headquarters Berlin from 1924 to 1927, Dönitz had his first experience of naval administration, being responsible for questions of maintenance of discipline and the application of military law. He also had to deal with internal political questions affecting the Navy. This brought him into contact with the Reichstag, the climate and atmosphere of which was highly distasteful to his well-ordered military mind. He found the 'parliamentary fauna' (Mauriac's words) and the parties' tactical manœuvring repellent. In particular, being used to short, factual reporting, the long-winded debates aimed at the electorate appalled him. These experiences, together with those of 1930–4 as Senior Staff Officer of the Baltic Station, led to an increasing anti-republican attitude and growing sympathy for National-Socialism. Initially, following the tradition of the Imperial era, Dönitz kept himself as far as possible aloof from politics. As Staff Officer of a Station, however, he had to concern himself with precautions in the event of internal disorders and so politics inevitably came into his purview. Undoubtedly the monarchy was still his ideal; its fall had been a real shock to him at the time. The Nationalist-Socialist programme now seemed to offer at least some guarantee of national purpose; the Party seemed to stand for stern ordered energy. Hitler's promises to build a true people's community, elimination of class warfare and unemployment and the prospect of a strong Germany, all seemed desirable to Dönitz; a strict regime directed from above was all in line with his ideas based on Prussianism and the monarchy. This trad-itional desire for leadership from above was common to broad sections of the population and of course accorded with the hierarchical tendencies of military and administrative circles. An additional factor was his naval officer's training which had instilled into him the ideal of a close-knit community of comrades on board ship; a similarly compact popular community eliminating class warfare therefore seemed a worth-while goal. This favourable picture of the new Party was reinforced by its militaristic character and authoritarian hierarchy, but above all by the prospect which it held out of rehabilitation of the profession of arms. Even before 1933 Hitler had given it to be understood that he would favour reconstruction of a fleet.[6] Soon after his assumption of power he confirmed this intention to the Chief of the Naval Staff, Admiral Raeder.

In short Dönitz' aversion to the Weimar Republic and attraction to National-Socialism must be regarded as one of the numerous illustrations of the Weimar State's failure to create a 'solidarity of interest between the officer corps and the State as a whole'. In the late 1920s and early 1930s a general trend towards National-Socialism was noticeable in the Navy, particularly among the younger officers.

The rapid deterioration on the internal political front after the Nazi seizure of power passed almost unnoticed by Dönitz; undoubtedly he was unaware of the true background. He spent the first six months of 1933 on an 'educational trip' to the Dutch East Indies (Sumatra, Java and Bali), Ceylon and Lower India – an annual gift from the Reich President to one officer from the Reichswehr.

On his return to Germany he found himself involved in difficulties and conflicts about spheres of authority with the SA; they were apparently even planning a *putsch* during which Admiral Otto Schulze, the Naval Station Commander, and Dönitz as his senior staff officer, were to be 'rendered innocuous'.[7] In the light of this the events of 30 June 1934, later given legal cover by the sophism of a 'State Emergency', seemed to Dönitz not only justified but necessary. Röhm had been an unpleasant perverted figure; the SA had included all the adventurers and unscrupulous rowdies – the worst elements of National-Socialism in fact. To many, therefore, the Party's action in eliminating them seemed like a house-cleaning and a clear swing to the side of the Reichs-wehr. Only a few realised[8] that the settlement of the conflict by gangster methods was indicative of the true nature of the new State; moreover the extent of the atrocities was generally unknown and was smothered by a wealth of propaganda phrases from Goebbels.

In November 1934 Dönitz left on another foreign cruise, this time as Captain of the cruiser *Emden*; the voyage took him round Africa into the Indian Ocean and he did not return until July 1935. During this period, he considered there had been a noticeable rise in German prestige abroad, evidenced particularly by a more friendly attitude on the part of the Royal Navy.[9]

When Commander Dönitz returned to Wilhelmshaven he found that meanwhile – in March 1935 – universal military service had been reintroduced and – on 18 June 1935 – the Anglo-German Naval Agreement had been signed. As he was a professional officer both these measures inevitably deluded him into giving even more enthusiastic support to the regime.

While still on board the *Emden* Dönitz was visited by Grand Admiral Raeder, the C-in-C of the Navy. After reporting on his voyage, Dönitz told the Admiral of his plans for further cruises. To his complete astonishment, however, Raeder replied that he was to take over the reconstruction of a German submarine fleet. At this point Dönitz' ambition got the better of him. Instead of being pleased that now at last he could put his plans for new attack tactics to the test, he was disappointed. He felt that he was being elbowed into a dead end, since every indication was that submarines could only form a very small proportion of the newly reconstructed fleet.

In fact the prospects were highly unfavourable. It was proposed to construct the most homogeneous fleet possible. The Versailles Treaty had left Germany with nothing but completely obsolete ships and new construction was subject to extraordinary limitations. In 1935 the German fleet comprised no more than two battleships, six light cruisers and twelve torpedo-boats, together with a few obsolete ships of the line, torpedo-boats, minesweepers and auxiliaries dating from the First World War. The personnel ceiling was 15,000 including 1,500 officers and the coastal defences.

According to the Anglo-German Naval Agreement Germany was permitted to rearm up to 35% of British tonnage, this percentage being applicable to individual categories of ship with the exception of submarines, for which 45% was allowed. In the Royal Navy, however, submarines played only a minor role, so, purely from the tonnage point of view, 45% or even parity, which the two governments had discussed in a friendly way, did not represent much compared to the other categories of ship.[10] In addition, technical innovations[11] and agreements under international law[12] seriously reduced the effectiveness of the submarine.

In September the first U-boat flotilla, 'Weddigen', was formed with nine small submarines, reinforced by a further nine in the following month. Commanding them was Captain Dönitz who, despite his initial hesitation, was soon 'body and soul a submariner once more' and, unhampered by instructions and directives, threw himself into the basic training of his crews, laying the main emphasis on 'war readiness'.[13] That the development of 'wolf-pack' tactics received due attention goes without saying.[14]

'War readiness' training in no way indicated systematic preparation for war; it did not even imply any aggressive intent; this was merely standard professional procedure. Even at Nuremberg Dönitz was acquitted under the heading of preparation for aggressive war. In fact the majority of the German officer corps, which 'in 1933 ceased to be a factor of importance in the political life of Germany',[15] were guilty of excessive complacency and obtuseness in face of a dictatorial government rather than of aggressive intent. Exaggerated nationalism and susceptibility to totalitarianism led almost 'the entire upper crust of society to fall victim to Hitler in one way or another'.[16] Dönitz was no exception.

Dönitz met Hitler for the first time in autumn 1934 before his cruise as Captain of the *Emden*. From then until the outbreak of war he saw him five times in all and from 1939 to January 1943 – the date of his appointment as C-in-C of the Navy – four times. Their meetings took place on military or social occasions; they never discussed anything other than military subjects.[17]

At Nuremberg Dönitz explained what had attracted him to National-Socialism. Its teaching was in line with his own ideas on nationalism and socialism – 'the ideas which found expression in the honour and dignity of the nation, its freedom, its equality among nations and its security; and the social tenets which had perhaps as their basis: no class struggle but human and social respect for each person regardless of his class, profession or economic position and on the other hand subordination of each and every one to the interests of the common weal. Naturally I regarded Adolf Hitler's high authority with admiration and joyfully acknowledged it when in times of peace he succeeded so quickly and without bloodshed in realising his national and social objectives.'[18]

This rather badly worded statement is quoted here because it is particularly typical of Dönitz and expresses genuine sentiments. At the time many others placed equal credence in the Nazi Party's statements on national and social questions. Moreover for Dönitz, the military man, 'honour and dignity' were no empty words; in fact they provide a key to any understanding of his character; they recur in many of his orders and proclamations. Social dignity and social equality of status were principles far more strictly observed in the Navy than the Army. In the confined space of a ship and on a long voyage class privileges were not so easy to maintain. An increasing number of naval officers were drawn from the bourgeoisie, the upper middle class. Professional efficiency rather than social status was the deciding factor.

Dönitz' admitted admiration for Hitler's authority, for the 'bloodless' achievement of his national and social aims, shows how oblivious he was to the criminal character of the regime, but it also indicates a certain moral complacency summed up in the words: 'That was none of my business.'[19] The fact that the Navy kept itself to a certain extent aloof, Hitler's masterly concealment tactics and Dönitz' complete absorption in his professional duties may be adduced as further reasons. The brutality of the regime's anti-semitic measures as evidenced in the events of 'Kristallnacht',[20] however, caused him to act. He protested to Admiral Boehm, his immediate superior. When similar protests arrived from other senior naval officers, Grand Admiral Raeder, the C-in-C of the Navy, made representations to Hitler.[21] The moral value of this step must not be rated too high, however, for Raeder based his case primarily on the damage done by such actions to German prestige abroad, though this may of course have been merely a tactical manœuvre.

Relatively little is known of Dönitz' attitude to anti-semitism but that little is symptomatic of the position adopted by many Germans at the time. When personally affected – in Dönitz' case when the Navy was affected – they opposed any excesses and took steps to maintain in their posts Jewish officers or those with Jewish wives. Anything which happened outside their own sphere they ignored and disregarded. Passively, therefore, they accepted the principle, breaking it only in individual cases. Practically everyone had his 'decent Jew',[22] on whose behalf he would intercede. On several occasions Dönitz himself intervened successfully with Hitler in favour of Jewish naval officers, but he nevertheless used the official Party phraseology, referring to the 'spreading poison of Jewry'.[23] Like the majority, he had not thought out the implications and effects of his attitude.

In May 1945, however, his reactions when the concentration camp ships arrived in Flensburg[24] and the concentration camp films were shown in Nuremberg, leave 'little doubt that he was honestly shocked by revelations of the brutality Hitler employed'.[25] Dönitz of course knew that concentration camps existed; he had himself agreed to the proposal to use concentration camp prisoners as shipyard labour. Clearly, however, he thought of them as a stricter form of arrest, in which severity would be the order of the day, but not atrocities or mass murder.[26]

On one occasion Dönitz is said to have asked Himmler for his views on the current rumours and the latter is supposed to have replied that there had been 'unworthy' conditions in certain camps; he had, however, initiated an enquiry and the culprits had been shot. With this Dönitz had to be satisfied;[27] little did he suspect that the death sentences had been pronounced for offences such as theft, embezzlement, murder for sadistic or selfish reasons and other breaches of the SS code of honour rather than for systematic murder.

Rumours about maltreatment in the concentration camps were also obviously and only too readily accepted as enemy war propaganda. On occasions welcome confirmation of this notion was provided by erroneous reports in foreign broadcasts, as for instance that Prien and Schulz, the two U-boat commanders, were under concentration camp arrest.

Is so much 'innocent ignorance' credible in the case of leading figures in the country?

In answering this question four factors must be taken into account:

1. The widespread habit of blinkered thinking. Everyone confined himself as far as possible to his own domain.

2. Hitler's fundamental Order (Grundsätzlicher Befehl) of 11 January 1940, supposedly drafted by Schellenberg and redrafted by Himmler,[28] ordering everyone to keep his duties secret and to ensure that he knew only so much as was essential for his job.

3. The tendency to regard apparently doubtful rumours and reports as untrustworthy – a self-preservation reaction comprehensible only to someone who has lived in the atmosphere of a totalitarian state and all the more tempting under the pressures of war.

4. The fact that 'chain-belt' murder represented a complete novelty in the catalogue of human atrocities and perversions; it was therefore something inconceivable to the normal mind.

In his reply to an article attacking him, Dönitz has said that those who criticise National-Socialism today are in general thinking of its crimes. 'These misdeeds were unknown to me. It is useless for me to try to say today how I should have acted, had I been informed of these crimes. Personally I am convinced that I would never have condoned them.'

Apart from certain 'superficial blemishes', therefore, the National-Socialist dictatorship presented itself to Dönitz in a positive light. The rape of Czechoslovakia does not seem to have ruffled his conscience. The abrogation of the Anglo-German Naval Agreement he rated as 'an exceptionally strong political measure' indicating that 'the policy of trying to reach agreement with Britain had been abandoned. Not merely temporarily but for a long time to come there was no likelihood of any improvement in Anglo-German relations.'[29] The conclusion which he drew proves how firm he was – and is – in his conviction that war is the natural continuation of policy and is inevitable, also his failure to grasp, or refusal to admit, that the conflict had been brought about by Hitler's megalomania. Writing in 1963 he says: 'The abrogation of the Anglo-German Naval Agreement was concrete evidence of the high state of tension that existed between Germany and Britain, and no political leader could with certainty guarantee that he could prevent this tension exploding into actual hostilities at any moment. An immediate and accelerated rearmament programme, based on the rapid construction of a large number of U-boats, was now the primary task which faced the German Navy.'[30]

His only worry was that, with the small number of U-boats available, the necessary successes would not be achieved in the event of war. He so informed his Commander-in-Chief, asking that Hitler be notified. The latter's reply, announced by Raeder to the officer corps assembled in Swinemünde on 22 July 1939, ran: 'He would ensure that in no circumstances would war with Britain come about. For that would mean "*Finis Germaniae*".'[31] Thereupon, that very day, Captain Dönitz went on leave, from which he was recalled on 15 August. At the end of the month he again drew his C-in-C's attention to his anxiety over the inadequate number of U-boats and handed him the draft of a memorandum which he submitted officially on 28 August entitled 'Thoughts on the expansion of the U-boat arm'.[32]

The primary object was described as 'the military defeat of Great Britain', since he believed that in the event of war England would be among Germany's enemies. In the light of the German arms shortage, however, he regarded war in 1939 as inadvisable, though in the long term he thought it inevitable. He did not think that this was Germany's fault: 'If before 1914 the other side found the existence of Bismarck's small German National State intolerable, it could hardly be expected now to tolerate the existence of the Greater-German Empire. If, therefore, we felt bound to regard an armed trial of strength between Germany and Britain as inevitable, it was essential that we should have pursued with determination an appropriately logical policy with regard to our naval armaments. But our leaders failed to appreciate the real situation.'[33] Even more clearly: 'Britain went to war in 1939 because Greater Germany, growing in strength and united with Austria, was becoming a menace to British imperial and economic interests. . . . The destruction of this political and economic power of Germany was Britain's war aim, an aim in which she was supported by the United States with a zeal even greater than her own.'[34] Here he shows himself as a supporter of the old tale of the clash of economic interests; obsessed by the friend-foe relationship theory and the philosophy of power, both basic tenets of National-Socialism, he disregards completely the overwhelming desire for peace characteristic of the Western democracies during the inter-war period.

Was Dönitz actually a National-Socialist? The question whether he was a Party member is irrelevant; on 30 January 1944 he received the Golden Party Badge as an honorary member of the NSDAP. He cannot be called 'a hard-core Nazi who had thoroughly identified himself with the ideology, aims and attitudes of the Nazi leadership',[35] since he knew nothing of their criminal methods and, as he says, would not have accepted them. He belongs more to the 'believers with reservations', who were 'nationalists rather than Nazis'.[36] In fact he was a misguided patriot who took ostensibly idealistic theories and fair words at their face value without realising that they were a façade behind which lay personal lust for power. A remark attributed to Alfred Rosenberg (the Nazi theorist) is applicable: 'The tragedy was that he really believed in National-Socialism.' The botched-up National-Socialist programme in many respects accorded with his own somewhat hazy political ideas. In addition Hitler exerted an enormous power of attraction over him – he was 'the great seducer', in the words of Percy Ernst Schramm (the German official historian). To form his own judgement Dönitz was often compelled to withdraw from Hitler's suggestive influence – and even then his own judgement frequently swung him over to Hitler's side.[37]

His nomination as Commander-in-Chief of the Navy was not, as many have maintained, due to his 'political reliability' but to his technical qualifications, his intelligence[38] and the fact that Hitler's initial predilection for large ships changed to aversion as a result of their lack of success in naval warfare; he then placed all his hopes in submarines. When Hitler decided to scrap the heavy ships, Raeder, whose relations with his Supreme Commander had long been strained, seized the opportunity to resign. As his successor he proposed either Grand Admiral Carls or Dönitz,[39] although his relations with the latter were cool and 'his somewhat conceited and not always tactful nature did not appeal to me'.[40] Hitler chose Dönitz and on 30 January 1943 – exactly ten years after the National-Socialist seizure of power – the new C-in-C of the Navy took office.

Dönitz brought to his new task his characteristic devotion to duty. He had longed for an opportunity to exert his influence in a wider field for, as a naval officer, he regarded German strategy as too exclusively continental. The best method seemed to him to be to bring personal influence to bear on the Supreme Commander of the Wehrmacht – memoranda had already proved ineffective.

The essential was to win Hitler's confidence, the only hope of influencing the self-willed Dictator, who regarded any advice with suspicion. Dönitz made a habit of spending long periods in the Führer's Headquarters in order to bring the necessary pressure to bear on important decisions and counter other influences. After a cool start the two men established a good relationship. As Commander-in-Chief of the Navy Dönitz had soon become convinced that the order to scrap the heavy ships was unwise and, to Hitler's surprise, pleaded for its cancellation. Hitler adopted the attitude of the calm, unprejudiced, thoughtful superior,[41] treated the new Head of the Navy with the greatest civility and largely allowed him a free hand. Hitler thought primarily on continental lines and had initially regarded the fleet purely as an instrument to seal off the continent; the sea was always something mysterious to him and he knew little about problems of naval warfare. He was personally interested mainly in heavy ships and technical innovations and on these subjects would frequently leave his listeners dumbfounded by his extraordinary memory and knowledge.[42] Dönitz enjoyed a degree of independence unparalleled by any other Wehrmacht representative. Hitler continued to have confidence in Dönitz even when, from April 1943, the U-boat war was brought practically to a standstill by the new Allied detection devices and Allied air superiority. Dönitz' position was sufficiently strong to enable him to check Nazi influence in the Navy. This he did, however, not so much on moral grounds as on principle; he was opposed to any outside interference in the internal affairs of the Wehrmacht in general and the Navy in particular. His predecessors too had always been jealous opponents of any external influences, from whatever quarter.

In summer 1943, for instance, Bormann attempted, via Dr. Thierack, the Reich Minister of Justice, to remove from the Wehrmacht jurisdiction over political offences and transfer it to the People's Courts. Dönitz immediately intervened personally – and successfully – with Hitler. After the 20 July 1944 coup Bormann returned to the charge. Neither the Chief of OKW nor the C-in-C of the Luftwaffe would take action, although both considered Thierack's proposal dubious. Although Dönitz protested both orally and in writing, on this occasion he failed. On 20 September 1944 Hitler signed an ordinance authorising the People's Courts and Special Courts to intervene in Wehrmacht legal cases. A teleprinter message from Dönitz immediately arrived raising serious objections and requesting delay. He was entirely undeterred by the machinations of Klemm, the State Secretary in the Ministry of Justice, who told OKW that 'he had listed a series of instances in which naval courts had either pursued cases of political subversion with insufficient energy or dealt with them too leniently; he proposed to show the Navy that his Minister's position with Hitler was at least as strong as that of the Grand Admiral'.[43] Neither the ordinance, even when signed by Hitler, nor its executive instructions were carried out in the Navy; they were simply pigeonholed. This was not a protest by Dönitz against the activities of the People's Courts in general. He was merely determined to keep his men under his own military jurisdiction.[44] He also succeeded in checking the influence of the 'National-Socialist Leadership Officers'. They were placed under the naval commanders concerned and allowed no say in operational matters.[45]

At Hitler's briefing conferences Dönitz confined himself as far as possible to his own subject, though occasions of course arose when he had to take a hand in questions of overall strategy, as they affected the Navy.

From January 1945 Hitler increasingly relied on Dönitz' advice since, as well as being C-in-C of the Navy, he was then appointed so-called 'coal dictator', responsible for the allocation of coal for all military purposes; in early April all merchant shipping, hitherto the responsibility of the Reich Commissar for Sea Transport, was placed under him. In addition, on several occasions he made naval troops available to Hitler for the war on land.[46]

At Nuremberg the prosecution reckoned that in something over two years Dönitz had visited Hitler on 119 days. Dönitz maintained that up to the end of January 1945 he had only had 57 interviews, all the rest being accounted for by his daily attendance at the briefing conferences in the final months of the war.[47]

'In the final phase of the war, when Hitler was in Berlin, Dönitz attended the briefing conference in the Reich Chancellery almost every day. This was essential owing to the pace of events and the close connection between naval and land operations. Courland and East Prussia had been cut off, as was later Danzig. Supply problems were in the forefront of all naval considerations.

In this situation Dönitz was the man who never lost his head and frequently came up with sound advice or a solution.'[48]

One of those present at the briefing conferences described Dönitz' attitude as follows: 'At the briefing conferences of the final weeks he was invariably dignified, thoughtful and determined. Even if it differed from that of Hitler, he put his point of view to the Führer tactfully but firmly and with vigour, and he put up a fight for it. Hitler had such confidence in him that on occasions he could openly criticise the Führer's proposals and attitude. . . .'

He must therefore be regarded as a clear-thinking, firm and dignified character, possessed of a natural authority. To these qualities he owed his influence, all the more remarkable in that 'it was not in any way in keeping with Hitler's peculiar disposition and personality to have advisers of that kind' and when real decisions were to be taken he would accept no advice.[49]

Dönitz' list of decorations also testifies to Hitler's appreciation of his services: on 16 September 1939 he was awarded the Clasp to the Iron Cross First Class for his submarine victories in the Baltic during the Polish campaign, on 21 April 1940 the Knight's Cross, on 7 April 1943 the Oakleaves to the Knight's Cross, and on 30 January 1944 the Golden Party Badge.[50]

There is no doubt that Dönitz always defended his point of view with tenacity, authority and competence.[51] This makes it all the more incomprehensible that he never broached to Hitler the question of ending the war. Instead, right to the end of April 1945, he was issuing fanatical exhortations to the troops and making available his last manpower reserves.

After careful analysis of the situation a Navy Headquarters appreciation dated 20 August 1943 had drawn the conclusion that 'in the light of the available forces and potentialities it seems doubtful whether Germany alone can win the war by military methods. . . . Since last year from the point of view of overall strategy Germany has become the anvil instead of the hammer.' This was tantamount to saying that militarily *no* solution could now be achieved. This estimate was nevertheless tempered later by a reference to defensive capabilities: 'The task of the Wehrmacht is to defend the European theatre of war long enough for the leadership to impose our political will upon the enemy.'

Although Dönitz had forwarded this appreciation to Hitler, he apparently never himself referred to the necessity for ending the war. What was his motive for this attitude? At Nuremberg he defended himself with the argument that this was a political problem and, as a military man, his sole duty was to obey.[52] But this does not hold water, since he was always outspoken on any problem which seemed to him important, and a reference to the hopelessness of the situation could hardly rank as 'disobedience'. Elsewhere, however, Dönitz stated that his attitude was conditioned by the enemy demand for unconditional surrender. This motivation is far more illuminating. The prospect of seeing Germany turned into a 'goat pasture' with no doubt as to the fate awaiting the Nazi and military élite, was not attractive. There may also have been a personal reason. Both Dönitz' sons had been killed on active service; his only brother, a businessman and naval reserve officer, had been killed in an air raid in Berlin in 1943. Had all these sacrifices been made for nothing but this dismal future?

In his subsequent memoirs Dönitz refers to 'unexpected political developments and similar occurrences' which may sometimes change even the most hopeless situations.[53] By 'similar occurrences' he meant his hopes of reviving the U-boat war and the earlier figures of sinkings. As early as September 1943 he had submitted construction proposals for a new type of U-boat with larger batteries and better streamlining, giving greater underwater speeds. Additional equipment proposed consisted of the schnorkel and the most modern offensive and defensive weapons. On 15 February 1945 he informed Hitler that 237 submarines were under construction, 111 old type, 84 Mark XXIs and 42 Mark XXIIIs. Moreover the total of 450 U-boats in service at the time was the highest ever achieved by Germany. The increasing severity of the Allied bombing and the consequential destruction delayed the commissioning of the new submarines; nevertheless at the time of the capitulation 120 were complete and fit for service.

Considering that in autumn 1939 the German submarine fleet comprised only 57 units and that Germany entered the war with only 23 submarines capable of operating in the Atlantic,[54] from the purely naval point of view Dönitz' hopes were perhaps not quite so absurd. They do, however, betray a lack of breadth of vision, as Dönitz himself admitted at Nuremberg. There he said that everyone kept to his own domain and Hitler alone had an overall view of things.[55]

It should be added that Dönitz had long been convinced – perhaps even before he became C-in-C of the Navy – that militarily the war could hardly be won. Even after the French campaign he had felt that the war would be long and at best would be brought to an end by general exhaustion and weariness. In his view it depended on who could hold out the longest. Obviously he could not voice such an opinion. His hope was that a revival of the shipping war with the new marks of U-boat would make the British 'ripe for negotiations'.

In his reference to 'unexpected political developments' Dönitz was counting on a split in the enemy alliance. He only seriously began to reckon on this, however, after capitulation.[56] Naval Headquarters appreciations of 20 May and 20 August 1943 had laid much emphasis on the disagreements within the enemy alliance, particularly between Great Britain and the United States. The Naval Headquarters War Diary of 13 April 1945 referred to the possible far-reaching consequences of Roosevelt's death. Both the appreciations and the war diary entry, however, were the work of Admiral Meisel, the Head of Naval Operations, and his staff officer, Captain Pfeiffer. Dönitz himself, in his Order of 11 April 1945, had warned against such wishful thinking:

> Capitulation means for certain the occupation of the whole of Germany by the Allies along the lines of partition discussed by them at Yalta. It means also, therefore, the ceding to Russia of further considerable parts of Germany west of the river Oder. Or does anyone think that at that stage the Anglo-Saxons will not keep to their agreements and will oppose a further advance of the Russian hordes into Germany with armed force and will begin a war against Russia for our sake? The reasoning: 'Let the Anglo-Saxons into the country, then at least the Russians will not come' is faulty too.[57]

This argument he was using merely to counter the danger of war weariness.

As a further explanation for his attitude Dönitz cited the number of soldiers who, in the event of capitulation during the winter 1944/45, would have fallen into Russian hands and probably been condemned to die a miserable death from hunger and cold.[58] This does not seem to have been an argument adduced *post hoc* in order to excuse himself. He had apparently already used it in late autumn 1944 against any idea of ending the war; at that time too he had referred to the vast areas which would fall to Russia in accordance with Allied plans known to the German High Command. The point, of course, begs the question whether a greater total of civilian and military casualties was not incurred by prolonging the war for several months. The fact remains, however, that during his short period as Head of State Dönitz did succeed in saving thousands of people from Soviet captivity and an unknown fate.[59]

All these considerations no doubt played some part in determining his attitude. The decisive factor, however, was his well-nigh limitless confidence in Hitler. He never made any secret of his admiration. In his secret order of 11 April 1945 already quoted, he said: 'At the latest next year, perhaps even this year, Europe will recognise that Adolf Hitler is the only statesman of stature in Europe' and again: 'In Hitler I saw a powerful personality who had extraordinary intelligence and energy and a practically universal knowledge, from whom power seemed to emanate and who was possessed of a remarkable power of suggestion.'[60] Since he had apparently never received an order from Hitler 'which in any way violated military ethics', he saw 'no reason at all to break with the Führer'.[61] This remark, made at Nuremberg, is not entirely truthful, since Hitler had ordered action against men in the water and denunciation of the Geneva Convention. Dönitz, who always insisted upon the observance of fair methods of warfare, refused to accept either order.[62] His code of honour, however, forbade him to vilify a man whom he had served for so long, even when his eyes had been opened to Hitler's true character: 'Of course we all know better now, but we cannot deny that we followed him then. That is why I did not want to attack Hitler.'[63]

Basically Dönitz was a completely non-political character who acknowledged the primacy of politics and whose concept of the soldier's duty to obey was absolute; accordingly he failed to distinguish between devotion to duty and unconditional loyalty to his superiors, between obedience and patriotism, particularly seeing that he regarded National-Socialism as a programme for the renewal of Germany rather than a party and Hitler as a being of mythical stature.

'I am a firm adherent of the idea of ideological education. For what is it in the main? Doing his duty is a matter of course for the soldier. But the full value, the whole weight of duty done, is only present when the heart and spiritual conviction have a voice in the matter. Doing his duty is then quite different from what it would be if he only carried out his task literally, obediently and faithfully. It is therefore necessary for the soldier to support the execution of his duty with all his mental, all his spiritual energy; and for this his conviction, his ideology are indispensable. It is therefore necessary for us to train the soldier uniformly, comprehensively, that he may be adjusted ideologically to our Germany.'[64]

A few sentences later it is quite clear: he equates ideology – National-Socialist ideology – with patriotism: 'The soldier embodies the State in which he lives; he is the representative, articulate exponent of his State. He must therefore stand with his whole weight behind this State.' For him therefore Hitler, National-Socialism, the State and Germany were one and the same notion. So he could say: 'From the very start the whole of the officer corps must be so indoctrinated that it feels itself co-responsible for the National-Socialist State in its entirety. The officer is the exponent of the State. The idle chatter that the officer is non-political is sheer nonsense.'[65]

As a result of this identification of Hitler with Germany and of the widespread naval complex about unconditional loyalty to those in authority, stemming from the memory of the 1918 fleet mutiny, Dönitz was categorically opposed to the German resisters and above all to the coup of 20 July 1944. This he regarded simply as high treason, all the more serious in that it was committed in the midst of a war which he considered a struggle of destiny. His proclamation on that occasion ran: 'Men of the Navy! Holy wrath and unlimited anger fill our hearts because of the criminal attempt which was to have cost the life of our beloved Führer. Providence wished it otherwise, watched over and protected our Führer, and did not abandon our German Fatherland in the fight for its destiny.'[66]

In his memoirs Dönitz' attitude to this problem is far less extreme. Politically he still considers the 20 July coup a mistake, since it carried with it too great a danger of civil war and might have led to the growth of another 'stab-in-the-back' legend. Nevertheless he respects the moral motives of the conspirators because 'they were aware of the mass murders that had been committed by the Hitler regime'.[67]

To the end of April, therefore, both in word and deed Dönitz supported Hitler's obduracy in refusing to admit the facts of military and political defeat. Moreover precise knowledge of the enemy plans reinforced him in his uncompromising attitude. During the Ardennes offensive the Wehrmacht had captured a copy of 'Operation Eclipse' giving Allied plans and preparations for the occupation of Germany. It included 'destruction of the military power of the Reich for all time' and 'complete suppression of the NSDAP'; on the attitude of Allied troops it said: 'From the outset it must be made clear to the Germans that they are a beaten nation.'[68]

When Dönitz took leave of Hitler on 21 April, he was determined to organise the defence of the Northern Zone down to the last detail. He worked on the principle of maximum simplicity and refused to deal with too many authorities. All civil affairs were dealt with by Paul Wegener,[69] the Gauleiter of Bremen; he had been appointed Supreme Reich Defence Commissar by Hitler on 23 April – at Dönitz' instigation – and took over his duties on 24 April. His subordinates were the Gauleiters, who worked in the closest possible contact with the Commanders-in-Chief of Army Groups and Armies, by-passing the Reich Minister. Certain of the Ministers had only left Berlin for Eutin on 20/21 April and at a conference held in the Eutin local council offices at 3.0 p.m. on 25 April they protested against these arrangements, pointing out to Wegener that 'the plenary powers conferred on the Grand Admiral were not compatible with the prerogatives of the Reich government, since his duties were confined to defence and his area to the Northern Zone'. Agreement was eventually reached that the work of the Ministries should continue and instructions affecting the Northern Zone should be passed to Gauleiter Wegener via Dr. Stuckart, the State Secretary in the Ministry of the Interior.[70] A few hours later (5.0 p.m.) Schwerin von Krosigk, the senior Minister, informed Dönitz of this arrangement, on which occasion the Admiral stressed the importance in the interests of the maintenance of order, of 'all military, State and Party authorities receiving their instructions from *one* source only'.

Even at this point, therefore, Dönitz was claiming for himself the authority of the Führer principle, according to which both political and military power of command lay in the hands of one man. In conversation with Schwerin von Krosigk he made a further significant remark. A little earlier Wegener had told Ministers that negotiations must be opened with the British in order that all available forces might be used against the Russians – a point of view which he says he represented to Hitler during the previous night; Dönitz, however, took another view: he was a soldier, he said, and was carrying out a definite task allotted to him by the supreme authorities of the State. So long as the political leadership thought it right, he would hold the Western Front against the British and send his U-boats out against England. If some different order was given, then he would act in accordance with that order. This was only the second time that the Finance Minister had met Dönitz – the first being in 1943 on the occasion of Dönitz' appointment as C-in-C of the Navy; von Krosigk pointed out that, in view of the severe fighting in Berlin, it would, in his view, shortly be necessary for Dönitz to act on his own initiative in political matters.

At the time Dönitz seems to have rejected this idea. He was still striving primarily for no more than a precise definition of his authority. Hitler's order issued during the night 24/25 April, laying down that his operational powers would not yet come into force,[71] he described as a serious disadvantage and arranged a discussion on the subject with OKW for 27 April.

OKW had meanwhile moved from Krampnitz to Neu-Rooten, south-west of Fürstenberg. In addition, during the same night 24/25 April Hitler had placed the General Staff of the Army (Operations) under the Chief of OKW, thus making OKW responsible for operations on the Eastern Front and putting an end to the perennial disagreements about the higher organisation of the Wehrmacht. In view of the general dispersal of authority and confusion of command channels, however, this order had no practical effect.

At the 27 April conference in OKW it was agreed that, as long as Hitler was exercising command from Berlin, OKW should remain responsible for operations in the Northern Zone; the Grand Admiral's plenary powers in regard to defence preparations in that zone, however, remained. The question of the succession to Hitler was also raised. Himmler behaved as if he was the established successor and was careful to say nothing of his capitulation offer to the West. He asked Dönitz if he would serve under him if Göring became Head of State and he (Himmler) became Reich Chancellor, as Göring had promised him.[72] Dönitz replied that he would place his services at the disposal of any government nominated by the Führer.[73] The answer shows Dönitz still firm in his conviction that the soldier owed unconditional obedience to the political leaders. The assurance came all the easier, however, in that he now no longer believed that any action could be effective. The discussions of the last few days had given him an overall view of the situation for the first time and shown him with horrifying clarity the inevitability of collapse.

On 24 April Ganzenmüller, the State Secretary in the Ministry of Transport, had stated that railway locomotives would have to be turned over to wood firing, since coal stocks had shrunk to a minimum. All passenger traffic had been cancelled to allow movement of troops, armaments and food to continue.

In the Navy the catastrophic fuel position had already led to drastic economy measures. All training of U-boat crews ceased. Only the most essential escorts were kept in service. The big passenger ships which had been carrying refugees and wounded in the Baltic also had to be laid off. The food position was more than critical. The Northern Zone's reserves of meat, fat and sugar were sufficient for a short time but the situation was bound to deteriorate rapidly with the loss of Mecklenburg, now clearly imminent.

On 25 April Dönitz had stated that decision on the question whether the struggle should be continued or abandoned was 'exclusively the business of the State leadership as represented by the Führer and no one had the right to depart from the line laid down by the Führer', adding: 'Since capitulation in effect means the destruction of the German people, it is from this viewpoint right to continue the fight.'

His visit to OKW followed by a briefing from Major-General von Trotha, Chief of Staff to Army Group Vistula, together with the miserable sight of the endless columns of refugees, must have extinguished his last hopes and illusions and brought him the bitter realisation that the enemy had won and that Germany *was* 'a beaten nation'. On returning to Plön Dönitz summoned his son-in-law, Commander Günter Hessler,[74] and told him drily and unemotionally that all resistance would shortly become impossible and therefore futile. In view of the situation in Berlin he did not think that there would be any successor to Hitler. He proposed to capitulate with the formations under his command and himself seek death in battle.

Hessler interposed to ask whether it would not be better, in the approaching chaos, for the Admiral to intervene on the side of discipline and order with all the weight of his authority. Dönitz, however, replied that defeat was so complete and the crash so great that it must bring with it the collapse of all values. Germany would take years to recover from this catastrophe and it might then be important for people to know that, even in so hopeless a situation, there had been men who had the courage to draw the correct conclusions without thought of themselves. His death would also be an act of atonement and remove from the Navy the slur which might attach to it if it capitulated on its own account. Dönitz then dismissed Hessler, asking him henceforth to regard himself as head of the family and take care of his wife and daughter. Hessler has never doubted Dönitz' sincerity on this occasion. For any military man in those days death was so close, so familiar that his father-in-law's decision seemed almost a matter of course.

Dönitz told no one else of his intentions, not even his aide, with whom he normally discussed everything. His nickname among his U-boat crews was 'The Lion' because of his courage, his efficiency and his fighting spirit; to raise their morale he had been prepared to use Goebbels' propaganda jargon, even though he might have his own doubts; he had radiated confidence in victory so long as even a glimmer of an improvement in the situation remained; but as far as his personal feelings and interests were concerned he was taciturn and reserved. He demanded much both of himself and others.

The last days of April can only have reinforced Dönitz' decision. On the 29th he received von Greim, the C-in-C of the Luftwaffe, who had left Berlin, wounded, before Hitler's last testament had been drafted. Greim was still harbouring illusory hopes – a further illustration both of the refusal to accept realities prevalent in the Führer's bunker and of the power of suggestion which the tyrant could still exert, even though physically and mentally a sick man.[75] Dönitz, not having been recently exposed to Hitler's direct influence, was more alive to the overall situation.

Also on the 29th the British captured a bridgehead over the Elbe; Army Group Vistula and Twelfth Army were both disintegrating and withdrawing westwards, so Dönitz thought it right to refuse them further reinforcements and use all available troops against the British in order to keep open a door to the west. Then arrived the news that coal stocks for shipping and shipyards would last only another ten days and no further supplies could be foreseen. Briefing conferences with Field Marshals von Bock and von Manstein completed the picture of misery.

On 30 April Dönitz decided to visit Himmler in Lübeck, where the latter had set up headquarters in the police barracks, show him Bormann's telegram about his 'treachery' and clarify the situation. Shortly before he left, a teleprinter message from Kaufmann, the Gauleiter of Hamburg, was shown to him.

Karl Kaufmann, Reich Commissar and Reich Defence Commissar, in a discussion with Hitler on 3 April had refused to turn Hamburg into a fortress and had thereupon been relieved of his offices as Reich Defence Commissar North Sea Coast and Reich Commissar for Sea Transport. All merchant shipping had been placed under Dönitz, who on 18 April nominated Rear-Admiral Engelhardt Head of Sea Transport.[76] Kaufmann, who was a friend of Speer's, wished to hand over the North Sea Coast area to the Western Allies and tried to rally to this plan the North German Gauleiter and Field Marshal Busch. He was only partially successful and was eventually reduced to attempting to arrange an independent capitulation for Hamburg. Using G. F. Duckwitz, the shipping expert in Copenhagen, as go-between, via the Danish Resistance he requested the British War Office to accelerate the advance of British troops towards Hamburg and Lübeck. Even the leader of Werwolf [the German partisan organisation], Obergruppenführer [SS General] Prützmann, seems to have tried to negotiate a peaceful hand-over of the city to the British.[77] In parallel, but initially independently, Riensberg, another shipping expert, started peace negotiations in Stockholm for the North German area. Eventually Riensberg's and Kaufmann's actions converged.

Dönitz had heard of Kaufmann's activities through Field Marshal Busch and Ohlendorf,[78] Head of Amt III in the RSHA, parts of whose intelligence service were functioning in the

Northern Zone. On several occasions he invited Kaufmann to a meeting but the latter refused, fearing that he would be arrested. At this point, however, his efforts to save the city of Hamburg from a final senseless battle – which he ultimately succeeded in doing – seemed to cut across Dönitz' aim which was to keep the Schleswig-Holstein area free for the flood of refugees from the east. He therefore told his aide to draft a telegram to Kaufmann setting out his view of the situation and the resulting requirements. While Dönitz was in discussion with Himmler in Lübeck (Himmler dismissed his negotiations with Count Bernadotte as rumour) Lüdde-Neurath drafted the reply to Kaufmann. Owing to delays in radio communications the telegram was not delivered until 9.0 p.m.; it stressed that the main concern of the military authorities was 'to save German territory and German people from Bolshevism'. To allow people to escape from the Russian troops they must be held in the Mecklenburg area as long as possible and a 'door to the West' kept open in the demarcation line agreed at Yalta. From this it followed that the Elbe position must still be tenaciously defended against the West and in this the city of Hamburg could make a contribution. Destruction of property was justified only if it was in furtherance of this object.

Dönitz and his aide returned to the Plön command post late on the afternoon of 30 April. Admiral Kummertz, Commander-in-Chief Baltic, was waiting to report on the situation in his area and on current sea movements. Speer, whom Dönitz regarded as a friend and who had the entrée to him at all times, was also in attendance. At 6.35 p.m. the first radio message from Bormann arrived, telling Dönitz that he was Hitler's successor.

CHAPTER TWO

The Private Office and Albert Speer

Dönitz' initial reaction was one of astonishment. Though others had perhaps foreseen the possibility,[1] to him the nomination was completely unexpected. The military was his natural milieu; his ambition was restricted solely to his Service. For its sake he had striven to the end and, when all his efforts had failed, had been driven to the conclusion that the only logical course was to capitulate with his Navy and then hope to die in battle. Now he was faced with a task for which he was unprepared and which was foreign to his nature. Naturally his thoughts turned at once to its military implications. He had already decided to surrender the Navy. Accordingly he conceived Hitler's arrangements for the succession as indicating that the entire Wehrmacht should now capitulate. 'His death was his final service to his people. He had realised that there was no military way of altering the outcome of the war. He therefore sacrificed himself to leave the way clear for someone else to end the war. This was what the Grand Admiral was commissioned to do.'[2] Solely for this reason, he thought, had the Führer selected him, the only available Commander-in-Chief now that Göring had been eliminated. He never saw the full text of Hitler's testament until Nuremberg.[3]

Later that evening he was visited by Admiral Godt, an old friend with whom he had worked on submarines since 1938.[4] Dönitz told him that he wished to end matters; the time for heroism was past. Fighting in the East could not, however, be ended at once; the refugees from Mecklenburg must first be got back and that initially implied continuing to fight on the Elbe. People like Field Marshal Schörner, moreover, would not easily abandon the struggle and very few troops would be prepared to give themselves up to the Russians.

To Godt Dönitz seemed a changed man. He knew nothing of the intention to surrender the Navy and had thought it likely that Dönitz would order a fight to the end. Was this sudden change, which even those closest to him found astounding, the result of some internal process which had long been gestating and had now come to the surface in a reaction of liberation and relief? Or was Dönitz hoping that Hitler's death would usher in a new phase in which, while continuing to employ some forces in the West, the fight in the East could be carried on, perhaps even with the support of the West?

In his conversation with Bernadotte on 24 April Himmler had equally stated that resistance on the Eastern Front should be continued for some time. Himmler and Dönitz both agreed that avoidance of chaos was the primary consideration. It was therefore essential to give both the refugees and the troops the possibility of withdrawing into areas to be occupied by the Western Powers. Horror and fear of the Russians were too great. In fact the Soviet troops' behaviour was no 'natural addiction to atrocities on the part of Asiatic hordes' but the answer to years of inhuman treatment of Russians by Germans; this does not alter the fact however that, in all his planning, Dönitz had to take account of this fear psychosis – and he knew that that fear was justified.

As Hitler's successor Dönitz initially relied on his own immediate staff. Like Admiral Godt, they were naval officers. First there was Rear-Admiral Gerhard Wagner, who had been liaison officer between the Commander-in-Chief of the Navy and Naval Headquarters since June 1944.[5] When Dönitz was appointed Head of State Wagner offered his resignation but Dönitz wished to keep him as a 'familiar face'. As his own successor in command of the Navy he nominated Admiral von Friedeburg, the Admiral Submarines,[6] and so he appointed Wagner Military Representative on his personal staff and a few days later Director of the Military Cabinet. Since the whole office consisted of one person only, Wagner thought this title too portentous and called himself 'Admiral Specially Employed, attached to the Grand Admiral'.[7] On 30 April Dönitz discussed the new situation with Wagner and his personal aide, Walter Lüdde-Neurath;[8] the latter had been with him since September 1944, accompanied him everywhere, took part in all naval discussions, and had usually been with him in the Führer's headquarters. Although Lüdde-Neurath kept strictly to his job, Dönitz always valued his opinion – perhaps the secret of his success as a commander was that he was always ready to listen to the views of others. He would accept only well-founded criticism, however; everything else he rejected, frequently in somewhat over-brusque terms.

Dönitz' real adviser in the early stages, however, was not a Navy professional but a civilian, the 'Führer's architect', the Reich Minister for Armaments and War Production, Albert Speer. In early May 1945 his influence was so great that a short description of his personality is not out of place. Trevor-Roper describes him as 'intellectually uncorrupted' but nevertheless 'the real criminal':[9] now forty years old, he had been one of the most powerful men in Hitler's State, the archetype of the 'blinkered specialist and amoral technocrat' (Joachim Fest's description). Had it not been for Speer, undoubtedly Hitler could not have carried on his war so long.

Albert Speer was born on 19 March 1905. Originally he had no intention of becoming an architect like his father and grandfather but leant more towards mathematics and physics. Finally tradition won the day, however, and he studied architecture at Karlsruhe, Munich and Berlin Technical High Schools (at the latter his grandfather had been taught by the well-known architect Schinkel). In 1928 he gained his diploma and from 1929 to 1932 was assistant to Professor Tessenow at the Charlottenburg Technical High School. During this period he became connected with the Nazi Party and joined it on 1 March 1931. Becoming a freelance architect in 1932, he undertook certain small jobs, mostly rebuilding, on behalf of the Party. Goebbels soon noticed him and took him on his staff. The May Day festival of 1933, which the new government had made official, gave Speer his first opportunity of demonstrating his ability to stage-manage vast mass demonstrations. Domes of light, clusters of flags and imposing façades produced an ideal setting for the art of demagogic seduction. A contemporary critic found it indicative that 'the National-Socialist era was the first to give new significance to streets and squares by filling large areas with ordered masses of men'. No wonder that Hitler's attention was soon drawn to the gifted young architect.

From this time on Speer had 'an absorbing task'.[10] He built the stadium on the Bückeburg where the Harvest Thanksgiving festivities took place; he designed the buildings for the Party Rally in Nuremberg; he became Head of the 'Beauty of Work' office in the 'Strength through Joy' organisation; he had a hand in the reconstruction and redecoration of the German Embassy in London, the German House and the International Exhibition in Paris. In 1937 Rudolf Hess, the Führer's Deputy, appointed him to his staff as 'Architectural Representative' and he thus became responsible for all buildings belonging to the Party and its affiliated organisations. Even more important was his nomination on 30 January 1937 as General Architectural Inspector for the Reich capital; he was now responsible for putting into practice Hitler's architectural fantasies. The result was a style which has been termed 'crazy monumentality', based on the Vienna classical form, which Hitler never ceased to admire. Between 1937 and 1939 the dictator and 'his artist' established a very close relationship. At Nuremberg Speer said: 'If Hitler had had any friends at all, I certainly would have been one of his close friends.'[11] During the early war years they drifted apart, but in 1942 Speer, now 36, was given a job which once more brought him into official contact with Hitler; he became Minister for Armaments and Munitions in place of Dr. Fritz Todt, who had been killed in an aeroplane accident on 8 February under somewhat mysterious circumstances. One of the main activities of this Ministry so far had been construction – hence Speer's nomination. The losses of the Russian winter campaign of 1941/42 had led to increased Army equipment requirements, but Speer found that in autumn 1941, on Hitler's orders, production had been deferred in favour of the Luftwaffe.

During 1942 Speer also took over the OKW Armaments Office and became Armaments Plenipotentiary for the Four Year Plan, which in effect gave him authority over the entire Plan. With Field Marshal Milch and Körner he directed the central planning. Following the Führer's decree of 2 September 1943 on concentration of powers in the war economy field, the authority hitherto exercised by the Ministry of Economics over raw materials and production for industry and manufacture was transferred to Speer, who was henceforth entitled Reich Minister for Armaments and War Production. He also assumed responsibility for distribution on behalf of the Reich Ministry of Economics and by 1943 was supervising certain sectors of production which placed him in complete control of coal and chemicals. By his totally unorthodox methods he soon succeeded in eliminating the worst bottlenecks. He proved to be a master of improvisation. He formed his own working staff of qualified experts[12] and rode roughshod over all bureaucratic obstacles and rules. Success seemed to prove him right. In 1944 he achieved record figures for production of ammunition, weapons, aircraft and U-boats.[13] If his published figures are to be believed production in that year could have equipped 225 completely new infantry divisions and 45 Panzer divisions for the Army. Such a level of production was only possible by concentrating exclusively on armaments at the expense of other branches of the economy, and by ruthless use and exploitation of the labour force provided by foreign workers and concentration camp prisoners.

By 1944, however, it was clear to Speer that, from the technical production point of view, the war was lost. All his expert improvisation could not conceal the fact that the German economy was being destroyed and that large sectors of industry were lying idle or had been demolished.

Between June and December 1944 he sent twelve memoranda to Hitler warning him of approaching catastrophe.[14] On 30 June he informed him that enemy action had raised the aircraft fuel shortfall to 90%; inevitably therefore by September 'the quantities required to cover the most urgent needs of the Wehrmacht cannot possibly be supplied any longer, which means that from that time on there will be a deficiency which cannot be made good and which must lead to tragic consequences'.[15] On 30 August he told his Head of State and Supreme Commander officially that in certain vital sectors all raw materials necessary for the further prosecution of the war were now deficient. In September an article in *Völkischer Beobachter* by Sündermann, Deputy Head of the Press Department, announced the 'scorched earth' policy and this caused Speer to act. He set out systematically to ensure that the measures of destruction planned by the political and military leaders were changed to ones producing temporary paralysis only.

On 5 September he wrote to Gauleiter Simon in Coblenz: 'Under *all* circumstances it must be ensured that, in so far as Lorraine, Luxemburg and other industrial areas fall into enemy hands, industries are paralysed only; in other words industry should be brought to a standstill for a few months by the removal of certain assemblies, usually electrical; the installation itself should not be damaged.'

He wrote in similar terms to all the Gauleiters. He gave the necessary instructions to the Reich Iron and Coal Board. He also took steps to ensure that there was no destruction in Upper and Lower Silesia, Czechoslovakia, Austria, France, Belgium, Holland, Finland, Upper Italy and Hungary.[16] All this was of course contrary to official policy and he could only work by subterfuge. Jodl was turning a blind eye but Hitler had to be won over by argument. On 15 September Speer sent the following to Bormann: 'The Führer has stated that he will shortly be able to complete the recovery of the territories now lost to us. Since, from the point of view of armaments and war production, the western areas are vital, the measures proposed in the event of evacuation should be cancelled in order that industry there may quickly resume activity.'[17] His high-handed actions earned him the enmity of Bormann and Goebbels, who described his Ministry as 'anti-Party' and 'a sink of reactionary businessmen'.

But Speer stood up to Hitler, arguing that his duties were non-political. He continued to bombard the Dictator with memoranda, to sabotage his plans for destruction and systematically to switch over from war to peace. When the Allies resumed their advance in mid-March, the official line became more stringent. On 18 March Hitler had eight officers shot for failing to blow up a bridge. On the same day Speer sent an outspoken letter to Hitler, stressing that no one had the right to destroy industrial installations, food stores, traffic facilities or bridges since 'they robbed the German people of further possibilities of existence'. 'We have no right', he continued, 'at this stage of the war to carry out destruction which might affect the life of the people.'[18] This missive he handed to Hitler personally. The Dictator countered with his famous disquisition about the people being lost if the war was lost, since they had proved themselves the weaker in face of the eastern peoples. In *Mein Kampf*, after all, he had said: 'The masses are but a part of nature herself. Their feeling is such that they cannot understand mutual handshakings between men who are declared enemies. Their wish is to see the stronger side win and the weaker wiped out or subjected unconditionally to the will of the stronger.'[19]

Hitler's ideology was a mere eclectic series of haphazard snippets from social-Darwinist theory, but its central tenet was the primacy of power. This was the background to his 'ice-cold' attitude to the fate of his people, demonstrated next day in his 'Scorched Earth' order of 19 March,[20] supplemented by Bormann's demolition and evacuation order of 23 March and the corresponding military directives.

Without compunction the Führer of the Great German Reich would have allowed the German people to go under, had not Speer assumed responsibility for counter-measures. He journeyed tirelessly to visit Gauleiters and Army Group Commanders; he brought pressure to bear on Field Marshals Model and Kesselring; he issued drafts of OKW orders prescribing preservation of communications and industrial installations; he ordered explosives to be dumped in coal shafts; in short he did everything to counter the official Scorched Earth policy.

He was the sole Minister who had the courage to oppose Hitler openly and sabotage his pathological thirst for destruction. He was helped by a number of professionals, being in close contact with the State Secretaries in the Ministries of Food, Transport and Propaganda, who co-ordinated all the necessary measures between themselves. Food supply to the population was given precedence over arms production and all provisions for destruction or paralysation of industry postponed until the last moment.

On 29 March Speer was summoned to Hitler and accused of sabotaging his orders. Had he not been 'his artist', Hitler said, he would have condemned him to death. Speer asked for no consideration for himself, merely saying that he did not wish to be one of those who thought as he did but had not the courage to say so. He refused to go on leave as Hitler suggested, saying that at this point he thought it his duty to remain. For both internal and external political reasons Hitler does not seem to have had the courage to dismiss him. The argument and a consequential letter from Speer on 29 March scored at least a partial success – in his executive instruction of 30 March Hitler in effect cancelled his Scorched Earth order and changed it into one for paralysation.[21]

Speer's sole concern really seems to have been to preserve some basis of existence for the German people; apparently he had no other purpose – unlike Schwerin von Krosigk, who thought the maintenance of a German potential might be a factor in future negotiations. Moreover, when he heard of Germany's catastrophic financial situation, Speer offered to make over to the

Reich all the income he had earned as an architect over the last twelve years.

During the closing months of the war Speer's circle frequently discussed assassination attempts against Hitler. Contacts were established with the SS. Only Speer's own preparations progressed beyond the planning stage. There is much evidence, however, that he was in fact relieved when his preparations were scotched by technical difficulties.

At the same time Speer also planned to eliminate Himmler and his circle. With the assistance of the State Secretary in the Propaganda Ministry, he drafted a speech to be broadcast on 9 April, but Goebbels intervened and it was never made. [22]

Thereupon, on 16 April, Speer drafted a further speech, intended to usher in the final phase, [23] the text of which was recorded in the Hamburg Radio Station on 21 April. In essence the speech called on the German people to take courage and exhorted them to avoid anything which might lead to a curtailment of their basis for existence – industries were not to be paralysed and detonators were to be removed from demolition charges on bridges. Simultaneously Speer called on the enemy to stop the air war on humanitarian grounds. He ordered all prisoners of war to remain where they were, political prisoners and Jews to be separated from common criminals in the concentration camps and the death penalty to be suspended. He called on officials to remain at their posts, describing the administration as a necessary instrument if difficulties were to be surmounted. He banned the partisan movement [Werwolf]. In addition the speech contained practical instructions for the avoidance of damage and the re-establishment of communications, which, Speer said, could be functioning adequately again in a short time. Industry and the farming community were encouraged to further efforts.

The speech was never broadcast in full. On 3 May Speer gave a revised version over Flensburg Radio relayed to Radio Copenhagen; it was also broadcast simultaneously from Oslo and Prague. The ban on the Werwolf was omitted, as were the instructions for concentration camps and prevention of destruction; the paragraph about officials and the administration had also disappeared. Instead Speer had inserted a few sentences about Dönitz' programme for rescuing the maximum number of people from the clutches of the Russian armies. The reason – on 30 April Speer had gone over to Dönitz' headquarters to help him deal with his initial problems, pending clarification of the question of who were to be his most important associates.

CHAPTER THREE

The Military Advisers –
Wilhelm Keitel and Alfred Jodl

FOR his duties as Supreme Commander of the Wehrmacht Dönitz could call upon the highest military organisation, the 'Oberkommando der Wehrmacht' (OKW)under Field Marshal Keitel, together with its operational section, the OKW Operations Staff under Colonel-General Jodl. Under the latter had been placed on 28 April the General Staff of the Army (Operations Division).[1] Further, Dönitz could call upon the Headquarters of Zone A (North) and Zone B (South) already mentioned.

On receipt of the first radio message from the Führer's bunker, however, and before exercising the powers of his office, Dönitz had to meet these senior Wehrmacht representatives and discover whether and to what extent they were willing to obey his orders. This was even more necessary in the case of Himmler, who commanded the Waffen-SS, the police and the Replacement Army. It was quite within the bounds of possibility that the Reichsführer-SS would contest the validity of the message and proclaim himself Hitler's successor. Late on the evening of 30 April Dönitz told his aide to call OKW, which had meanwhile moved to Dobbin, and summon Keitel and Jodl to Plön with all necessary documents. Himmler, still in Lübeck, was also informed. At first the Reichsführer-SS refused to come. After a personal appeal from Dönitz, however, he appeared about midnight with an escort of six gigantic SS men. On the urgent advice of Gauleiter Wegener Dönitz had equally provided himself with a guard of reliable submarine sailors, who surrounded the C-in-C's hut. On his table, hidden under files, he had a revolver with the safety catch off. There could be no more striking illustration of their mutual distrust.[2] Dönitz' arrangements, moreover, show that the problem was one of pure power politics, not differing views about future policy or even moral considerations.

Himmler reacted quickly to the new situation. On reading the message appointing Dönitz the successor, he blenched for a moment but recovered himself quickly and asked whether he might be Number Two in the State. It is impossible to say whether this was a tactical manœuvre in the hope of seizing power later, or his habitual subservience to any decision of Hitler's – even this final one; alternatively it may have been lack of force of character to oppose the Grand Admiral's authority or the result of life-long submission to the precept of the 'good of the State'. Dönitz on his side played for time. He could not ignore the realities of power; Himmler was in command of the SS, the police and the Replacement Army and could mobilise them for his own purposes; against them Dönitz could only set a few naval units. He therefore pointed out the necessity for non-political leadership and suggested that initially the problem of Himmler's further employment be left pending.[3]

The discussion with Keitel and Jodl took place on 1 May, by which time Dönitz knew that Hitler's testament was in force. Being no expert in land warfare, he had wished to replace Keitel by Field Marshal von Manstein, whom he had met a few days earlier and who had stressed the necessity of withdrawing the eastern armies and bringing them nearer to the Western Front.[4] Owing to a misunderstanding or a failure of communications, however, the appointment was never made.

Wilhelm Keitel, Hitler's 'chef de bureau',[5] Dönitz considered ill-equipped to deal with the pressing operational problems of the time, since he had long been away from troops; he also knew that Keitel was unpopular in many Wehrmacht circles. Jodl, on the other hand, he rated high and considered his experience in tactical and strategical matters and his mastery of the technical machine to be indispensable. Since Jodl declared that, if Keitel were dismissed, he would go too, both the previous 'operational assistants' remained.

Both these two highest-ranking professional officers of the Third Reich were hanged in Nuremberg, but the latest German historical interpretations have partially rehabilitated Keitel. Walter Görlitz, for instance, in his picture of the Field Marshal, shows clearly the dilemma in which 'Hitler's Berthier' was placed, acting partly as a War Minister, partly as a State Secretary, partly as Chief of Staff to a non-existent War Minister, and with no command authority of his own.

Keitel came from the Hanover countryside, had originally been an artillery officer and had risen to the rank of Captain during World War I when he had held a junior staff appointment. In the 1920s he had served in the Organisation Section of the Reichswehr Ministry and become a Section Head. After the usual period of service with troops as artillery regimental commander, he had been given a division. In 1935 the then Reichswehr Minister and Commander-in-Chief of the Wehrmacht, Field Marshal von Blomberg, selected him to succeed von Reichenau at the head of the Wehrmacht Office, confident that he would not be cantankerous or have any too original ideas. For these same reasons when Blomberg had to retire on 4 February 1938[6] and Hitler took over command of the Wehrmacht, Keitel was retained as Chief of OKW.

Keitel has been habitually portrayed as a typical product of the cadet corps and military training, but Görlitz throws considerable doubt on this somewhat trite judgement. Nevertheless, the standard picture is confirmed rather than denied by Keitel's undoubted organisational ability (he has been referred to as a 'military management virtuoso') and by a loyalty to his Head of State, rooted in tradition and recognising no mutual obligation or scale of values.

Keitel's most outstanding qualities were his incredible industry and a conciliatory manner. He was almost painfully conscientious, the typical obsequious, pliable subordinate. He was not suited to be a military commander. He regarded himself as insignificant and did not therefore dare to voice a contrary opinion. He could not stand up to a dictator like Hitler.

It is of course to Keitel's credit that he consistently opposed Himmler's claims to power – but this he did, not on moral grounds, but because he wished to keep military power in the hands of those qualified to exercise it.

Keitel does not seem to have realised the full implications of what he had done until in the dock at Nuremberg. Not a strong personality, he buried his head in the sand in the face of distasteful facts foreign to the concepts of a German officer brought up in the strict traditions of dignity and good order, and this escapist complex was reinforced by Hitler's frequent remarks about 'things which were nothing to do with him as a soldier' and the trappings of Prussianism with which the Dictator deliberately surrounded himself in order to simulate a regime based on the traditional values. Keitel's workload was almost inconceivable, subjecting him to intense nervous and mental strain; he was exposed daily to the Führer's monologues; so he gladly left all responsibility to Hitler and regarded himself merely as a mouthpiece.[7] His anxiety to please was exemplified by the 'Keitel trot', a double-quick-time gait which he adopted when summoned by Hitler or Bormann. His nickname was even more revealing – 'Lakai-tel'.*

In his defence it should be recorded that, when later confronted with his responsibility at Nuremberg, he made no attempt to deny that morally a share of the blame was his. The criminal orders of which he was accused,[8] he said, had seemed to him 'disputable' even at the drafting stage. He had tried, if not to stop them, at least to water them down, in some cases by the usual procrastination tactics and in others by amendment. Hitler had then acted on his own. Nevertheless, as Erich Kordt has put it, 'by participating in and tolerating this monstrous misuse of the command mechanism, he destroyed the moral foundations of the army to which he had belonged for 40 years'.

Keitel was no criminal by nature; he was guilty simply of weakness and gullibility. That he suffered terribly when the whole enormity of the Hitler phenomenon was made clear to him is illustrated by an admission he made to the American psychologist, Gilbert: 'I suffer more agony of conscience and self-reproach in this cell than anyone will ever know. I believed in him so blindly.'[9]

In his testament Hitler vouchsafed no word of recognition to Keitel for his years of service; in fact everything goes to show that in the last few days he had fallen into disfavour.[10] Yet on 30 April (the exact time cannot be established) he drafted an informatory order for issue down to Commanders-in-Chief of Armies expressing complete devotion to the Dictator. Addressees were told that the Führer with his immediate entourage was remaining in Berlin to conduct the defence in person, whereas he, Keitel, would be outside the capital and direct the overall operation in accordance with Hitler's instructions. The order continued: 'The fate of Berlin will be the fate of the Führer. Should the Reich capital fall, the Führer, after a struggle of unparalleled heroism, will have sacrificed his life for the German people. The essential condition for the survival of the German

* Lakai in German = lackey.

Reich and people is therefore our political and military solidarity.'

Keitel then called upon the German Wehrmacht for 'unconditional obedience to the Head of State' and declared that continuation of the struggle was the sole means of preventing millions of German soldiers sinking into Bolshevism. Any unauthorised initiative and any surrender were strictly forbidden, both being characterised as treason. The order ended with the words: 'The Führer has staked his life for the German people. The fate of the German people depends on the steadfastness and loyalty of the German Wehrmacht.'

In a radio message to General Winter on the same day, however, Keitel admitted that the attempt to relieve Berlin had failed. He ordered concentration of all forces in the Northern Zone in order to keep open communications with Denmark. The Southern Zone was ordered to concentrate all its forces into a large area suitable for all-round defence, so as to save the maximum number of men and the maximum territory from the Red Army. If communications with the North were cut, they were to fight on in order to gain time politically. Any signs of disintegration were to be dealt with most severely. In the interests of better co-ordination Army Group South was placed under Army Group Centre.[11]

This directive fitted Dönitz' programme. Keitel noted at the same time that he and Jodl were agreed that the war must be brought to a rapid end as soon as they had succeeded in withdrawing major portions of the Eastern army.

No comprehensive biography so far exists of the Number Two in the military hierarchy, the far more interesting character.[12] Both his experience and his views in general ran parallel to those of Dönitz in many ways, which explains why Dönitz rated him so high that he was prepared to stomach Keitel.

Alfred Josef Ferdinand Jodl was another who 'fought the war in the belief that it was inevitable'.[13] He was oblivious to the fact that one of a soldier's responsibilities may be to prevent war.

Jodl was the son of a Bavarian artillery officer, born in Würzburg on 10 May 1890. He was therefore brought up in an atmosphere of military discipline and conformity, both at home and in the Munich Bavarian Cadet Corps, which he joined at the age of thirteen. In 1910 he was gazetted to 4 Bavarian Artillery Regiment in Augsburg, served as a young officer at the front in World War I and was wounded once.

As for most men of his generation the war was an over-whelming experience which coloured all his subsequent thoughts and actions. 'Battle as an inner experience' (Ernst Jünger's phrase) and the 'comradeship of the front' were no empty clichés to him; they signified a deep-felt sense of unity, to be preserved as transcending war and social barriers. The counterpart to the communal experience of battle should, in his view, be a true people's community and a new order of social life between human beings.

In an autobiography begun in Nuremberg Jodl described, in words characteristic of his generation of Germans, his reaction to the end of World War I: 'In summer 1918, when it became obvious that, in spite of all our victories and exertions, we were losing the war, I tried to explain to myself the reasons. I thought that they could be ascribed primarily to two facts: neither the social nor the State problems had been solved in Germany. The existence of the German *Länder* as independent states seemed to me ridiculous, and dangerous too; the party struggle, in particular that between the conservatives and social-democrats, I regarded as the cause of the complete cleavage among our people and of the munitions strike. The State had given the people no co-ordinated leadership. I thought that both the monarchy and the Kaiser himself had failed.'

Like so many others therefore, he felt that the war had been lost for internal political reasons – an error or a refusal to recognise the truth, the clearest expression of which was the 'stab-in-the-back' legend.

Young Jodl supported the Ebert Government in the hope that it would succeed 'in eliminating the anachronistic princely houses ... creating a unified Reich, perhaps even including Austria, and negotiating a tolerable peace'.

As with so many Germans of his generation, Jodl's political ideals were the creation of a 'popular community,' abolition of social barriers, revision of the Versailles Treaty and a greater Germany – all postulating a 'policy stemming from the heart', which National-Socialism so adroitly made its own.

When the republic proved an increasing disappointment, he turned to anti-liberal, anti-democratic and racialist ideas: 'There it was, this freedom-loving, democratic republic; there were no limits to its freedom. Blockheads and criminals fought for power;

nihilist eastern Jews and Spartacist fanatics were well on the way to domination of the leaderless decadent German citizenry. They were Moscow's first emissaries, though fortunately still without military power behind them.'

Jodl joined the 100,000-man army not entirely without hesitation. For a time he toyed with the idea of studying medicine but eventually turned professional soldier in the belief that a disciplined military force would be a factor in reinforcing the State's authority. He passed the 'Assistant Commanders' course (corresponding to the old Staff College) and in 1924 was given his first staff appointment in the headquarters of Wehrkreis [Military District] VII in Munich. Then he spent four years as instructor on the Assistant Commanders' course, during which time he gained a thorough grounding in military theory, and in 1932 was appointed to the Reichswehr Ministry.

Jodl's career (he was now a Lieutenant-Colonel) had so far followed a normal course but thenceforth promotion was rapid. In August 1935 he became Colonel, in April 1939 Major-General, on 19 July 1939 General (jumping the Lieutenant-General grade)[14] and on 1 February 1944 Colonel-General. From 1935 to autumn 1938 he had been Head of the National Defence Section in the Operations Branch of the German Armed Forces, the task of which was 'to prepare the operational employment of the Wehrmacht in accordance with the directives of the political leadership and to draft the basic directives and instructions for the organisation and supply of the Wehrmacht'. In October 1939 he was appointed Head of the OKW Operations Staff, into which the National Defence Section had developed.[15]

As soon as he joined the Reichswehr Ministry, Jodl found himself in conflict with the Army General Staff. His views on the true task of OKW and its Operations Staff were the direct opposite of those of the Army with its traditional continental outlook on strategy and its claim to overall strategic direction as its hereditary privilege. Pursuing the reorganisation of the higher echelons initiated by Field Marshal von Blomberg and General von Reichenau, the Head of the Wehrmacht Office, and in agreement with Keitel he insisted upon the equality of all three Services and their co-ordination by and subordination to a superior Wehrmacht headquarters.[16] This he frequently did with his customary asperity, earning himself many enemies in the process, a fact still detectable today in contemporary statements and literature. For instance, he had originally been on very good terms with Colonel-General Beck, the Army Chief of Staff, who had recommended him for the Wehrmacht Office in the belief that he would support the position of the Army staff. Their relations cooled noticeably, however, and ended in increasing estrangement.

Outwardly these disagreements were concerned purely with the principles of organisation, though the arguments used were frequently other than professional; in fact, however, they touched the fundamental question of ultimate command authority. Theoretically Jodl was right; he had realised the necessity for centralised military command in modern war and its subordination to political requirements – Roon's formula: 'Armed forces do not deliberate; they do as they are told.' His concept was invalidated, however, on the one hand by the deterioration of political leadership under totalitarianism and the fascination which Hitler exerted over the senior officers of oĸw, on the other hand by the moral factors which weighed with conservative Army opinion, quite apart from its outdated claim to predominance, and apart from military considerations and national or personal interests.

In the event Jodl did not succeed in pushing his reforms through and unified direction of the armed forces became further away than ever. Instead the leading military authorities became increasingly estranged both professionally and personally, the oĸw Operations Staff possessed no authority over the three Services and the command headquarters for which Jodl strove developed into a sort of bureau for the transmission and despatch of Hitler's orders. Keitel and Jodl made numerous attempts to reach a compromise between Hitler's requirements and the demands formulated by the military staffs. In general, however, the Services only accorded the oĸw Operations Staff some limited command authority when it was to their own advantage to do so.

The reason for this development lay partially in the disproportionately strong position of the Commanders-in-Chief of the Luftwaffe and Navy,[17] who guarded their interests jealously. The decisive factor, however, was that in 1941 Hitler himself took over command of the Army, and this resulted in the exclusion of the oĸw Operations Staff from the conduct of the war in the East apart from a few basic decisions. The Staff became less and less capable of fulfilling its real duty as the Supreme Commander's working staff for major decisions on allied strategy and as co-ordinator of the three Services. In fact it developed into a second Army operations staff for the so-called OKW theatres of war – Finland, Norway, Denmark, the West, the South-West and the South-East. For this the staff was in no way organised, whereas the Army General Staff, the body really qualified to do it, was con-fined to the Eastern Theatre. This illustrates how adroitly Hitler implemented in the military sphere the policy of *divide et impera* which he pursued so consistently in internal politics. As a result of this arbitrary and unrealistic division of responsibility Jodl found himself in a dual position; he was both the high-level adviser and the staff officer responsible for the operational requirements of 'his' theatres of war. Inevitably, therefore, he could not be impartial in many of his decisions. Since the responsibilities of the Army General Staff and the OKW Operations Staff overlapped, his position was incredibly difficult,[18] particularly when dealing with a dictator who was often impervious to factual argument and obsessed by boundless mistrust of Generals. In a memorandum written at Nuremberg Jodl described the 'tragedy of Hitler's leadership' as follows: 'They (the Generals) and the entire German Wehrmacht with them were facing an insoluble problem – how to fight a war which they did not want, under a Commander-in-Chief whose confidence they did not possess and in whom they had only limited confidence, using methods frequently contrary to their strategic principles and established views and with troops and police forces over which they did not have full command.'

This dilemma was one of the reasons why Jodl failed to achieve his initial aim of a centralised Wehrmacht command and equally failed to oppose with sufficient energy the disastrous dispersal of command authority.

Jodl's disposition was another reason for his failure. Though no one who knew him was in any doubt as to the uprightness of his character or his operational and organisational ability, people still wonder whether he was really up to his job. He was taciturn and gruff, so that conversation was reduced to the strictest minimum, but in addition he has been accused of lack of breadth of vision and strategic perception.[19] A final judgement on Jodl's capabilities must await a detailed examination of his contribution to all the important strategic and operational decisions, which is outside the scope of this book.[20] The fact remains that, perhaps knowing his own limitations, he confined himself to tactical problems and left to Keitel and others all questions of allied strategy and the supply and administration of occupied territory, generally acknowledged to be politico-military matters. By so doing he reinforced Hitler's tendency to meddle in Army operational and tactical details and remove any independent initiative from commanders. Jodl concentrated increasingly upon making himself a second Army Chief of Staff without having the necessary working staff to do so. He evaded the majority of the 'big questions', convinced that, having overcome so many difficulties already, he would be able to deal with one more when the time arrived. He was a procrastinator, but not merely because he was a born optimist, who would cheerfully confront even the most hopeless situations. The real reasons were his lack of political acumen and his relationship to Hitler which, though it passed through several phases, was irrational rather than rational.

Before the Nazi seizure of power Jodl's attitude to Hitler was one of aversion, if not actual enmity.[21] His aversion stemmed from a natural defensive reaction to Hitler's negative attitude towards the bourgeoisie, from which Jodl originated, and the aristocracy, to which he felt himself connected by marriage.[22] To this was added the built-in antipathy between the traditionally schooled General Staff officer and the revolutionary who denied all traditional values, an antagonism never entirely overcome and evidenced in Hitler's permanent distrust of military experts. Jodl himself mulled over the question why the military professionals subordinated themselves unresistingly to Hitler. His explanation was the nature of total war, which can no longer be conducted by a military commander but demands a statesman employing all the various specialists. In such a war elaboration and direction of purely military strategy was no longer enough; an overall strategy was required embracing both the political and military machines. This *post hoc* conclusion partially explains Jodl's concentration on operational and tactical matters. He regarded himself as a technician placing his ability and intelligence at the disposal of the superior statesman – and he rated Hitler as such. By so doing, however, he was rejecting Moltke's ideal of the General Staff officer as the co-responsible adviser of his commander-in-chief, as well as executive technician. Moreover he placed his services at Hitler's disposal before the outbreak of war. From 1933 to 1942 his admiration for the Dictator increased continuously. He appreciated the internal and external political 'successes' of totalitarian leadership. He was aware of the regime's illegalities and excesses but thought he must accept them as inevitable accompaniments of a revolution. Had there ever been a mighty cultural and governmental upheaval, he argued, without its obverse of cruelty and horror? This view of the regime's 'infant maladies' was common at the time – and not only among its supporters. Unpleasantnesses were ascribed to the Party, which was not yet identified with the State. Jodl's original aversion changed gradually into admiration until eventually he regarded Hitler, whom he had not yet met, as a real genius. His diary and notebooks contain many references to his almost mythical faith in the man. On 10 August 1938, for instance, he records a discussion with Hitler in the Berghof when – for the umpteenth time – the Dictator's views and those of the Army clashed on the possibility and advisability of war. When General von Wietersheim commented that the western fortifications could only be held for three weeks, Hitler replied that in that case the Army as a whole was of no value: 'I tell you, General, the position will be held, not for three weeks, but for three years.' Jodl's comment: 'There are a number of reasons for this pusillanimous attitude, which is unhappily fairly widespread in the Army General Staff. To begin with the General Staff is obsessed with memories of the past and, instead of doing what it is told and getting on with its military job, thinks it is responsible for political decisions. It does get on with its job with all its old devotion, but its heart is not in it because, in the last analysis, it does not believe in the genius of the Führer. It is all very well to compare him to Charles XII. As sure as fate the result of all this belly-aching will be not only enormous political damage – for all the world knows about the differences of opinion between the generals and the Führer – but also some danger to the morale of the troops. However, I don't doubt that in an incredible way the Führer will raise the morale both of the troops and of the nation when the time arrives.'

The increasing severity of the Sudeten crisis, however, found him 'not without anxiety . . . when one considers the volte-face in the estimate of the political and military possibilities shown by the latest statements as compared with the directives of 24 June, 5 November, 7 December 1937 and 30 May 1938'.

Nevertheless he soon took refuge in the specious heroic phrases which Hitler knew how to use so adroitly[23] – this test must be withstood. On Hitler's speech of 12 September he commented: 'A great day of reckoning with Czechoslovakia. . . . I hope that many in the country and in the officer corps will blush with shame at their pusillanimity and smugness.'[24] Comparing these remarks with the scruples voiced by General Beck and his successor, General Halder, they show a lack of political insight and moral rectitude which shed a different light on the arguments about higher organisation of the Wehrmacht.

In all this Jodl knew that he had the support of Keitel, who had already emphasised to him that 'he would not tolerate any officer in OKW giving voice to criticism, doubts or complaints'. Jodl's opinion of the senior officers of the Wehrmacht was that 'only by action can they now atone for their faults of lack of character and discipline. It is the same problem as in 1914. There is only one undisciplined element in the Army – the generals, and in the last analysis this comes from the fact that they are arrogant. They have neither confidence nor discipline because they cannot recognise the Führer's genius. This is, no doubt, to some extent due to the fact that they still look on him as the Corporal of the First World War instead of the greatest statesman since Bismarck.'[25]

Jodl was incapable of realising that the generals' so-called indiscipline was based on a sober analysis of the situation; still less could he grasp the deeper reasons for the sceptical attitude of the senior officers. Hitler thought that he could bend facts to his will, Jodl that it could be done by 'strength of character'.

When the Sudeten crisis ended in autumn 1938 Jodl was posted as Artillery Commander Vienna, whence he was recalled on 23 August 1939 to his mobilisation appointment as Head of the OKW Operations Staff. He returned to Berlin and on 3 September met Hitler. From this moment he was a committed disciple and his admiration became even greater. His confidence in victory was unbounded: 'We shall win this war even if it is 100% contrary to General Staff doctrine, because we have better troops, better equipment, stronger nerves and purposeful co-ordinated leadership.'

During the Polish campaign Jodl accompanied Hitler in the 'Führer Special' and immediately thereafter he and Keitel took up residence in the 'Old Reich Chancellery'. They were therefore exposed to the direct and continuous influence of Hitler, while their own staff and the Army staff were accommodated elsewhere – an outward and visible sign of their increasing divorce from their colleagues.[26]

The part played by Hitler in the planning of the French and Norwegian campaigns (to the latter Jodl had originally been opposed) reinforced his conviction that in matters of military strategy the Dictator was a 'phenomenon'.

The French campaign in particular led him to regard Hitler as a 'classic commander' and for this there is only one explanation. Like Hitler, Jodl was too caught up in the problems of the moment; so absorbed were they in small technical questions that they did not perceive the big strategic issues. Moreover some of Hitler's ideas, surprising to a professional, dazzled Jodl. Finally it must not be forgotten that the daily routine, consisting of dealing with a vast number of files and six to eight hours in conference with Hitler, left no time for real staff work, still less for long-range thinking.

Jodl had his first doubts during the Russian campaign, particularly about the vast extent of the objectives. But then Hitler's intervention during the winter 1941/42, when by sheer will-power he put a stop to the talk of imminent catastrophe and withdrawal, seemed to Jodl the acme of the commander's art. In 1942, however, even Jodl at last began to see the unrealism of Hitler's plans. He felt that he was dealing with a changed Hitler, an impression which increased after the move of the Headquarters to Vinnitsa. Maybe the Dictator's nerve was failing; with increasing frequency he failed to conceal his true nature behind one of his manifold masks; his orders became more erratic and unrealistic, his attitude more obdurate. Probably he first saw the spectre of a lost war during the summer of 1942, but instead of drawing the military and political consequences, he simply clung on. Disagreements between the Commander-in-Chief and his senior technical adviser became more frequent. Jodl talked less to the Army about Hitler's genius and his 'sixth sense', attempted to forestall Hitler's false moves, used delaying tactics and finally took refuge in a sort of passive resistance.[27] His relations with Hitler gradually deteriorated, for (in the words of an unpublished account) 'Jodl was not one of those who crept and crawled to Hitler. He spoke his mind openly, without mincing words and often in strong terms. . . . He saw matters clearly and soberly. His semi-cynical expression showed unmistakably that he considered himself better than Hitler at directing operations. . . . He would not give way, sometimes even asking Hitler the question who was the idiot, Hitler or Jodl. But Hitler would never reply. He shrugged off everything Jodl said without reacting. . . .'

Operations in the Caucasus finally led to severe differences of opinion between Jodl and the Dictator, resulting in 'a crisis which shook Supreme Headquarters to its foundations'.[28] From this time on Hitler ordered the proceedings of the daily briefing conferences to be recorded in shorthand. This was the time too when he himself drafted in all its detail the notorious 'commando order'.[29] Jodl was to be relieved by Field Marshal Paulus after the capture of Stalingrad, but the situation there and Hitler's aversion to seeing new faces around him put an end to the proposal. Jodl himself asked for a transfer to the front but Hitler refused with the words: 'I am the one to decide whether and when you go.' For a long time Hitler no longer greeted Jodl, did not attend the briefing conferences and refused to eat in the mess. Jodl later described life in the Führer's Headquarters as 'martyrdom'[30] and said that he was one of the few 'who dared look the Führer in the eye and say things to him which made the onlookers hold their breath for fear of a catastrophe'.

The old relations of confidence were never entirely re-established though Hitler must have realised that he was unlikely to find another General Staff officer who would carry out his duties so selflessly, with such devotion and with so complete an absence of personal ambition. Jodl's somewhat gruff blunt manner also probably suited him better than that of the typical Prussian General Staff officer. Accordingly in January 1943 Hitler awarded Jodl the Golden Party Badge – partly to show that the 'Vinnitsa crisis' hatchet had been buried; it was the only decoration Jodl ever received from his Supreme Commander. At the end of that year Jodl felt himself obliged to apply for membership of the NSDAP and was accepted on 1 January 1944. Being a member of the Wehrmacht, however, his membership was held in abeyance.

Jodl cannot be described as a friend of Hitler – he has himself

specifically denied it. Hitler was incapable of friendship. Nevertheless Jodl felt that he was more capable of handling the growing
doubts and fears than anyone else. Just as the 1918 mutiny had
produced a lasting shock effect in the Navy, he had lively memories
of the 'stab-in-the-back' legend. Germany's defeat in World
War I he considered the result of a cleavage between the home
country and the front. In World War II therefore he regarded as
dangerous any criticism by the Wehrmacht of their Supreme
Commander, who was also Head of State. In his view this could
only lead to disintegration. In the case of decisions which he felt
he could not prevent, he retired with increasing frequency into
stony silence, giving many to suspect that he was imitating Field
Marshal Moltke, who was known as the 'Great Silent One'.
He confided only in a few friends;[31] he had always been reserved.
He now became increasingly isolated; without personal contact
with Hitler and increasingly divorced both from his own staff
and that of the Army, he began to live in a vacuum; the increasing
angularity and illegibility of his handwriting testified to his
loneliness and seclusion. No one knows whether his private
doubts about Hitler were military only or whether eventually he
had moral scruples; assassination of Hitler certainly never crossed
his mind; being oblivious to any moral motives, with his absolute
concept of discipline and loyalty and identifying himself with the
Army and the State, such a thing was pure 'American gangster-
dom' in his eyes. The bomb plot of 20 July, when he was slightly
wounded, therefore, came as a great shock and produced 'a
discipleship complex if possible more unquestioning than
before'.[32] He called it the blackest day in German history and the
deed an enormity; Hitler he referred to as 'the highest and most
valued type of mankind, devoted to an ideal'.

The revelations of the crimes committed by the Nazi regime,
however, caused him to revise his original totally hostile attitude
to the conspirators. From Nuremberg he wrote to his wife:
'You know that I will offer my hand to anyone who strives for
something higher. I respect anyone prepared to sacrifice himself
for an ideal, even if I agree neither with his ideal nor his methods.
The only ones I hate are the self-seekers who sail with the wind.
My ultimate goal was always the same: love of our country.
There will always be differing opinions about this attempt and
they will revolve, not so much around its moral and ethical

background, as around the question whether, had it resulted in Hitler's death, it would have been advantageous or disadvantageous for Germany. Today I have no doubt that the object of men like Beck, Witzleben and Olbricht was solely the good of Germany. It is certainly wrong to say, however, that these officers alone drew the only possible conclusion from the fact that Hitler was a criminal. With my knowledge of the circumstances I say that is not true. Hitler's accomplices in crime were few and he was a master of secrecy; the conspirators knew as little as did the officers of the Wehrmacht. Had the latter known, it would have been an argument strong enough to bring the majority of the officer corps over to the side of the conspirators.'

This is tantamount to an admission that he was oblivious to the moral motives of the German resistance and considered only the treasonable aspect of the affair.

While in prison Jodl on several occasions emphasised his ignorance of the mass shootings and killings. 'The secrecy concerning the annihilation of the Jews and the events in the concentration camps was a masterpiece of concealment. It was also a masterpiece of deception by Himmler, who showed us soldiers faked photographs about these things in particular and told us stories about the gardens and plantations in Dachau, about the ghettos in Warsaw and Theresienstadt which gave us the impression that they were highly humane establishments.'[33]

The case for the prosecution at Nuremberg, therefore, hit him 'like a smack in the face', since he was completely oblivious of 90 % of the counts; the remaining 10 % he regarded as excusable in total war. The concentration camp culprits he described as brute beasts and found it inconceivable that such grisly tales were really true.[34] From Nuremberg he wrote to his wife: 'I am now hearing of these disgusting crimes for the first time and that seems incredible.'

His well-known description of the Führer's Headquarters as 'a cross between a monastery and a concentration camp'[35] may be taken as proof of his ignorance of the real conditions in the camps – even though the remark was only made at Nuremberg. A concentration camp meant to him confinement, surrounded by barbed wire and sentries.

He was not entirely free of anti-semitic sentiments, however, and agreed with the principle of discrimination against the Jews.

In a note on the nature of the military profession, for instance, he said: 'Here pride of profession and pride of race meet and in this sense the German officer has always been anti-semitic.' There could be no more damning admission.

Jodl made several statements about ending the war once the military situation had become hopeless. As late as autumn 1944 he was still placing great hopes on the new weapons, primarily the new U-boats; negotiations seemed to him fruitless 'since it had been made quite clear on all hands that the war could only be ended by unconditional surrender and the ultimate destruction of everything German. The normal conditions for negotiations in previous wars when one could say: We have lost, we lay down our arms and cede a province, did not obtain in this war.'[36]

Capture of the Allied 'Plan Eclipse' reinforced the determination to resist to the end. An additional consideration, also emphasised by Dönitz, was that, should the war end in winter, millions would have to camp in the open and would freeze miserably to death. 'It was our endeavour to save as many people as possible by sending them into the western area. That could only be done by drawing the two fronts closer together.'[37]

Jodl fails to mention the fact that, like Hitler, he believed that the Ardennes offensive would so change the position in the West that the Western Allies would be more ready to negotiate. Although, after the failure of this offensive, he must have realised that there was no prospect of the military situation improving, he continued up to the end to issue exhortations to fight couched in the sternest and most rigid terms. A Top Secret instruction signed by him and addressed to Commanders-in-Chief of Army Groups and Military Districts reads: 'In the next few days the enemy must be made to realise that he is penetrating into a land inspired with a fanatical determination to fight. Only thus can we succeed in re-establishing continuous fronts based on suitable natural features. The Führer expects all Commanders-in-Chief and Commanders to address themselves to this task with the whole weight of their personal influence and – without waiting for orders or directives or adhering to dividing lines and spheres of responsibility – to conduct the most fanatical struggle against the enemy now moving upon us. No consideration for the population can be allowed to affect the issue at this stage.'

He subsequently stated that he had hoped to die in the final battle for the Obersalzberg, but this somewhat juvenile romanticised picture, reminiscent of the Goths' last stand on Vesuvius, need not be taken too seriously. In fact, when Hitler decided to remain in the capital, he left the Berlin 'mousetrap' and moved to the north. Moreover in a note on principles, obviously written at the time of the collapse or shortly thereafter, he said: 'For a people of 80 million a fight to the death, like the Goths on Vesuvius, is not practicable.'

We do not know what he thought of Dönitz' nomination. Although the appointment of a naval officer as Supreme Commander of the Wehrmacht must have seemed to him unusual, he no doubt welcomed it as a transitional arrangement, preferring Dönitz to either Göring or Himmler.

CHAPTER FOUR

The Political Adviser –
Johann Ludwig (Lutz) Graf
Schwerin von Krosigk

FROM Bormann's first radio message Dönitz drew the conclusion that he should take over all the offices held personally by Hitler. Military advisers being already available, he did not therefore look for a Chancellor or Head of Government but for a foreign policy expert.

On the evening of 30 April he told his aide to make enquiries concerning the whereabouts of the ex-Reich Foreign Minister, von Neurath, whom he had known ever since 1915.[1] At 11.0 p.m. Admiral Wagner transmitted Bormann's message to Rear-Admiral von Puttkamer in the Southern Zone, asking him to inform Freiherr von Steengracht von Moyland, the Foreign Ministry State Secretary, and order him to move at once to the Northern Zone with a small staff.[2] When the enquiries concerning von Neurath's whereabouts proved fruitless, Ribbentrop, who was near Plön, was asked for his address. Hitler's Foreign Minister insisted on speaking to the Admiral personally and pressed his own candidature.[3] Rumour has it that Dönitz eventually banged down the receiver with: 'He's really too stupid to be borne.' Time was pressing; Dönitz had no wish to be dependent solely upon the advice of military experts for the outstanding important decisions, nor did he want to form a purely military dictatorship, of which there was now every indication. He accordingly asked Graf [Count] Schwerin von Krosigk, the senior Reich Minister present, to take over foreign affairs. During a short interview von Krosigk had impressed him favourably; his friend Speer had advised in this sense and even Himmler, on Schellenberg's advice, had apparently proposed von Krosigk.[4] Such unanimity in suggesting the ex-Finance Minister as foreign policy adviser to the new Head of State was remarkable and indicates that his abilities and character are worth examination.

As already mentioned, Schwerin von Krosigk was a fringe figure in the National-Socialist regime. He and Franz Seldte were the only survivors of the conservative members of Hitler's 1933 cabinet, the 'respectable element'. To understand the combination of errors, illusions and weaknesses which led an offspring of the old-established aristocracy to serve the Dictator for twelve long years, one must look at his family background and career. Though the latter was very different from those of Dönitz or Jodl, the Admiral's and von Krosigk's political views coincided in many respects.

Lutz von Krosigk was born on 22 August 1887 in Rathmanns-dorf, Anhalt. He was the youngest of the family, something of an afterthought.[5] His father, Erich von Krosigk, had six children by a previous marriage and three sons by Lutz' mother. Lutz did not carry the title of Count until adopted in 1925 by an uncle who had no children.

The Schwerins had taken root towards the end of the 12th century as Governors of the island fortress of Schwerin built by Henry the Lion as a defence against the Wends; the 'von Krosigk' came from Krosigk Castle near Halle on the Saale. Both sides of the family could cite famous ancestors – bishops, soldiers and statesmen, but also outstanding administrators and country noblemen. Lutz von Krosigk had inherited the industry and devotion to duty of the administrator, the piety of a bishop and a small infusion of martial blood.

After matriculating in 1905 he studied law, first in Lausanne and then for eighteen months at Oriel College, Oxford, to which he had been awarded a Rhodes scholarship.[6] While in England he gained an Economic Diploma and returned to Germany full of the ideas of the Fabian Society, to which he had been introduced by his tutor, Professor Sidney Ball. He announced that he was a 'convinced socialist' but his later career shows that this was mere youthful enthusiasm. His father hit the nail on the head, saying on hearing the news: 'Any true conservative must have been a radical socialist in his young days.'

In 1909 he began to practice as a junior barrister in Halle with his two elder brothers, Wilfried and Anton. By July 1914 he had become a barrister in Stettin and had been promised a move to Upper Silesia but was then swept up into the First World War.

Von Krosigk took part in the Belgian campaign, earning the Iron Cross Second Class, a decoration in which he took more pleasure than all the numerous subsequent orders awarded him as a Minister. He continued on the Western Front and by the end of the war was serving as divisional administrative officer.

Back in civil life von Krosigk offered himself to the newly-formed German National People's Party as an election speaker – though he did not join the Party. He longed to sweep away narrow-minded ideas and was convinced that 'we, the youth, are called upon to alter many things in the State and society one day'; he therefore wished to become active in politics. Hitherto he had not felt attracted to any party. Now, however, the German Nationalists seemed to him 'to be trying to pursue a sensible social policy suited to the changed times'.

After a few electoral speeches he was forced to realise that he had not the slightest aptitude for politics and in fact found party political demagogy and everything to do with it distasteful. He ceased attending electoral meetings altogether and henceforth devoted himself entirely to his profession.[7] A pre-war promise of an appointment to Zabrze (Hindenburg) in Upper Silesia was still open, but he was soon disillusioned by life in this remote locality where professional prospects were unpromising. He was then offered the Directorship of 'Welfare and Economics Ltd' in Rügen (a sort of forerunner of the Pomeranian Farmers' Union) and accordingly asked for a year's leave and moved there.

Von Krosigk's career now took an unexpected turn with the arrival of a telegram from Lippert, the Stettin Government Recorder, offering him the post of 'Assistant' for financial and economic questions in the Reich Finance Ministry. Although he had 'always dreamt of a post in the Ministry of Culture' and, as he admitted, knew little of financial matters, he decided to accept.

The familiarisation period was accordingly laborious. He was placed in the 'Peacetime' section, where he had to deal with dry and highly complex subjects such as liquidation of German property abroad, compensation and the settlement of debts and claims. In 1920, however, he was appointed *Regierungsrat* [Counsellor], thus becoming a regular civil servant, and thenceforth his rise was rapid; by 1929 he was a *Ministerialdirektor* [Ministerial Director] and Head of the Budget Section. A National-Socialist appreciation of 1936 says of him: 'Thanks to his extraordinary accuracy, objectivity and clarity in the evaluation even of the most difficult questions, together with his upright character and great modesty, an out-and-out patriot who had always stood aloof from party political squabbling, von Krosigk was very soon entrusted with greater and greater responsibilities.' In this environment of sober factual work he felt at home and developed into an outstanding expert.

Hilferding, the social-democrat Finance Minister, appointed him Director of the Budget and he thus became responsible for the passage of all budgetary and currency measures, since the office carried with it the chairmanship of the 'Combined Financial and Budgetary Committees' of the *Reichsrat* [Upper House]. At the end of a month he frequently did not know where to find the money for salaries and interest payments, for Germany was several times near bankruptcy. Tax payments were in arrears while the cost of unemployment insurance was rising. In addition there was an alarming reduction in the in-flow of foreign capital and a flight of capital abroad. Loans and debts, granted short-term, though repayable long-term, had to be honoured, and this against a background of rising social expenditure.

At the Reichstag elections of 14 September 1930 the National-Socialists captured 107 seats as against their previous 12. Here was the first unmistakable danger signal and it caused the Brüning Government to enter 'the transitional phase towards totalitarianism'. The Reich's financial position meanwhile deteriorated rapidly and the climax of the crisis came with the bank crash of summer 1931. At the London Conference in July, at which Schwerin von Krosigk was present, Brüning and his delegation managed to obtain a credit extension, but then came Britain's departure from the gold standard in September. An experts' conference on reparations was called in Basle, at which von Krosigk represented the Reich Government. This looked like a further step in controlling the crisis but before the conference assembled two decisive events had taken place in Germany: at the Presidential elections of 10 April 1932 Hindenburg emerged the victor with 53% of the votes – but only on the second ballot; Hitler scored 36·8% and Thälmann (communist) 10%; secondly on 30 May the President accepted the resignation of the Brüning cabinet.

Von Krosigk heard of Brüning's resignation in Paris, where he was taking part in talks on Austria. On the evening of 31 May, when the formation of a new cabinet under Papen was already under discussion, von Hoesch, the German Ambassador in Paris, called him to find out what sort of a person the new Chancellor might be. Von Krosigk could tell him little except that he was right of centre and 'a man who indulged in extravagances and was therefore not popular with his party'. Before von Krosigk left Paris the Ambassador called again to tell him that he was being proposed as a candidate for the post of Finance Minister. During a sleepless night on the train he decided to refuse the offer under all circumstances. He remained firm in this decision even when von Papen explained to him in urgent terms the necessity for a presidential cabinet.

When, however, Meissner, the President's Secretary, called him to say that the President hoped that an officer and a nobleman would not leave his old Field Marshal in the lurch, von Krosigk felt that his honour as an aristocrat and a soldier was at stake, and accepted. One may laugh, but for von Krosigk, as for many other Germans, Hindenburg, the hoary old Field Marshal, was a venerated figure, on whom all hopes rested now that the monarchy was gone. With hindsight this hero-worship may seem mistaken but it was nevertheless responsible for the fact that the majority of republican officialdom remained at its post, even when the constitutional outlook was at its most unpromising. Hindenburg represented both tradition and the State, and service was to him. Schwerin von Krosigk's attitude to the Republic was similar to that of many civil servants of his age group in a number of Ministries, the technocrats who kept the State machine functioning; he described it as follows: 'Though we had never discussed it among ourselves, we were united in our efforts to serve the Republic and its new Ministers with absolute loyalty, to make the Republic independent externally and strong internally, to free it from the fetters of the Versailles Treaty and to revive in it something of the best old Prussian tradition. For us the word "Prussia" denoted an attitude of mind – incorruptible devotion to duty.' The strict Prussian concept of service, combined with Hindenburg's request, was therefore decisive.

Moreover, being non-political, von Krosigk found the prospect of an extra-parliamentary government of experts, 'an independent cabinet of officials', attractive rather than the reverse. The idea had been repeatedly aired in Hindenburg's circle and was in fact widely supported, since the unstable structure of the parliamentary republic and the quarrels of the main parties frequently led to

insuperable difficulties in governing the country. The Finance
Minister's position illustrates the general trend. Originally, under
the Weimar Republic, his position was very strong, though never
the equivalent of that of his colleagues in the Western democracies.
From the Imperial Treasury he had inherited responsibility for
the budget, customs and taxation, but not for the vital problems
of banking, credit and currency which were under the Minister of
Economics – a particularly important point in connection with
von Krosigk's later position under the National-Socialists. The
Reich Budgetary Ordinance of 31 December 1922 had given the
Finance Minister a right of veto, although this was not provided
under the Weimar constitution; he could not therefore be out-
voted by a Cabinet majority, always provided that the Reich
Chancellor was on his side. On several occasions the Reichstag
had amended the Budgetary Ordinance, partially to give Parliament a greater voice in budgetary matters and partially to give the
Finance Minister greater responsibility *vis-à-vis* departments.
Under Brüning there was a tendency to demote Ministers to the
level of departmental heads, in other words technical executives
as under Bismarck, and this trend became more marked. Gradually,
and even more so after 1933, their constitutional and legal
responsibility to the Head of State and to Parliament for the
signature of laws and ordinances was reduced to a limited
responsibility for the legality and expediency of the drafts submitted. Simultaneously, during the Republic's final phase, the
influence of powerful pressure groups became noticeable.

It is hard to say how far this change of function was dependent
upon individual personalities. As a typical representative of
professional officialdom, technically highly qualified but non-
political, Schwerin von Krosigk undoubtedly contributed
unconsciously to this 'technological' development, which ended
by 'reducing political problems to technical administrative
duties'. He was a man of great charm, personally modest and an
undoubted patriot; all his life, however, he showed a lack of
political insight which blinded him to the dangers inherent in
over-concentration of power at the top. Moreover he frequently
required the support of the Chancellor to ensure acceptance of his
practical requirements in face of opposition from other departments or the Reichstag. The German national ideal of those years
was a strong powerful State, above party strife and individual

economic interests, maintaining order within and radiating power without, led by a governing élite. Von Krosigk supported this ideal and felt that he belonged to this élite.

Under the von Papen Government, nicknamed the 'Barons' Cabinet', a whole series of measures were taken to revive the economy and reduce unemployment. Armed with plenary powers by Hindenburg – something he had refused to Brüning – von Papen dissolved the Reichstag, called new elections for 31 July and raised the ban on the SA and SS. The result was to inflame the internal political situation until it was not far short of civil war.

Externally an event took place during von Papen's chancellorship which might have made a major contribution to stabilisation – the Lausanne Reparations Conference arranged by Brüning for 16 June to 9 July. Extremely tough bargaining took place, during which (in the words of Schmidt, the interpreter) von Krosigk, who was of course a member of the German delegation, was 'a sort of German counterpart to Chamberlain', reeling out figures with brilliantly sober objectivity. Agreement was finally reached on a payment of 3 milliard marks, but Germany did not achieve her other object – settlement of the war guilt question. Von Krosigk showed himself particularly adept during the discussions on methods of payment. With British assistance he succeeded in reaching an arrangement which, for all practical purposes, meant the end of reparations. In his memoirs he said that 'it had been worth becoming a Minister, if only because of Lausanne'.

In the Reichstag elections of 31 July 1932 the National-Socialists returned with 230 seats, thus becoming the strongest party in the House. Democracy had now lost control, not only of the government but of parliament as well. In his book *Die Weimarer Republik* Albert Schwarz says: 'The question now was, not whether the National-Socialists would participate in a government, but the extent to which *they* would tolerate the participation of other parties in a government to be formed by them.' Hitler was demanding not only the offices of Reich Chancellor and Minister-President of Prussia, but also the Reich and Prussian Ministries of the Interior and the Ministries of Justice, Agriculture, Aviation and Education. No wonder that the negotiations initiated between the National-Socialists, von Papen and General von Schleicher soon failed. Only after the Nazis had suffered a 2-million-vote set-back at the 6 November elections did hopes revive.

Schwerin von Krosigk, who had entered the von Papen cabinet in the conviction that it was a transitional regime only, combined with Gürtner, the Minister of Justice, to support Hitler's entry into the government. He considered that 'the economic programme, the success of which was decisive for the continuance of the government, could only succeed with a strong government; there was also grave danger that, if they remained in opposition and were driven to increasingly violent propaganda, many of the Nazis, including the youth, would drift into the communist camp'. After a detailed briefing by Schleicher, in fear of a Nazi/communist alliance and in view of the increasing trend to extremism, if not the drift into civil war, all members of the cabinet voted against another von Papen government.

Schleicher was therefore appointed Chancellor and in this von Krosigk played no small part. Even today he still maintains that, with the information available to him at the time, he could not have acted otherwise. Although he found it hard to place much confidence in this devious and inscrutable character, he declared himself ready to work with him.

By the end of 1932, however, Schleicher had isolated himself totally and towards the end of January 1933 there began a confused bidding match between the politicians and the military, from which Hitler emerged the victor on the 30th. Like the majority, von Krosigk was convinced that there was no alternative but to appoint Hitler provided that he could form a parliamentary government, and he refused to participate in a von Papen-Hugenberg rival cabinet. Hardly a soul realised the devilish nature of the National-Socialist movement, certainly not an aristocrat like von Krosigk. Both by origin and character he was poles apart from the upstart new Chancellor, the power-seeker – but had not Brüning said that he 'lacked even the most elementary experience or instinct for party political manœuvring or political tactics'?

Much has been written about the failure of the German Right and its readiness to collaborate with Hitler; criticism has been devastating. Thirty-five years later and knowing the criminal nature of Hitler and his regime, so complete a misjudgement of the situation seems barely comprehensible. Transposing oneself into the atmosphere of those days, however, the actions of these people seem to be governed by an almost fatal inevitability. Any generalised judgement based on research into individual cases proves unsatisfactory. It is no good talking of 'failure to look facts in the face', 'breakdown of the spirit of conservatism', naïveté or exaggerated nationalism and holding them up as signs of degeneration in the German character. In each case one must differentiate between general European phenomena, specific political traditions, concrete historical facts and particular individual situations. The single-party State, the tendency to autocracy and the monopolisation of power are not specifically German developments. Even exaggerated militant nationalism is not purely a German speciality. It was the combination of these general trends with a particular German situation – the aftermath of a lost war and a topsy-turvy economy – which produced a predicament such that wide circles regarded a temporary dictatorship – and hardly anyone thought of it as anything other than temporary – as a necessary evil.

All this does not alter the fact that failure there was. Nevertheless, worldwide there can have been few men with the brilliancy of political acumen demanded by the situation. It must also be remembered that Hindenburg was the embodiment of the State – and not only in Reichswehr eyes. And Hindenburg's State had now acquired a National-Socialist government.

As we all know, in the early days Hitler played his cards very cleverly; he buttered up the Generals; he staged the Potsdam comedy; in the initial Cabinet meetings he presented an exterior quite different from the popular picture of him. Von Krosigk noted: 'He did not present himself as the uproarious demagogue whipping the masses into a frenzy, but as the calm polite negotiator; he was familiar with the subject in hand and, with the aid of his extraordinary memory, could quickly pick out the essentials of a problem; he could summarise the conclusions of a long discussion and was able to present in a new light a question which had been argued from all angles.'

Von Krosigk had stipulated that he would only co-operate if left to continue his practical work undisturbed, and before the new cabinet was sworn in on 30 January 1933, he reiterated this demand to von Papen, the Vice-Chancellor. Von Papen took him straight to Hitler, whom he then met for the first time. Von Krosigk faced the new Chancellor with his conditions: secure balance of payments, no currency manipulation, acceptance of tax certificates. Hitler agreed the last point in principle, though he said that he might wish to make changes of form. He said nothing about the first two points – and the swearing-in ceremony cut short the interview.

During their first discussions on budgetary matters Hitler seemed somewhat embarrassed. He invariably addressed von Krosigk as 'Herr Reich Minister', a formal title which he never dropped. Possibly he wished to emphasise thereby the distance which separated them; or perhaps it was the expression of a certain respect for his Finance Minister's technical competence – he respected Dönitz, for instance, and always addressed him as 'Herr Grand Admiral'. Basically, however, Hitler loathed routine government business in general and financial questions in particular. In his eyes the Finance Minister existed merely to provide him with the resources to carry out his plans. He therefore relegated him to the status of a 'Reich Paymaster' (Himmler's contemptuous description) and regarded him as a pure executive. The Weimar Republic may have given indications that the technocrats were in the ascendant, but under National-Socialism there was a general down-grading to pure technical specialisation with the resulting constriction of outlook. The effects were a general lack of insight and a reduction of the will or power to command. It was a creeping, almost imperceptible development affecting all important authorities.

As far as actual Finance Ministry work was concerned, the measures initiated under the von Papen government were continued. They were tantamount to abandonment of the deflationary policy; investment was the central feature, priority being given to transport; apart from some insignificant concessions the tax increases introduced under Brüning were perpetuated. To stimulate the economy, direct government spending was increased, the additional investment being financed by raising the floating debt and use of the device of 'creation of work credits'. These were three-month credits extendable to five years and backed for re-discount by the Reichsbank. All these measures had to some extent been initiated by previous governments, but by 1933/34 they were producing a noticeable decrease in unemployment and thus contributed to Hitler's prestige. In fact, up to 1935, Nazi financial policy was well suited to the situation. When full employment was achieved in 1936, however, the increasing budget deficits produced an inflationary effect. Then, instead of curbing this trend, deficit spending continued and the Finance Minister's tax increases were entirely inadequate to deal with the situation.

The worst feature was Germany's foreign trade, which encountered foreign export barriers resulting in a catastrophic shortage of foreign currency, a situation aggravated by the considerable loan and interest requirements. Purchase of the essential raw materials and foodstuffs became a matter of extreme difficulty. To deal with this problem Dr. Schacht, who became President of the Reichsbank in March 1933 and Reich Minister of Economics in August 1934, initiated an ingenious system of bilateral barter agreements, used later in a perverted form to exploit the occupied territories. In addition a policy of prices and wages control was adopted, which checked the symptoms but did not deal with the root causes of the disease. These of course lay primarily in the continued increase in arms spending. During the period 1934 to 31 August 1939 this totalled about 60 billion marks, almost 40 % of all government expenditure.

What part did the Reich Finance Minister play in all this and to what extent can he be accused of consciously furthering Hitler's bellicose expansionism? As already mentioned, he had no authority in questions of banking, credit or currency policy but was restricted to the budget, customs and taxation. His main activity amounted to little more than preparation of the budget, in other words he was responsible for the overall budget, ensuring that receipts were adequate and checking the various authorities' proposals for expenditure. This measure of control by the Finance Minister had led to considerable argument even during the Weimar Republic days; at that time, however, he could count on the support of Parliament or the Chancellor or both; in Hitler's totalitarian state neither was available. A further factor was that by a cabinet decision of April 1934 the Wehrmacht was accorded a privileged position, in that it did not have to present its budget under individual votes. It simply demanded a global sum and this was negotiated at the start of the budget year between the Chief of OKW, the President of the Reichsbank and the Finance Minister. In addition, by the secret Reich Defence laws of 21 May 1935 and 4 September 1938 warlike expenditure was placed under the economic plenipotentiaries, initially Schacht and later Funk. In all this Schwerin von Krosigk played only a passive subordinate role;

he was a technical executive with no say in the important decisions.

Ought not the mere size of the sums demanded, however, have taken him aback and led him to suspect warlike intentions? At the Wilhelmstrasse trial his defence counsel maintained that an expenditure of 60 billion marks (equivalent to 25 billion dollars) over a period of six years[8] on a rearmament programme starting practically from zero did not *ipso facto* indicate preparation for aggressive war, if compared with nations' present-day annual expenditure on armaments. The argument cannot be rejected out of hand. There is no doubt, however, that von Krosigk welcomed rearmament; he has never made any secret of it. Re-introduction of military service (he was a co-signatory of the relevant law) he regarded as a 'deliverance' because it ended the period of the 'black budget' for secret rearmament.

As a supporter of the concept of the powerful State, von Krosigk was all for revision of the Versailles Treaty; rearmament seemed to him to guarantee the necessary reinforcement of the Reich's foreign policy position. A secret Naval Headquarters memorandum of 1937 includes him among those whose services in the struggle against the Peace Treaty deserve mention. Nevertheless he never visualised anything other than a peaceful settlement. In his memoirs he says that he believed that 'a Party wedded to systematic increase of the Germanic race, to a demographic policy based on leaving a healthy stock behind it, must be opposed to any warlike policy'. Even when, in autumn 1936, Hitler addressed a secret memorandum to the relevant Ministers saying that Germany must arm for the decisive struggle against Bolshevist Russia, he read it only as referring to military security. If he had any doubts, they were dispelled by a statement of Hitler's to Reinhardt, the Permanent Secretary of the Finance Ministry. The Dictator promised 'a long period of peace, the end of rearmament within a year and the re-establishment of the Finance Minister's budgetary prerogatives *vis-à-vis* the Wehrmacht'. Today we know with what cynical disregard Hitler treated the truth, but at the time a Minister could hardly be expected to realise at once that his Chancellor was a shameless liar. Von Krosigk certainly did not believe that Hitler was bent on a war of aggression; his doubts began only when it was too late. Blind to the real background of Third Reich policy, he took the peaceful assurances with which Hitler was so free only too seriously.

Like most other important events, von Krosigk heard of the
Austrian *Anschluss* only through the radio – and was overjoyed.
He did not realise that the dictator had used a combination of
bluff and threats and he 'allowed himself to be dazzled by the
heartfelt joy with which the Germans were welcomed into
Austria'. No one had asked him for special financial provision for
the move. The increasingly severe Sudeten crisis, however, seems
to have horrified him.

In spring 1938, on the occasion of the Blomberg crisis, Ministers
were summoned to Hitler for the last time, and von Krosigk
subsequently decided to write him a letter. On 1 September he
committed his anxieties to paper. Following the general convention in totalitarian states described by Buchheim as 'structural
opportunism', he cloaked his admonitions behind factual arguments – Hitler would have accepted nothing else from him. He
pointed out that between 1932 and 1937 taxation had risen from
6·5 billion to 14 billion marks, whereas arms expenditure had
risen from 750 million to 11 billion. As a result the Reich's
indebtedness had trebled (from 12·5 to 35·8 billion). During 1938,
he continued, there had been a fundamental change, with the
'recovery' of Austria, the western fortifications and a further
acceleration of rearmament. Expenditure on these counts amounted to 14 billion. After these technical financial arguments came the
real warning: 'Since any future war cannot be fought by military
methods only but must inevitably be an economic war of a major
order, I consider it my irrefutable duty, knowing our economic
situation and that of foreign countries, to express to you, my
Führer, frankly and openly my serious anxiety about Germany's
future. Whether in the event of a showdown with Czechoslovakia the war can remain localised or becomes general, depends
primarily on England. . . .'

Von Krosigk emphasised that the repeated British declarations
were certainly no bluff, a statement intended as a counter to
Ribbentrop's fatal misinterpretation of British intentions. Revert-
ing to his own field, he stated that economically Germany was in
a position comparable to that of 1917. The Western Powers
would not attack the Siegfried Line but would simply wait until
Germany's economic position worsened. Eventually, as a result of
American deliveries of arms and aircraft, she would be inferior
militarily. As his final and decisive argument von Krosigk cited

the attitude and opinion of the German people. They had hailed
the reoccupation of the Rhineland and the liberation of Austria
because they were 'convinced of the justice of our cause'. 'On
the Czech question, however, our people feel quite differently at
heart. Should this affair develop into a world war, the German
people's confidence in you, my Führer, will be shaken to its
foundations.' Time was working for Germany, he went on; one
should wait until Czechoslovakia placed herself in the wrong –
'We can only gain by waiting. Hence the fanatical efforts of the
communists, Jews and Czechs to drive us into war *now*. They
regard this as the *last* chance of turning the Czech problem into a
world conflagration and, as a result of this conflagration, bringing
about the annihilation of their hated Third Reich.' Better therefore, he said, 'with the calm of strength to await one's moment in
face of these provocations', to make good armaments deficiencies
and use the demand for self-determination to deprive England of
any 'cogent argument for war against Germany'. Then, he felt,
the day would come when 'the Czechs could be given the
coup de grâce'.[9]

This passage, arguing only for postponement, von Krosigk
tries to pass off as 'diplomatic verbiage'. At Nuremberg the
prosecution read it to mean that he was interested not in *whether*
there was to be a war of aggression, but *when* – unlike Schacht
who from an initial admirer of Hitler turned into an enemy and
suffered the consequences thereof. Von Krosigk's letter to
Hitler shows that he was opposed to any action which might
lead to world war; it also shows, however, that he both welcomed
and supported any measure leading to an expansion of the German
Reich or an increase in its power and prestige – even at the
expense of smaller and weaker parties. Whereas Schacht did
everything he could to re-establish proper control of financial
policy and opposed inflationary expenditure, being dismissed in
January 1939 as a result, von Krosigk allowed himself time and
again to be lulled into security by Hitler's peaceful assurances and
so contributed to a further increase of the Dictator's powers.
For instance, on 15 June 1939 he signed the Reichsbank law,
Section III of which laid down that: 'The German Reichsbank will
be managed and administered in accordance with the instructions
and under the supervision of the Führer and Reich Chancellor';
Section XVI removed from the Reichsbank the right to withhold

credits from the government.[10] This meant that in the financial field all decentralisation was gone and the Führer principle was paramount. Von Krosigk would have us believe that he had many scruples and frequently considered resignation, that all his professional advice was against the course pursued by Germany, primarily with a view to reducing armaments expenditure; if this were really so, however, he ought to have lined up with Schacht and come out in support of independence for the Reichsbank.[11] By 1939 he must long since have realised that he was serving a government and putting his name to measures which could not be made to accord with his conscience or religious convictions. That he played a part in the consolidation of Hitler's power cannot be denied. He says that he remained in office, at first from a sense of duty, later to check injustices and hardships within his sphere of responsibility, and finally because it seemed to him cowardly to leave the sinking ship. François-Poncet says that he and von Neurath simply did not wish to lose their jobs. What therefore was his true role in laying the foundations of Nazi power and how far did he participate in the regime's illegal measures?

As we have seen, in January 1933 he considered a Hitler government inevitable and his participation in it quite natural, provided that he was left to do his practical work. In the end he had even agreed to serve von Papen, the unknown 'amateur jockey', and Schleicher, the inscrutable 'socialist General'; his technical ability had scored one or two successes when Germany was in a difficult financial situation. For centuries his family had belonged to the ruling upper class – was he now to be a renegade?

During the preparatory work on the Enabling Law von Krosigk and Popitz (Finance Minister of Prussia, later an active member of the Resistance) attempted to limit the scope of the subjects to which the Law was applicable. They proposed formation of a special committee of representatives of the Reich and Prussian Finance Ministries and the Reich Ministry of the Interior, to draw up a list of measures to be formulated immediately on promulgation of the Law. Hitler at first gave his agreement, but at the next cabinet meeting withdrew it, saying that the political parties wanted neither a catalogue nor restrictions and were content with regular information being passed to a Reichstag committee!

This was a typical von Krosigk manœuvre, motivated less by opposition to the Nazi regime than by a natural bureaucratic caution. He seldom took open or spectacular action but preferred to use administrative channels in an attempt to shade off the more extreme developments and check excessive severity. He later used these indirect methods on many occasions with success and in a totalitarian state they were often the only practicable solution; they led him, however, into the fatal error of accepting illegal measures *in toto* and in principle, while attempting to mitigate or cancel them in individual cases.

He therefore signed a whole series of discriminatory laws which he then attempted to water down in so far as his own Ministry was concerned. A law of 7 April 1933, for instance, signed by Hitler, Frick and von Krosigk, prescribed that all officials of non-Aryan origin should be retired and that officials, whose previous political activity did not guarantee unquestioning support for the National-Socialist State, should be dismissed; the first executive instruction on the subject, issued on 11 April, was signed by Frick and von Krosigk alone. On 30 June 1933 followed a law changing the regulations on salaries and social security, again signed by Hitler, Frick and von Krosigk; this also contained drastic measures for the removal of persons of non-Aryan origin. On 20 July 1933 came a supplementary law ordering the dismissal of persons who had been active communists or had belonged to communist auxiliary or reserve organisations. Finally on 26 January 1937, once more with Hitler and Frick, he signed the law on German officialdom; this prescribed a personal oath to Adolf Hitler and laid down, first that no one married to a non-German or 'non-Germanic' might be employed in official positions, and secondly that such marriages were forbidden. On 30 April 1938 he signed a further ordinance in the same sense. The laws suppressing the trades unions also carried his signature.

In applying legal regulations within his own domain von Krosigk reserved to himself the right of decision in each individual case. Thanks to him many a member of the Centre Party, the Bavarian People's Party or the Social Democrats remained at his post or was 'favoured with a posting to Thuringia'. When there was the danger of infraction of the professional sphere he remained inexorable; in personal matters he occasionally made a 'concession'. One victim, for instance, was Dr. Zarden, the long-established head of his Tax Department; he was a half-Jew and married to a Jewess; von Krosigk salved his conscience by saying that 'Zarden himself realised that he could not remain'. On Hitler's personal advice he was replaced by Fritz Reinhardt, the Party's tax expert. Though von Krosigk took steps to ensure that Zarden had enough to live on (as he did in many other cases) the incident is typical of his acceptance of a discriminatory principle, while mitigating it in individual cases. We have seen that Dönitz also did likewise.

Von Krosigk described himself as 'a stranger to any anti-semitism'. Nevertheless he wished to see as many Jews as possible removed from Germany and, together with Schacht, worked on a plan 'to enable German Jews to emigrate, assisted by world Jewry and taking their possessions with them. World Jewry should provide Germany with the necessary credits to be covered by proceeds from increased exports.'

On 25 November 1941 and 1 July 1943 Reich citizenship laws were promulgated giving rise to a number of executive ordinances, to Nos 11 and 13 of which von Krosigk was a co-signatory; their purpose was discriminatory and they deprived the Jews (who after all were Germans) of various rights; criminal proceedings could now be taken against them by the police – implying that the normal processes of law were closed – and on death their possessions reverted to the State. The Finance Minister was a co-signatory only for procedural reasons, since the ordinances affected his sphere of responsibility; the contents were the work of the Minister of the Interior and the Führer's Deputy, who also issued the legal and administrative regulations to supplement and implement the law. The Finance Minister was responsible only for technical execution. Nevertheless, though not an instigator, he was a willing minion. This was his position too in the matter of Jewish property in the occupied territories. They were under the sole authority of the military commander and the Finance Minister was only implicated in respect of the property of German Jews who had emigrated.[12]

Von Krosigk was also involved in the 'settlement' following the bloody events of 'Kristallnacht' in November 1938. He attended Göring's meeting on 12 November when Heydrich reported that 101 synagogues had been damaged and 76 destroyed; 7,500 shops had been damaged at a total cost of about 25 million marks. Notoriously Göring decreed that the Jews should pay an additional 'fine' of 1 milliard marks, payable to the Reich Finance Ministry.

Von Krosigk thereupon issued an ordinance the same day assessing this sum at 20% of Jewish property and calling for payment in four instalments. On 21 November he issued an executive instruction raising the contribution to 25%.

Von Krosigk says that at this time he asked himself once more whether he should remain in office. He had had similar doubts after 30 June 1934 and during the Sudeten crisis. He was persuaded to remain, he says, by Dr. Zarden, his former Permanent Secretary, and von Manteuffel, a Director in the Ministry, both of whom urged him to introduce moderating clauses in the measures concerned. Indirect confirmation of this is given in a statement by Walter Donandt, von Krosigk's long-standing Personal Assistant; he says that, in dealing with the assessment regulations for the levy on Jewish property, von Krosigk tended 'to be conciliatory in individual cases and therefore concentrated all important decisions as far as possible within the Ministry'. In fact he did contrive to arrange that the assurance payments, which under Göring's original instructions were to be paid directly to the State, should be regarded as part of the individual Jew's contribution.[13] Here was another of his typical 'technical dodges' – acceptance of the measure as a whole while attempting to mitigate it in individual cases.

Nevertheless there is good reason to doubt the seriousness of his thoughts of resignation, at least at this time. At the 12 November meeting he said: 'We must do all we can, as part of an increased export drive, to get the Jews out of the country, abroad. The important point is that we should not be left solely with the working-class Jew. That would be a fearful burden'; and later: 'I do not view with relish the prospect of driving them into ghettos. . . . Our aim must therefore be, as Heydrich has said: Out with anything that can be got out.'

This statement shows that von Krosigk, while wishing to eliminate Jewish influence from Germany as far as possible, was opposed to incarcerating them in ghettos and was searching for methods of excluding them from public life, but in the most humane manner possible. He was all for discrimination but not for extermination. He was not to know that, in Hitler's State, the one implied the other. He cannot, however, be regarded as free from racial prejudice.

The subject of treatment of the Jews leads naturally to that of the concentration camps. From 1936 onwards their cost was borne by the Reich budget – and again von Krosigk raised no objections. In so far as his responsibilities allowed – and even in the judgement of the American Military Court they were of a 'pure bookkeeping' nature – he attempted to restrict the expansion of the camps and alleviate the lot of their inmates. He refused to disburse for expansion and new construction or for an increase in guard personnel; but these tactics soon had to be abandoned since, with the increasing number of prisoners, restriction of the camps' budget became impossible and the opposite of that intended was being achieved. He also raised the prisoners' daily allowance. Both these measures were completely ineffective and, in view of the real situation in the camps, derisory.

Undoubtedly prior to 1945 von Krosigk had no detailed knowledge of conditions in the camps. He only visited a concentration camp once, on which occasion he was accompanied by von Manteuffel, who described the Camp Commandant as 'a beast in human form'. Von Krosigk, on the other hand, gained 'not the slightest impression of anything horrible'. One is left wondering whether this was a case of being 'shielded against reality by self-deception, lies and stupidity' (Hannah Arendt's description)[14] or whether he was simply burying his head in the sand. One suspects that he was merely working on the old-established principle of 'hunting with the hounds'. On 30 January 1937, for instance, together with von Neurath, Gürtner and Schacht, the other non-Party members of the cabinet, he accepted from Hitler the Golden Party Badge.

Nevertheless von Krosigk was a devout Christian. His wife was related to Friedrich von Bodelschwingh, Head of the Bethel Institute, who was proposed for the office of Reich Bishop by the *Land* churches in 1933 but was not elected on representations from the 'German Christians'. The Krosigk house was a frequent meeting place for private discussions between senior evangelical dignitaries. With Hindenburg as sponsor he became a member of the Order of the Knights of Malta and, at the request of the Abbess, senior trustee of the Convent of the Holy Sepulchre, an evangelical nunnery which ran a girls' school. He retained all these offices even after receipt of the Golden Party Badge. The best proof (if there is one) of the truth of his argument that he remained a Minister solely to 'avert something worse', lies in his continued activity in Church affairs. On many occasions he spoke out in support of religious interests. On 22 September 1941, for instance, he protested to Lammers, the Head of the Reich Chancellery, against the seizure of the Bethany Central Deaconesses' House and was bold enough to quote the question being asked by people returning from Warthegau (ex-Poland): 'What's the difference between this and Bolshevism?'

By adroit delaying tactics von Krosigk also defeated a Party proposal sponsored by Bormann, the Head of the Party Chancellery, to prevent the State finance offices administering Church taxes by making them a percentage surcharge on State revenue. He dealt similarly with attempts by the Party to abolish tax concessions for Church undertakings and establishments and to confiscate Church property. The evangelical Church in particular had good reason to be grateful to him. In a statement on oath Koch, the prelate, said: 'In those dark days for the Church I considered it a great advantage that he was a Minister and could therefore bring some influence to bear on the Church's side'. Many have testified emphatically to his kindness and readiness to help, describing him as 'a man and a Christian' and 'a shining example'. His private life was known to be impeccable; his tastes were simple and his manner modest. He never used his official position for personal gain. In fact, in autumn 1942 with the money paid him as expenditure allowance he set up the 'Graf von Krosigk Trust' for needy families of Finance Ministry personnel who had fallen in action. Colonel-General Fromm is said to have described him as one of the most upright men he had ever met. That such a man should become involved in the machinery of a totalitarian state and lend his name to illegal measures inevitably produces a sense of shock.

To accuse him of 'imbecility' or 'ineptitude'[15] or sheer servility is an oversimplification, as it is to describe him as a courtier, a 'ninny'[16] or 'puerile'.[17] There is no question of his ability as a civil servant and finance expert. His post-war books also show such an estimate of him to be untenable. The problem is of quite a different dimension. Listing the pros and cons of von Krosigk's behaviour under National-Socialism, one is immediately struck by the sharp contrast between his public and his private code of morals. In certain respects Dönitz and Jodl are parallel cases but they belong more to the category of the degenerate phenomena of total war. Nowhere is this moral dichotomy so glaring as in the case of von Krosigk. In private life he was true to his character, upright, charitable, impeccable. In public life he not only tolerated but participated in the illegal practices of the regime. These double standards had a double reason: worship of the nation as an absolute concept; an exaggerated sense of duty and an exaggerated notion of loyalty. Anything which was to the benefit of the nation, whether legal or not, was justified. The idea of the community was so transcendent that it overrode all norms and codes of values. So long as Hitler was leading the nation from defeat to recognition, success and victory, so long was he accepted and his measures tolerated. When the gulf between the traditional code of morals and that of the State became too wide, the resultant conflict of conscience was salved by tempering and mitigating those measures thought to be over-extreme. An exaggerated sense of duty forbade withdrawal from an office increasingly felt to be burdensome.

Von Krosigk did not equate Hitler with Germany, as did Dönitz and Jodl. As scion of an ancient family he did not place an upstart like Hitler on a level with the Reich, which had its roots in very different traditions. The demagogue thrown up by history had his role to play (as Schwerin von Krosigk had his role in his appointed place), but if he failed, he should disappear.

Differences and similarities between Dönitz and Jodl on the one hand and Schwerin von Krosigk on the other become more comprehensible if set against the behaviour of Albert Speer. In 1944, after a period of illness and realising the inevitability of defeat, Speer could no longer bring into consonance his loyalty to Hitler and his loyalty to the nation, nor did he equate the two. During the last month of the war, however, he found it impossible to sever his ties with Hitler and the result was an ambivalent attitude.

The comparison was even closer in the case of these men's reactions to the events of 20 July 1944. Though neither Speer nor von Krosigk questioned the Dictator's right to rule, both doubted whether his continued presence was desirable.

Dönitz and Jodl condemned the coup unequivocally – and were regarded as enemies by the conspirators. Von Krosigk was also an opponent, although many of the resisters were his personal friends – von Hassell the Ambassador, Johannes Popitz the

Prussian Finance Minister, Fritz von der Schulenburg, Graf Peter Yorck, Graf Helldorf, General Stülpnagel, General Wagner, Colonel Graf Stauffenberg and Field Marshal von Witzleben. He was friendly with Goerdeler and related both to Ulrich-Wilhelm Graf Schwerin von Schwanfeld and Kurt Plettenberg. Nevertheless, in spite of appeals from their relatives, he refused to intervene with Hitler in favour of his cousin Schwerin-Schwanfeld or Schulenburg or Peter Yorck. He did, however, write to Kalten-brunner and later to the People's Court requesting release from arrest for his brother-in-law Friedrich Karl von Zitzewitz, since he was convinced that the extent of his complicity was limited to knowledge of Goerdeler's plans. On 19 September 1944 he asked Lammers to bring the matter of his arrest before Hitler either verbally or by showing him the following letter: 'Since the case concerns a close relative, I feel it my duty to inform you of this fact and leave it to you to decide whether you wish to retain me as a Cabinet Minister. I assure you that my brother-in-law has never discussed Goerdeler's plans with me. Heil, my Führer! In abiding loyalty.' The Finance Minister remained in office, his duty to confiscate the conspirators' property. Once again he attempted to mitigate hardships and ease the lot of the relatives.

Speer also condemned the coup – and then busied himself later with similar plans. His reason was deep-rooted devotion to Hitler. When he realised that the tyrant was becoming a disaster for his people, he thought to render service both to Germany – and to Hitler himself. Probably he could not bring himself to destroy his picture of Hitler. Nevertheless, because of their technical qualifications and without their knowledge, both he and von Krosigk were considered by the resisters as potential allies.[18]

Von Krosigk's reactions were, in fact, astoundingly consistent. His attitude to the war, for instance, shows a similar pattern. He tried to warn Hitler against world war, particularly at a time when it seemed to him inopportune. On 23 August 1939, after an official visit to Italy, he wrote to von Ribbentrop (of whom he had no opinion) that Hitler would be proved wrong in his views on the British attitude and that Britain and France would go to war if Germany intervened in Poland. When war had become a fact, however, and he had no choice but to accept it, he tried to prevent it spreading. On 6 November 1939, for instance, he wrote a long letter to Göring, Germany's Number Two, pointing out the weaknesses in the Reich's economy, not yet even recovered from the effects of World War I. He warned against any move into neutral countries and against war in the West. Even at that time he did not believe that Germany could win a major war: 'If England does not *win* the war, she has lost it. If we do not *lose* the war, we have won it.' Some years later this point of view led many people, Dönitz among them, to continue a war which, militarily, had long since been lost. Von Krosigk also realised that attack in the West would mean that 'we had finally turned our backs on a peaceful settlement'. His fear at the time was of over-dependence on Italy and Russia; that Hitler would embark on a war on two fronts never entered his head.

The fact, however, that the German press played down the conclusion of the Russo-Japanese Pact, merely reporting it tersely on an inconspicuous page, shed a new light on an earlier remark by Göring that Germany's relationship to Russia might change, since the existence of this Bolshevist state was not helpful to the reconstruction of Europe. Von Krosigk had hitherto believed Göring's statements to imply that 'in pursuance of the Führer's policy we must be prepared against all eventualities and take all precautions to facilitate any possible change in Russia whether in personalities or in the political views of authoritative quarters there'. In a letter to Göring of 19 April 1941 he listed a whole series of facts arguing against war with Russia, the first of which was the food situation; in contrast to the majority view he considered that this would seriously deteriorate rather than improve. Current delivery agreements, he pointed out, could not fail to be affected by the resultant destruction and transport chaos. He reminded Göring of his remark on the outbreak of war that maintenance of the people's morale and power of resistance would be one of the most difficult problems. Would not the prospect of a war on two fronts, he asked, together with total uncertainty regarding the war's end, constitute a test too severe for large sections of the population? Moreover Germany would be bring-ing about precisely that turn of events which the enemy, despite all his wiles, had failed to achieve, namely to bring Russia over to his side. 'It would be the "Miracle of the Marne" for which they are still hoping without knowing whence it may come. Are we to make a present of it to them?' Attack on Russia would raise the hopes of all those in the occupied territories still looking for a

German defeat; a wave of sabotage would ensue. Finally he asked: 'If, within a period of two years, Germany swings from bitter enmity through loudly trumpeted friendship back again to enmity leading to armed conflict, do you not think that she will forfeit the confidence essential to her if she is to be the ruling power in Europe and the leading world power in the post-war world? Do you not think that a second complete change of front would rob our foreign policy of any basis for the present Axis policy which must be founded on confidence?'

The existence both of a Bolshevist Russia and a National-Socialist Germany did not seem to von Krosigk to imply a danger necessitating armed conflict. He pointed to the traditional Anglo-Russian differences and opined that world-revolutionary tendencies would 'gradually die away in favour of a socialism with its eye on Russian domestic requirements'. He even adduced the biological argument so dear to National-Socialism, questioning whether the Germans could really colonise the conquered areas. The German population growth rate was inadequate, he said, whereas the strength of the Slavs lay in their fertility and willingness to emigrate. Inevitably therefore the Slavs would win in the end.

Von Krosigk did not believe that Russia would default on her treaty obligations and in fact the Russians fulfilled them to the very day before the outbreak of war. He therefore saw neither necessity nor occasion for war with the East and considered that far better prospects were offered by a blow 'at that position which England still holds but where she is most susceptible, the Suez Canal; this would place us in a dominating position *vis-à-vis* Africa *and* Asia Minor'. It would put an end to any weakening on the part of Italy, and Turkey too 'could hardly evade the great pincers'; if the air and submarine war against England were then intensified, 'the time could not be far distant when England would be weak and America would hardly take the suicidal step of declaring war on both Japan and Germany. At the moment when the guns go off between Russia and Germany, however, such a possibility is lost for ever.'

Von Krosigk did not know that the decision had already been taken. Though a member of their cabinet, the Nazis did not tell him of their plans; he was of value only as a useful tool. Nevertheless when war with the East came, he once more bowed to the inevitable and did his utmost for a German victory. Ultimately he even hailed exploitation of the conquered territories as a 'relief from the financial and economic points of view'. On the other hand, as already mentioned, he opposed the policy of stripping the East, pleaded for decent treatment for Eastern workers and even referred to the steadfastness and endurance of the Russian people in terms of admiration which, coming from a Minister of the Reich in December 1943, would have made many people wonder. Von Krosigk wanted Germany to appear in the East as liberator, not conqueror. He urged the abolition of all the machinery of Bolshevism, reintroduction of private property and a pro-Church policy.

When finally the star of the 'political gambler' (as von Krosigk privately called Hitler) began to wane and he seemed to be bent solely upon Germany's ruin, von Krosigk found himself at one with Speer in an effort 'to bring about the inevitable end as soon as possible and with the minimum casualties and damage'. In his capacity as Minister for Armaments and War Production Speer used to hold regular meetings with the Permanent Secretaries from various ministries and in the wings of these a circle of Ministers took to meeting in Speer's house at three- to four-weekly intervals during the winter 1944/45. In addition to von Krosigk there was Dorpmüller (Transport), Backe (Food) and less frequently Franz Seldte (Labour).[19] Bormann heard of these gatherings and told Hitler, who is said to have forbidden these 'defeatist club evenings'. The Ministers, however, let it be known that, although he could dismiss them, he could not forbid them to meet and talk to each other. Nothing more was said.

As already described, in the final months von Krosigk initiated a lively correspondence in the hope of easing Germany's position by negotiations. This he did, in the words of his defence counsel to the American Military Tribunal, 'for the sake of his country in its mortal struggle'.

When the 'unobtrusive' move from Berlin of Ministries and senior Reich authorities produced the increasingly frequent comment that the rats were deserting the sinking ship, von Krosigk approached Goebbels with the suggestion that 'an explanatory word over the western radio might perhaps be salutary'. Hitler thereupon forbade any further move by Ministers and their immediate staff before mid-April. The great Russian offensive of 16 April, however, and the inexorable move of the

Russian advanced guards on Berlin soon made it clear that there would shortly be no further possibility of an organised evacuation southwards. On Hitler's birthday, therefore, Kritzinger, State Secretary of the Reich Chancellery, enquired cautiously of Bormann whether new instructions on the subject were to be forthcoming. After checking with Hitler the reply was: 'No change.' Later that evening, obviously when Hitler had decided to move to the south himself, Bormann called Kritzinger to say that those Reich authorities due to move to the Southern Zone must leave within the next two hours or they would not get through. In view of the dangerous situation, however, the order did not apply to Ministers. They were to remain in Berlin and, if necessary, move to the north and fly south from there. Major Büchs of the OKW Operations Staff, who was responsible for organising the air transport of the Führer's Headquarters, advised that, if possible, they should move to Schwerin and Eutin, where radio and air communications were still available. Four-engined Condor aircraft were held ready to transport the Führer and his immediate entourage. Shortly thereafter came another telephone call from Bormann: According to Göring the proposed air move of Ministers to the south created difficulties; they were to leave for the south by road that same night. Hardly had the necessary instructions been issued than a further call arrived, this time from Högel, a criminal police officer in the Führer's apartment: Road movement southwards must be stopped forthwith, since no passage through to the south was now possible. Kritzinger at once informed all offices concerned. Only one did he fail to reach: Göring with a column of trucks had already left Berlin for the south. The move had been authorised by Hitler personally.

Late that evening Stuckart, the Permanent Secretary of the Ministry of the Interior, told Kritzinger that Soviet troops had already reached Bernau. Was not this the moment for the move north? A call to Bormann elicited the necessary authorisation, with the proviso that the move should be made as unobtrusively as possible or the Führer would later call the Ministers to account when they reached the Southern Zone. Kritzinger immediately passed on this new instruction, initially by telephone but later, during the night, in writing. After checking with Bormann, Ministers were 'recommended' to leave.[20] That night or during

21 April the following left for the North: Backe (Food), Dorpmüller (Transport), Ribbentrop (Foreign Affairs), Rosenberg (Occupied Eastern Territories), Rust (Science, Education and Training), Schwerin von Krosigk (Finance), Seldte (Labour) together with a number of civil servants. The meeting-point was the local government office in Eutin, which had the advantage of being near Dönitz' command post. In the Southern Zone were Funk (Economics), Ohnesorge (Posts), Lammers (Head of the Reich Chancellery), and Göring. Supreme military and political direction still lay nominally in the hands of Hitler and the OKW Operations Staff North, but with transport in chaos and communications difficult the division of staffs and authorities into northern and southern groups made any central direction illusory. The head was now separated from the limbs.

The difficulties associated with this division of authorities and staffs is illustrated by a minor incident. After von Krosigk had laboriously extricated himself from Berlin, threading his way through columns of refugees, and had finally reached the Northern Zone, he was held up first by a military check-point and then by a police captain because he had no pass signed by Field Marshal Busch. To control the continuous infiltration of refugees into the Northern Zone and ensure that it was ready to defend itself, Busch had given strict orders that no unauthorised persons were to be allowed in; the captain who held up von Krosigk had already received a 'rocket' for letting through another Minister, Rust. Only with the greatest difficulty did von Krosigk reach the local government offices in Eutin under escort and thence telephoned Field Marshal Busch.

Meanwhile – morning 21 April – Kritzinger had informed Bormann that the move was complete and that he himself would leave at 5.0 p.m. To his query how long they intended to remain in Berlin Bormann replied: 'The Führer desires to continue to organise the defence here.' When Kritzinger again reported to Bormann from Dönitz' command post after his move and said that he had initiated preparations for the flight southwards, Bormann told him that this was no longer necessary since 'they were remaining in Berlin'.[21]

The Ministers who had moved north therefore established themselves provisionally in Eutin; they met almost daily with the exception of Himmler who was in Lübeck, and Ribbentrop who set himself up in the neighbourhood of Plön. Shortly thereafter Rust and Rosenberg arrived in the Flensburg area. The only Minister who frequently drove over to see Dönitz was Speer. The only other contact was the conversation between Dönitz and von Krosigk already described. Work was practically impossible. All were waiting for the end. When the truth of Göring's 'illness' filtered through, discussion turned to the reasons for this catastrophe and the problem of the succession. Göring was regarded as primarily responsible for the military defeat owing to the failure of the Luftwaffe. Political errors were laid at the door of Ribbentrop and criminal types like Erich Koch and Bormann. Hitler, the real culprit, was never discussed. His death was counted upon daily. The most likely candidate for the succession was thought to be Himmler. Had it been passed to him in Hitler's testament, no one would have disputed the legality of his claim. Even in the absence of a testament he was thought to have the best prospects; it seemed futile to refer to Para 51 of the Weimar Constitution, which designated the President of the Reich Court as successor, since the whereabouts of the latter were unknown. An emergency regulation passing executive authority to the armed forces seemed more suitable. No one, however, thought of Field Marshal Keitel, who was regarded merely as Hitler's creature. Himmler, on the other hand, as Chief of the German Police, Minister of the Interior and Commander-in-Chief of the Replacement Army, held 'in his own hands the greatest actual power'. In order to avoid conflicts and misunderstandings between the Reich Government and the senior military authority in the Northern Zone, the members of the 'Northern Cabinet' thought it indispensable that Dönitz and Himmler should be in constant contact, primarily to check separatist tendencies. Von Krosigk noted in his diary: 'In Hamburg and Bremen people are already thinking of a North-West German Reich, possibly under an English Prince; to them the Reich equals Hecuba.'

Although under the circumstances he could see no other solution, von Krosigk had the gravest doubts about Himmler as the successor, since the name of the Reichsführer-SS was 'rightly or wrongly linked with the murkiest chapter unfortunately ever to be found in recent German history'. He thought it essential that, on assuming office, Himmler should announce a whole series of measures amounting to 'a change in previous policy and a rejection of much that is repugnant to people both externally and internally'.

The composition of the new cabinet was also discussed in Eutin. Seldte, Backe, Dorpmüller and Speer all told von Krosigk that he was the only possible candidate for Foreign Minister, if not for Chancellor.

On 1 May arrived the news of Hitler's death. This was now 'hardly shattering', but with it came 'the surprising news that he had nominated Grand Admiral Dönitz as his successor'.[22] Von Krosigk thereupon drove over to Dönitz' headquarters to discuss matters with Speer. The latter, who was in and out of Dönitz office, told him that the Grand Admiral was looking for a Foreign Minister and that he (Speer) had proposed him (von Krosigk). Von Krosigk immediately drafted a radio speech which he considered that the Foreign Minister should make, but stressed his lack of qualifications for the office, saying that he was 'a Minister foreign to Foreign Affairs' and too colourless a personality for his name to be associated with any programme abroad. Dönitz, who was busy drafting his call to the German people and the Wehrmacht, asked him via Speer to accept the post. Von Krosigk asked for a day to think it over.

That evening he paid another visit to Himmler at the SS Command Post between Eutin and Plön. Similar to the festival atmosphere in the Führer's bunker after the death of Hitler, he found the SS leaders in the best of spirits – laughing and drinking on the principle of '*Le roi est mort, vive le roi*'. Himmler himself indulged in the wildest fantasies. He was convinced that he was secure in his role as Number Two in the new German state and already saw himself accepted by Montgomery and Eisenhower as 'an indispensable factor for law and order' in the fight against Bolshevism.

After hearing Dönitz' appeal over the radio and therewith the outline of his programme, on the morning of 2 May von Krosigk gave the Admiral his agreement, but only after a long discussion during which Dönitz appealed to his sense of duty and gave him to understand that there were no laurels to be gathered.[23] With the nomination of von Krosigk as the new Foreign Minister Dönitz had now assembled all the most important members of the staff which he considered necessary for the implementation of his policy. During the next few days he formed his cabinet.

CHAPTER FIVE

The Acting Reich Government

THE formation of a government to succeed Hitler was a complex and gradual process. Although the more important appointments were made between 2 and 5 May, the government was still incomplete when its members were arrested on the 23rd. The real starting-point was the third radio message from Berlin giving details of Hitler's testament.[1] The delay in transmission of Hitler's instructions seemed suspect to Dönitz and the list of Ministers contained therein a restriction of his freedom of action. Initially therefore he ordered his aide to keep the document secret.[2] Later he discussed it with Keitel and von Krosigk, who both supported his view that, though Hitler might nominate his successor, he could not dictate the choice of that successor's staff. So far Dönitz had been content to work with a Foreign Minister as adviser. Now, however, he decided on the formation of a regular government.

In doing so he accepted Hitler's division of the office of Führer and never claimed this title for himself. During the drive from Plön to Flensburg on the evening of 2 May he discussed the formation of a cabinet with von Krosigk, his newly-appointed Foreign Minister. In his memoirs von Krosigk says that Dönitz wished to appoint him Chancellor and had prepared an announcement to that effect; he felt, however, that to use this title, which had once been Bismarck's, in defeated Germany was 'akin to sacrilege.' Both the office and title had also been Hitler's – a fact which von Krosigk does not mention. He preferred the designation 'Chief Minister' for himself and 'Acting Reich Government' for the Cabinet, in order to emphasise its provisional and transitional nature, also the restriction of its responsibilities to the task in hand. Von Krosigk's concept of the new government's task was described by Walter Donandt, a member of his staff, as follows: 'This collection of people must feel themselves to be representatives of the Reich in its entirety; they should regard as their task, however, not to make policy but to save the German people from the supreme economic crisis implicit in a breakdown of food supply, transport, the social order etc.'

On 2 May the members of the Reich cabinet handed in their resignations. The President (Dönitz) and his Chief Minister therefore now had to decide which of the previous ministers they would retain and which should be dismissed. The simplest problem was that of the Party dignitaries who were not present – Göring, Goebbels and Bormann. Von Krosigk proposed that, should they appear, Goebbels and Bormann should be arrested. Göring was already under arrest and a query from Kesselring on 5 May whether he could be released into the unoccupied zone was answered in the negative on 6 May on the advice of OKW.[3] Meanwhile, however, Göring had contrived to escape and in a letter to Dönitz he proposed that he instead of Jodl should negotiate with Eisenhower 'Marshal to Marshal'. When this letter arrived, however, Jodl was already in Reims and it was pigeonholed. Göring surrendered to the Americans.[4]

The other Ministers in the Southern Zone, Funk, Ohnesorge and Lammers, equally presented no problem in the formation of the new cabinet. They were recommended to hand themselves over to the Allies in proper form. The most difficult case was that of Himmler, Reichsführer-SS, Minister of the Interior and Commander-in-Chief of the Replacement Army. On several occasions he appeared unannounced in Dönitz' office and took part in the discussions. Accompanied by a strong SS escort, he attempted to maintain his aura of power. Dönitz had given him to understand that he would have no post in the new government, but it was not so easy to dismiss him from his existing offices. The variety of the wordings proposed to this end shows how uneasy the situation was; Reichsleiter Bohle arrived from the south and attempted to explain to Himmler that he would have no further function; following this a meeting was held during the night of 4 May from which the following draft emerged: 'While retaining command of the Waffen-SS, the Reichsführer-SS, Heinrich Himmler, has assumed responsibility for the maintenance of law and order as Chief of the German Police'. This was in line with an order issued on the same day prescribing that responsibility for the maintenance of law and order lay with Field Marshal Busch, Commander-in-Chief North-west, for the Schleswig-Holstein Zone and with the Reichsführer-SS for all other areas.

On the next day, 5 May, when the local surrender in the north came into force,[5] Dönitz proposed a much looser wording: 'The Reichsführer-SS, Heinrich Himmler, has placed himself at the disposal of the Grand Admiral.' Himmler obviously did not agree with this and so von Krosigk produced a new formula: 'The Reichsführer-SS, Heinrich Himmler, has placed himself at the disposal of the Grand Admiral to assist in the maintenance of law and order.' Even this did not satisfy Himmler. Clearly he wished to take over some office which would serve to rehabilitate him and allow him to demonstrate the 'humanitarian aspirations' which he had been emphasising for some months. He proposed the following: 'The Reichsführer-SS, Heinrich Himmler, has placed himself at the disposal of the Grand Admiral for the solution of the refugee problem and the maintenance of public order.'

On 6 May, when the overall capitulation began to take effect, the vital steps were finally taken. Letters of dismissal prepared by von Krosigk were despatched to Rosenberg, Rust and Thierack telling them that the Grand Admiral had decided to dispense with their further services and thanking them for their service to the Reich; a similar letter to Himmler was 'cancelled on the orders of the Grand Admiral'. In an interview at 5.0 p.m. Dönitz told Himmler personally that he was dispensing with his services as Minister of the Interior, Commander of the Replacement Army and Chief of Police and that he regarded all relations between him and the present government as severed. The office of Reichsführer-SS was not mentioned. Himmler was also told not to visit Dönitz' headquarters in future. At the same time the Admiral seems to have issued some general instruction forbidding leading National-Socialists to visit the government building in Flensburg. In fact, Himmler wandered about for several days, under a false name and in disguise, accompanied by a number of senior SS officers. Captured by an Allied patrol, he committed suicide on 23 May, the day of the government's arrest.[6]

Police General Wünnenberg initially took over the police; Obergruppenführer and Waffen-SS General Jüttner was ordered to assemble all members of the SS in a collecting camp. On 17 May, however, he and the majority of SS headquarters were arrested at Arenholz, north-west of Schleswig. OKW thereupon informed the Allied Control Commission that it regarded itself as 'absolved from responsibility for the consequences to be anticipated from the dissolution of the reception organisation'.

Ribbentrop, the ex-Foreign Minister, appeared in Hamburg under a false name and was later arrested. Rust committed suicide in a hospital to which von Krosigk had sent him at the request of Zschintsch, his State Secretary.

The arrest of Rosenberg, the ex-Minister for the Occupied Eastern Territories, was almost a music-hall turn. He first had to be forcibly reminded of Dönitz' ban on entry into the government building (he arrived drunk); then he sprained his ankle after a drinking match and was handed over to the Military Hospital in Mürwick. There he learnt through the press and radio that the British authorities were looking for him. The perfect bureaucrat to the last, he summoned Professor Gebhardt, the notorious Hohenlychen doctor, who had carried out experimental operations on prisoners and was now, at the instigation of his friend Himmler, acting President of the German Red Cross;[7] he was persuaded to draw up a certificate that Rosenberg was 'confined to bed with severe bleeding as a result of torn joint ligaments' and was under doctor's orders. On 12 May, via the German Liaison Staff to 21 Army Group, Rosenberg sent this certificate with a covering letter to Field Marshal Montgomery. At the same time came a letter from Thierack, the ex-Minister of Justice, who also placed himself at the disposal of the Allied command. Dr. Brandt, the Inspector General of the Health Service and for many years Hitler's doctor, also wrote to the Allied Control Party which had meanwhile arrived in Flensburg.[8] On 13 and 14 May the Acting Reich Government announced the arrival of Rosenberg's letter. On 18 May, with considerable fuss, Rosenberg's hospital was surrounded by British troops and the staff accused of harbouring the ex-Minister. Kritzinger, State Secretary to the Acting Reich Government, immediately protested to the Control Party against this accusation.

Von Krosigk insisted that Ministers in the Acting Government should be chosen primarily for their technical competence. In view, however, of the chaotic situation in Germany with practically all communications cut, this was hardly feasible. Von Krosigk was forced to include in his cabinet such ex-Ministers as had escaped to the Northern Zone and to replace those who seemed too incriminated by their only slightly less incriminated State Secretaries. Ministers were dropped for purely practical rather than ethical reasons, as is proved by the notes of a ministerial discussion of 13 May: 'For political reasons highly "incriminated" persons should, as far as possible, not be employed in individual departments.' The only senior minister to be retained, at Dönitz' express wish, was Speer as Minister of Economics and Production. Speer made it plain, however, that he only wished to take over this office temporarily. The real head of the Economics Department (six members and eight office staff) was Otto Ohlendorf, Head of the Internal Intelligence Service of the RSHA; since 1943 he had double-banked this appointment with those of Section Head, Director and finally acting State Secretary in the Reich Ministry of Economics. He was a cold ideologist, protagonist of a peculiarly National-Socialist economic theory based on the maintenance of small- and medium-sized businesses.

Apart from his experience as an economic expert Ohlendorf placed at the disposal of the Acting Reich Government those parts of his intelligence service which had escaped to the Northern Zone; they included in particular the ex-Heads of the sections 'Ethnology' and 'Economics' and the desks 'Popular Culture and Art', 'Occupied Territories' and 'Legal Matters'. These were incorporated into the Reich Government's Intelligence Office set up on 13 May under the temporary leadership of Captain (Navy) von Davidson. An instruction issued by von Krosigk set out the duties of this office as follows:

'The duty of the Intelligence Office is to obtain and evaluate the necessary political, economic and military information and reports, both external and internal, for the benefit of all members of the Reich Government and their offices. It will also distribute and publicise such speeches, announcements and reports of all types as may be issued or desired by individual Reich ministers and their offices.'

The Intelligence Office was manned partially from the Wehrmacht ('National-Socialist Leadership Staff', Propaganda Office and Propaganda Troops), partially from the late Foreign Ministry and partially from Section III of the RSHA.

Whereas the Acting Government offices were in general short of personnel, the strength of the Intelligence Office, according to a strength return dated 23 May 1945 from von Krosigk's State

Secretary, was 59, with in addition 109 NCO's and men, 26 male and 33 female employees, 2 drivers and 1 member of the Women's Naval Service.

Ohlendorf wrote to von Krosigk enclosing a report explaining the advantages of the 'spheres of life intelligence service' which he had created. This, he said, was of particular importance in a Führer State which lacked the corrective of parliamentary and publicity institutions. It was intended to be a source of information for the leaders of the State concerning the mood and views of the people – practically a substitute for public criticism. To ensure that it remained objective, it was desirable that it should be independent of the government, the administration and all pressure groups. The material should be evaluated and summarised by a small number of experts; the actual informers, however, should be unpaid workers drawn from all walks of life. It should be modelled not on a Fouché-type spy system but on the British Secret Service, a sort of 'gentleman's affair' such as Heydrich had planned.[9]

Ohlendorf's report was discussed by Dönitz and von Krosigk. Both agreed that its transmission to the Allies, as Ohlendorf had proposed, was 'initially inadvisable'. They were content to receive the evaluation of reports from former members of the SD now employed by the Intelligence Office.

As Minister of the Interior Dr. Wilhelm Stuckart, the State Secretary, succeeded Himmler on 3 May. He was a highly qualified civil servant who had carried out in exemplary fashion any task given him by the government irrespective of its morality. Both his professional career and his devotion to his country show him as a typical example of those German officials who climbed on the National-Socialist bandwagon and not only welcomed but promoted the regime's measures.

As the fortunes of the Reich declined, even this gallant patriot came to the conclusion that the time had arrived to put an end to National-Socialist domination. His conviction did not, however, lead to any action.

As Minister of the Interior in Flensburg Stuckart headed the second-largest office (thirteen members and nine office staff). One of his subordinates was his ex-colleague as State Secretary, Dr. Leonardo Conti, who committed suicide when threatened with arrest. In general Stuckart's activity in the Acting Government was confined to the preparation of a few legal memoranda[10] and discussions with the Control Commission.

By far the most important department in Flensberg was the Reich Ministry of Food. Dönitz proposed, and von Krosigk agreed, that the previous Minister, Herbert Backe,[11] be retained. He was both an expert and a staunch National-Socialist, whose services to the regime had been inestimable.

As already mentioned, during the winter 1944/45, he became alarmed by the rapidly deteriorating situation and held meetings with von Krosigk and Dorpmüller. The Soviet break-through at Baranov and their subsequent advance compelled him to take drastic measures on the food front and to cut the ration. A teleprint of 25 January 1945 to all *Land* Agriculture Leaders gave priority to food supply for towns and industrial areas.

To assist him Backe had Hans-Joachim Riecke, his State Secretary, also an old Party member with a career in many respects similar to those of Stuckart and Backe. From autumn 1944 he had been a member of Speer's circle. As early as 18 September he had issued instructions to the *Land* Food Offices to refrain from destruction and keep production going as long as possible. A memorandum entitled 'Economics of the Food Situation' and dated 24 February 1945 set out the catastrophic food position and forecast a 35% reduction of rations from 9 April, which implied that 'the Wehrmacht would remain capable of fighting but the majority of the civil population would no longer be fully fit for work'. When this produced no reaction from Hitler, Riecke, together with his Minister and Speer, decided on further measures. Within his department he did all he could to ensure that people would be fed, even should the anticipated transport catastrophe occur. In accordance with the instructions already issued to the *Land* Agriculture Leaders priority in the build-up of reserves and food stocks was given to the towns and industrial areas. Everyone was urged to restrict destruction or paralysation measures in so far as food production was concerned. As a follow up to Speer's executive instruction on Hitler's decree of 30 March which ordered 'production to continue to the last possible moment even under the most difficult circumstances', Riecke urged that food supply to industrial concerns be maintained whatever the situation; it was for consideration, he said, whether the object could not be achieved by paralysation measures as opposed to destruction and whether supplies which could not be moved should not be handed out to the population. Priority over arms production was given to the maintenance of nitrogen works producing fertilisers for agriculture, to fuel production and the repair of agricultural machinery.[12]

On 7 April Speer extracted an order from Hitler that bridges were only to be blown if operationally necessary, that transport was to be kept moving up to the last moment and that all installations, railway lines, industrial stocks, workshop installations and the communications facilities of the Posts, railways and private companies were to be paralysed rather than destroyed. Riecke immediately followed with an order applicable to his domain, demanding that transport for foodstuffs be maintained as long as possible. Both Speer and Riecke elaborated and underlined their instructions by personal visits to the *Land* Agriculture Leaders in the west.

Encouraged by Speer, Riecke did not confine himself merely to measures designed to ease the lot of the people; he was also aiming at an early end to the war and internal changes in the Reich. Discussions took place in his office with SS-Obergruppenführer Hildebrandt together with Backe, Speer and Dr. Hupfauer of the Armaments Ministry, when plans were concocted to eliminate Bormann and Keitel and force Hitler to end the war. They foundered on the indecision both of the participants and of the Reichsführer-SS.

As Ministers in the Acting Government both Backe and his State Secretary[13] devoted themselves wholeheartedly to their job.[14] Their entire staff consisted of a single Assistant Secretary whom Riecke had brought with him from Berlin.

The next in line among the disillusioned patriots was Julius Heinrich Dorpmüller, whom von Krosigk confirmed in his office as Minister of Transport, giving him in addition that of Postmaster General. Under him as State Secretaries were Ganzenmüller (Transport) and Nagel (Posts), each with two staff officers and a clerk. His assumption of office was only notified to the Allied Control Party on 22 May, by which time Dorpmüller had moved back to Malente in the Eutin district. Politically Dorpmüller was the least conspicuous of the Ministers in the Acting Government.

The Ministry of Labour and Social Security was left in the hands of its previous incumbent, Franz Seldte, a typical representative of conservative nationalist circles with large-scale upper-class political and industrial interests.

As already mentioned,[15] towards the end of the war Seldte established contact with Himmler and Schellenberg and planned to eliminate Hitler. Probably he hoped to recapture some political role. His department in Flensburg was staffed by his personal assistant, two staff officers and eight clerks. There is no record of any activity on his part.[16]

Other leading members of the Acting Reich Government were the State Secretaries Kurt Klemm, Werner Zschintsch and Baron von Steengracht von Moyland.

Klemm was provisionally placed in charge of the Ministry of Justice. Theoretically he was under Dr. Bumcke, the President of the Reich Court, whose whereabouts, however, were unknown.[17] As State Secretary in the Ministry of Justice he had supported for years the policy of Thierack, his Minister. In Flensburg he hardly appeared in the forefront at all; his department was the smallest of all – he was the only member of it.

Although Stuckart was in charge of the Reich Ministry of Education, the real head of it was Werner Zschintsch, who had one staff officer. Since on Allied instructions schools and colleges initially remained closed, the department was superfluous and did nothing at all during the short period of its existence. It was intended later to take over ecclesiastical affairs.

Von Krosigk, the Chief Minister of the Acting Government, was also both Finance and Foreign Minister. In his capacity as Head of Government and Finance Minister he had eight staff officers and five clerks. His State Secretary was Friedrich Wilhelm Kritzinger, late of the same post in the Reich Chancellery. For financial matters he used Walter Donandt, his personal assistant from the Reich Finance Ministry.

The Foreign Department formed an entirely separate office. It consisted of the State Secretary, von Steengracht, one Under-Secretary – Andor Hencke, one minister [Gesandte] 1st class – Schnurre, two counsellors [Legationsrat] 1st class – Freiherr Dietrich von Mirbach and Lohse, two counsellors, one administrative officer [Oberregierungsrat] and fourteen clerks. The real head of the Foreign Affairs Office was Baron von Steengracht.

His attitude was similar to that of von Krosigk, though he lacked the latter's technical qualifications. A weak and unstable character, he had, thanks to Ribbentrop's protection, reached a position to which he was not equal and which led him into collaboration in illegal measures. In Flensburg his activity was confined to a few routine matters.[18]

In addition to these nine Ministries plus the Intelligence Office, the Acting Reich Government had a 'Government Bureau' under a Principal [Ministerialrat] – Herrmann. This was responsible for the supply of office equipment, accommodation, food and welfare, transport (the government still possessed a few cars), passes, telephones, office staff and drivers. The 'bureau' consisted of four officials and six clerks.

Including ancillary personnel, therefore, the total strength of the Acting Reich Government was about 350.

The following were disbanded: the Ministry of Popular Enlightenment and Propaganda, the Ministry of Armaments and War Production, the Ministry of Aviation, the Ministry for the Occupied Eastern Territories.

Dönitz' Military and Civil Private Offices did not belong to the Government. Both were shown, however, in the 'Personnel Report of the Acting Reich Government' of 23 May 1945 and they are therefore mentioned here to complete the picture.

The Head and sole member of the Military Private Office was Rear-Admiral Wagner.[19] At the head of the Civil Private Office was Gauleiter Wegener with the title of State Secretary. He had one assistant, Dr. Helmut Stellrecht, together with one male and two female clerks.

Paul Wegener[20] was present at the majority of the important discussions; all press and radio announcements had to be submitted to him. He was also responsible for assembling material for the archives and subsequent official history. This was later sifted by Dönitz and von Krosigk and passed down to history as the 'White Book'. Wegener was calm and efficient. He and Stellrecht were responsible for most of the memoranda on the Reich's external political prospects.[20]

The composition of the new cabinet therefore shows that it consisted of two interlocking groups: the national conservatives who had proved susceptible to National-Socialism partly through mistaken idealism and partly through opportunism (von Krosigk,

Seldte, Dorpmüller, von Steengracht, Zschintsch, Klemm); the real National-Socialists who, primarily for reasons of patriotism, were striving for reform of the system and were at one with the first group on the necessity for this (Speer, Backe, Riecke, Ohlendorf, Stuckart, Wegener). The reformist tendency was therefore far stronger than the restorationist. Evolution was to succeed revolution.

Part Two

THE GOVERNMENT'S ACTIVITIES

The three weeks of the new government's activity were clearly divided into two distinct parts. Until the signature of general capitulation Dönitz and his team acted as, and felt themselves to be, a legitimate sovereign German government. After general capitulation the new Head of State, OKW and the Acting Reich Government were subject to the orders of the Allies. In practice they were nothing but prisoners of war, enjoying a certain freedom within their 'enclave'.

Up to capitulation Dönitz was primarily occupied with military matters; the business of forming a cabinet, already described, went on in parallel. With one or two exceptions, activity in the civil field only began after the capitulation of 8 May.

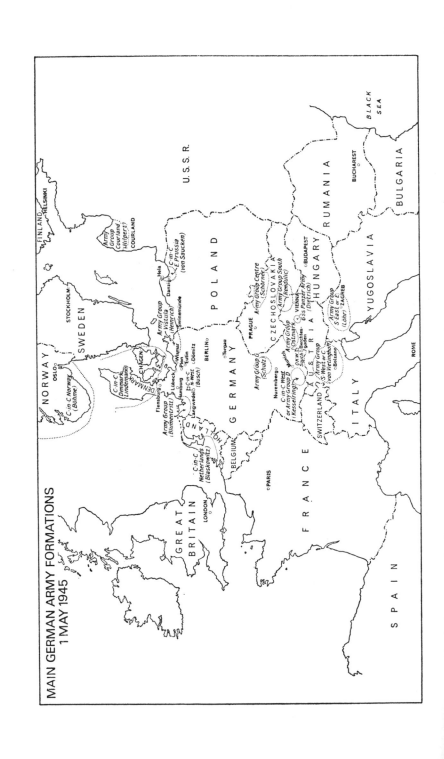

MAIN GERMAN ARMY FORMATIONS
1 MAY 1945

CHAPTER SIX

Pre-Capitulation

ÖNITZ' most urgent task on receipt of the radio message
from Berlin telling him that he was the designated successor
was to draft a reply to the Führer's bunker. In view of
Hitler's previous reactions to the steps taken by Göring and
Himmler, the wording required careful consideration. Dönitz'
telegram clearly had to express readiness to assume the office
conferred on him, but it must also contain a last word of
encouragement since everyone was anticipating Hitler's early and
final disappearance from the scene.

Albert Speer and Captain von Davidson, the Head of the Naval
Intelligence Section, were charged with the production of a
suitable draft.

The naval draft was short and to the point, leaving the Grand
Admiral all possible freedom of action: 'My Führer! I have
received your charge. I will justify your confidence by doing my
utmost to act for the good of the German people, faithful to your
own concept.'

Dönitz, however, preferred Speer's proposal, drafted on his
instructions, and amended it only in minor detail. This was far more
emotional: 'My Führer! My loyalty to you is eternal and unconditional. I shall therefore continue to make every effort to relieve
you in Berlin. Should, however, fate compel me to lead the
German Reich as your designated successor, I shall conduct this
war to the end in the mannner demanded by the German people's
unique heroic struggle.'

This telegram has been characterised as ambiguous,[1] and has
been read as indicating that on the evening of 30 April Dönitz
was not yet prepared to end the war. It has already been shown,
however, that for some days he had been clear that Germany's
hopeless situation made a cessation of hostilities inevitable. In
the early hours of 1 May, while Dönitz was interviewing Himmler,
Speer produced a draft of a proclamation to the German people:

German people!
The Führer has remained in Berlin fighting against Bolshevism. By

133

this voluntary decision he has provided further striking and imperishable confirmation of his entire life's purpose and the import of his tireless creative activity. We hope that, after his death, both Europe and the world will come to recognise, not only his personality, but also his prophetic insight into the danger threatening all mankind from the East. . . .

There followed arguments for the continuation of the struggle against the East, whereas in the West only 'screening' operations should be continued. Demolitions should be restricted to the essential minimum. Since they were bound by their agreements, it was not to be expected that 'our enemies will support us individually in our intentions'. The draft then called for discipline and comradeship, referred to a 'united people', to the hope of a better future, and concluded with the words: 'Germany will remain for ever and aye. God protect Germany!'

The wording clearly reflects Speer's own conflicting emotions as regards Hitler and shows that he was not yet entirely free from the spell of the Dictator. The hope expressed that the Eastern danger would be recognised in time is not entirely incompatible with the view that initially no reversal of alliances was to be anticipated. The reference to Hitler's death skirts cleverly round the problem of suicide. After Hitler's statements to him on 23 April, Speer can hardly have been in any doubt regarding the manner of his death.[2]

Dönitz looked at the situation in an entirely different light. Hitler seems to have given him no indications. He himself would have nothing to do with suicide, regarding it as an admission of guilt. To him it was self-evident that one should seek death in battle – and he assumed that Hitler would think likewise.[3] Accordingly in his call to the German people and his Order of the Day to the Wehrmacht of 1 May the words used are: 'The Führer has fallen.' Today Dönitz admits that it would have been better to say 'is dead'. When drafting his proclamation of 1 May, however (he used very little of Speer's draft), he still had no doubts; he says that he discussed the subject with no one.[4]

Whether any subsequent disagreements on the subject arose, we do not know. Jodl, in any case, used the same wording in the Wehrmacht report on 2 May, although Hitler had on several occasions told him of his intention to commit suicide. Probably, however, when Dönitz, not realising their implication, used the words 'has fallen' in his proclamation, Jodl simply followed suit, perhaps relieved that some form of words had been found. Even in ordinary notices of death a suicide was normally concealed and Hitler had set the stage to present his death as that 'of a soldier'. Jodl was also a believer in Hitler's story of the inevitable fateful conflict with the East. In his case, therefore, a statement that Hitler had 'fallen' in battle seems to have been, not so much a deliberate lie, as complacent acceptance of a convenient formula, quite apart from the fact that at this stage he still regarded Hitler as a 'hero'.

On 1 May at 3.18 p.m. arrived the third telegram from Berlin containing the words: 'The Führer died yesterday at 3.30 p.m.' This could mean suicide and Dönitz discussed it on the morning of 2 May with Keitel, von Krosigk and Wegener. Jodl was present only for Dönitz' first briefing conference at 1.0 p.m.

The gulf between Dönitz' views and those of the hardened Nazis, though they were in some respects similar, was well illustrated by the proclamations discovered in the fortress of Breslau and issued by the local National-Socialist 'Leadership Officer'.

Both for the Nazis and Dönitz the most difficult problem was to announce Hitler's death and at the same time justify the continuance of the struggle, which most people already considered senseless. One of the Breslau documents says that the Führer had deliberately remained in Berlin 'because he was convinced that, at this stage of the struggle, he could do more for the German people there than anywhere else'. It continues: 'Our situation offers us the choice only between deportation to Siberia or, by fighting on, creation of an opportunity for that political turn of events which would mean that the German people's struggle had not been in vain.' Another proclamation refers to Moeller van den Bruck's book '*Das Dritte Reich*' [*The Third Reich*] which opens with the words: 'A war can be lost. An unfortunate war is never irrevocable. The harshest peace is never final. But a revolution must be won.' After a lengthy disquisition on the meaning of struggle, the proclamation ends with the call: 'We must win the revolution.'

The 'savage' Field Marshal Schörner's order as C-in-C Army Group Centre struck an even more uncompromising note: 'Adolf Hitler has fallen fighting against Bolshevism to his last breath as a martyr to his concepts and beliefs and a soldier for our European mission. His work and his mission will form a sacred legacy for future generations. We who survive have the duty to pursue the struggle as he would have wished and to finish his work. The battle for Germany's freedom and her future continues.'

Dönitz' proclamations and orders, on the other hand, were comparatively moderate, apart from the perpetuation of the Führer cult which shows through in the first paragraph of his announcement. The usual Nazi platitudes are still there – 'proud reverence and sorrow', the 'hero's death' and the 'Bolshevist flood'. The most important passage, however, reads as follows: 'The Führer has nominated me as his successor. In full consciousness of my responsibilities I therefore assume the leadership of the German people in this fateful hour. My first task is to save German men and women from destruction by the advancing Bolshevist enemy. It is to serve this purpose alone that the military struggle continues. For as long as the British and the Americans continue to impede the accomplishment of this task, we must also continue to fight and defend ourselves against them.'[5]

There then follows an attempt to lay on the Allies responsibility for the continuance of fighting in the West, the object of which is described as 'the expansion of Bolshevism in Europe'. This is both crude and, in contrast to Speer's draft, takes no account of existing circumstances. It appears, however, only in the proclamation to the German people, not in the order to the Wehrmacht, which was similar in content, though slightly different in wording.

In Part 3 of his proclamation Dönitz has words of encouragement for the German people and calls upon them to do their duty and remain orderly. In the Wehrmacht Order of the Day this passage is replaced by a call to discipline and obedience and a statement that the oath of allegiance sworn to Hitler is now applicable to him (Dönitz).[6] This unilateral declaration was intended to solve an extremely difficult problem. According to the oath sworn on 21 August 1934 soldiers were pledged not only to faithful service to 'People and Fatherland' but to 'unconditional obedience' to Hitler personally; they were pledged not to the Head of State as such and certainly not, as under the Weimar Republic, to the constitution. Strictly, therefore, there should have been a new formal oath-taking ceremony, something obviously impracticable under the conditions of 1 May 1945.

Apart from a few exceptions[7] the Wehrmacht followed their new Supreme Commander. Colonel-General Heinrici, Commander-in-Chief of Army Group Vistula, noted: 'We welcome Dönitz' nomination as Hitler's successor because we wish to see no Party dignitaries in that position' – but Heinrici had been relieved of his post by Keitel on 29 April for using divisions earmarked for the relief of Berlin to cover his own flank and ordering the abandonment of Swinemünde on his own initiative.

The Military Situation

When Dönitz assumed office the military situation was broadly as follows:[8]

In various areas Hitler's Reich had collapsed. In East Prussia were some 150,000–180,000 men of all three services.[9] Here and in West Prussia they were faced by overwhelming Russian superiority. Certain 'Eastern fortresses' were still standing amid the Red flood but finally only Breslau remained. Kolberg had fallen in mid-March, Danzig-Gotenhafen and Pillau at the end of that month. The Hela peninsula and a narrow coastal strip at the mouth of the Vistula were still in German hands; in addition an area was occupied by the Courland Army, still 200,000 men strong including Navy, Luftwaffe and ancillaries. Complete collapse was inevitable in the very near future owing to shortage of ammunition and fuel, of which no further supply was possible. Army Group Vistula in the northern sector of the Eastern Front was withdrawing into Mecklenburg in complete disorder. Ninth Army under General Busse and Twelfth Army under General Wenck, after failing to relieve Berlin, were also withdrawing westwards.

In North-west Germany Eastern Friesland and Schleswig-Holstein were still unoccupied but contained insufficient forces to defend themselves. The divisions in Eastern Friesland and west of the Elbe were accordingly moved to Holstein to keep at least that area open. Some Anglo-American forces had pushed forward to the area Hamburg–Kiel–Lübeck (Bremen had fallen on 26 April). No fighting was taking place in Holland, Denmark or Norway, where the military formations were still completely intact.[10]

In Central Germany the Americans were on the Elbe and Mulde and had already linked up with the advancing Russians at Torgau.

In the south the French had broken into the Alps on a broad

front on 30 April. The Alps massif, however, still remained the last stronghold for Army Groups South-West, South-East, G and parts of Army Group South in Austria. It was to be held as long as possible, until the Eastern Army Groups had disengaged from the Russians. The withdrawal of Army Group E (South-East – 180,000 men) in the Balkans presented particular difficulties, since its movement had to be co-ordinated with that of Army Group C in Italy (200,000 men), Army Group South in Austria (450,000 men) and Army Group Centre in Czechoslovakia (600,000 men).

The Army in the West (250,000 men under Field Marshal Kesselring) was fast disintegrating under continuous pressure from the French and Americans. Owing to shortage of ammunition and fuel resistance could only continue for a short time in the south.

In early May German troops were still holding the outposts of the western fortresses, the Biscay ports, Dunkirk and the Channel Islands. In the eastern Aegean they held Crete, Rhodes and Milos.

In the final days of the war the OKW Operations Staff estimated the strength of the Army in the East at 1,850,000 men and that of the remaining theatres at 1,230,000 – total Army strength 3,080,000.

Owing to shortage of fuel the Luftwaffe could hardly use its few remaining serviceable aircraft.[11] In recent months the Navy had regarded the movement of troops and refugees as its primary task. Of its heavy ships only *Prinz Eugen* and *Nürnberg* were intact. The new-type U-boats were not yet serviceable.

In a speech in Flensberg on 9 May Dönitz said: 'As a result therefore of the enemy's overwhelming material and numerical superiority and of the strength of his air forces to which we had no answer, fighting had everywhere either been stopped or had ceased or had become futile. There was therefore no possibility of changing the fortunes of this war in our favour by military action. It was therefore the duty of the leaders of the State to end the war as quickly as possible.'

Expedients

Dönitz' programme did not visualise an immediate end to the war; he was aiming at the earliest possible cessation of hostilities in the West, while the troops fighting in the East withdrew to the western demarcation line. This operation was calculated to require eight to ten days, approximately the period for which coal stocks would suffice.

There were differing views on the form in which surrender to the West should take place. For a soldier capitulation is a bitter experience. The demand for unconditional surrender was regarded as intolerable. Keitel and Jodl therefore urged that surrender be piecemeal, with restricted capitulation negotiations conducted by individual formations, the intention being to 'confront the enemy with a vacuum'. No central authority was to accept or fulfil his conditions. Such an attitude would have been no surprise to the Allies; for some time they had assumed that, in the event of capitulation, they would find no political or military authority in Germany.[12]

Both by training and tradition Dönitz was naturally inclined to accept this idea. Other considerations, however, had recently begun to weigh with him and these were supported by the arguments of Speer and von Krosigk, who pointed out that, if this procedure were followed, it implied continuation of bombing, the death of refugees in thousands and further destruction of bridges, buildings, ports and industrial installations, furthermore that wherever some hope of success seemed to remain, battles to the death would take place. Even before Hitler's death Dönitz' main preoccupation had been the avoidance of chaos and the rescue of the refugees. Moreover, now that the fate of the Reich lay in his hands, could he sit idly by and watch its final shipwreck? It was not in his nature, nor did it accord with his conception of the task he had inherited. On 1 May therefore Dönitz decided on local surrenders by military formations, roughly on an Army Group basis, but under his central direction and using already established contacts. His decision was unaffected by von Krosigk's international law arguments to the effect that capitulation was tantamount to a treaty binding on both victor and vanquished but applicable only to the armed forces, not to the State.

The impulse to try for local surrender was provided by the situation in North-West Germany. Continuance of the struggle in this area was dictated by three compelling considerations:

    1. maintenance of a 'loophole' through the demarcation line

2. preservation of a free area in which Dönitz could operate
3. security of the necessary disembarkation facilities for returning sea transport.

On the morning of 2 May orders in this sense were issued to Army Groups. Field Marshal Busch, Commander-in-Chief North-West, whom Dönitz had promoted to Commander-in-Chief North, was told to fight a delaying action 'in order to gain time for OKW's negotiations with the British concerning the north-west German area'. A radio message was sent to Army Group Vistula 'to conduct operations so that the greatest possible proportion of the Army Group could fight back in an orderly manner into the British and American zone west of the line Dömitz-Wismar. Local opportunities should be seized for negotiations with local British and American commanders.' Gauleiter Kaufmann was told by teleprinter that it was not intended to defend Hamburg and he was authorised to despatch a flag of truce on the morning of 3 May in accordance with the British offer made as a result of his earlier initiative. A supplementary order instructed Army Groups to blow only the minimum number of bridges in face of the Russians and none at all in the west.

That same afternoon, however, the first·reason for continuing to fight in North-West Germany was overtaken by events. During Dönitz' briefing conference his aide had to telephone to Lübeck and learnt by chance that British tanks were already in the streets. Early that morning parts of Field Marshal Montgomery's 21st Army Group had broken out of the Lauenburg bridgehead, overrunning weak German opposition, and had pushed on to Lübeck. Further south the Americans had made a surprise crossing of the Elbe and had reached the Baltic at Wismar, meeting no resistance since no one had expected the Allies to cross the agreed zone boundaries. The advance had been ordered by Eisenhower as early as 7 April to forestall a Russian occupation of the Schleswig-Holstein area.[13]

The Allied advance removed all real reason for the continuance of fighting in this area. In his capacity as Supreme Commander of the Wehrmacht, therefore, Dönitz immediately informed Admiral von Friedeburg, the new C-in-C Navy. He had already told von Friedeburg on the previous day of his intention to try and initiate negotiations with Montgomery in the first instance, since he seemed the least involved politically. Dönitz now moved his headquarters to Flensburg, since Plön could be reached within an hour by tanks from Lübeck. He arranged to meet von Friedeburg at the Levensau bridge over the Kiel Canal which he must cross on his way to Flensburg and which von Friedeburg also had to use on his way westwards. Owing to continuous attacks by British low-flying aircraft their conversation could not take place until 9.0 p.m. OKW's proposals not having met with his approval, Dönitz gave von Friedeburg points for discussion with Montgomery set out in note form as follows:

'Attempt to save the maximum number of German soldiers and Europeans from Bolshevisation and enslavement. Army Group Vistula therefore to withdraw into the Anglo-Saxon zone. Rescue from destruction and starvation of the men concentrated in the Schleswig-Holstein area. Medical supplies for this area. Prevention of destruction of major localities by bombing. In addition attempt to discover an arrangement to save Central and Northern Europe from further chaos.'

Admiral Wagner, General Kinzel, Chief of Staff to C-in-C North-West, and Major Friedel were detailed to accompany von Friedeburg. General Winter was informed that an OKW delegation was on its way to British Headquarters to discuss far-reaching matters with Field Marshal Montgomery on the basis of the British offer to spare the city of Hamburg.

Occupied Holland, Denmark and Norway

In Holland the Allies and Seyss-Inquart, the Reich Commissar, had been negotiating about the population's food supply since early April. On 30 April agreement was reached: the Allies to refrain from further military operations in the area and Seyss-Inquart from reprisals against the Dutch; food to be supplied with the help of the Red Cross.[14] On 2 May a telegram arrived from Seyss-Inquart and Blaskowitz, the C-in-C Netherlands, reporting the successful conclusion of their negotiations with General Bedell Smith, Eisenhower's Chief of Staff, and asking for further instructions, Smith having proposed armistice negotiations which might form the basis for wider contacts.

This was entirely in accordance with Dönitz' ideas. An immediate reply was sent to Seyss-Inquart as follows: 'All possible soundings on the lines indicated, highly desirable. At the same time I would ask you to be here tomorrow as agreed, if at all possible. If you think fit, indicate that you wish to gain contact with the Reich government tomorrow.'

The interview took place on 3 May at 3.30 p.m. with von Krosigk and Wegener present. Seyss-Inquart gave his report but showed himself sceptical about local surrender, stressing that the Allies were mutually bound to accept only general capitulation. It was agreed, nevertheless, to try. Dönitz laid down that, until an armistice had been concluded, existing operational instructions held good but that demolitions and inundations were not to be undertaken.

The Wehrmacht Cs-in-C Norway and Denmark, Generals Böhme and Lindemann, had also reported to Dönitz by telegram on 1 May concerning the situation in these areas. Böhme reported minor enemy air activity and increased propaganda from Sweden about possible action by the Swedish armed forces against the occupying power. He considered unilateral action by Sweden unlikely but participation in an Allied invasion possible, although at present there were no signs of any such invasion. In the event of a major operation he anticipated that the main blow would fall on southern Norway with subsidiary actions against Trondheim and possibly Narvik. Böhme drew particular attention to the Norwegian resistance organisation, saying that it had 'good human material' available and was 'formidably armed'; he stressed that 'with large impenetrable areas served by only a few vulnerable roads and railways conditions for resistance operations were ideal'. He reported German forces available as: 11 divisions and 5 brigades, 9 fighter squadrons, 1 night fighter squadron, 6 ground attack squadrons, 3 transport squadrons, 1 naval transport squadron and a few naval units. Apart from units withdrawn from Finland, he said, the majority of these troops were without battle experience. Supplies were available till mid-November, petrol till 1 August, coal and fuel oil till end May. Ammunition was enough for a few weeks' fighting. Böhme ended his report with the words: 'In Norway we can accept any battle.'

Although General Lindemann in Denmark was a supporter of a fight to the end, his report had a somewhat less martial tone. He did not foresee any major Anglo-American landing – no more than minor raids in support of operations in the North German area. There were no indications of Russian landings on the eastern

Danish islands and in any case German forces were inadequate to defend them. He stressed that the troops in Denmark lacked mobility; their battle-worthiness was limited as a result of continuous withdrawals of personnel and equipment. The attitude of the Danish population was described as anti-German and in some cases actively hostile; both the King and the political parties, however, wished to avoid active operations in Denmark. The current rumours about Himmler's negotiations via Sweden and an imminent capitulation had led to all sorts of enquiries from local authorities. 'Rumours about capitulation have been most energetically denied.'

Lindemann estimated the strength of the resistance movement at 25,000–30,000 men, half of whom were well armed. He reported increased sabotage activity, primarily against railways and communication installations. Danes working for the Germans were being increasingly terrorised. Nevertheless he did not think that there would be an overt rising except in combination with attack from outside. It could be suppressed at any time; in the event of simultaneous Allied attack, however, guerilla activity must be reckoned with owing to shortage of German forces. According to the latest reports Sweden intended to preserve her neutrality but would give 'passive support' to the Danish resistance movement.

Lindemann emphasised that the large number of refugees and wounded constituted a special problem; he estimated them at 230,000. This restricted the use of his troops and complicated his relationships with the Danish authorities and population as well as his measures in the event of internal unrest.

The supply position Lindemann described as 'in general assured'. He was still, however, largely dependent upon Danish sources, since the Army supply installations were only in course of construction. In the event of prolonged major operations a shortage of ammunition and fuel was inevitable. The clothing situation was bad and that of transport difficult owing to lack of trucks, petrol and locomotive coal.

Lindemann's telegram gave no details of strength available. Notes for a conference, dated 8 May 1945, by the Deputy Chief of Staff of the Wehrmacht, however, show a total of 231,700 men, of which 102,000 (including foreign personnel) belonged to the Army, 35,000 to the Navy, 30,000 to the Luftwaffe, 3,300 to the police and 1,400 to the Todt Organisation. The same source gives the number of wounded as 60,000.[15]

Both Böhme and Lindemann together with Dr. Best, the Plenipotentiary for Denmark, and Terboven, the Reich Commissar for Norway, were ordered to Flensburg for a discussion with Dönitz. This took place at 11.0 a.m. on 3 May with Keitel, Jodl, von Krosigk and Speer present.

In view of the relatively large forces available Dönitz, in his capacity as Supreme Commander of the Wehrmacht, posed the question whether the war could and should be continued in Denmark and Norway. In discussion two points of view emerged: Böhme, Lindemann, the OKW representatives and Terboven spoke up for continuation, Lindemann even referring to 'the last decent battle of this war'; Speer, von Krosigk and Best took the opposite view. The latter stressed the numbers of refugees and wounded (he estimated them at 300,000), the possibility of a rising in rear of the troops and information which had filtered through to him from Per Albin Hansson, the Swedish Prime Minister, to the effect that Sweden would not tolerate a 'frivolous' struggle and would intervene with armed force.

Dönitz' decision took account of both viewpoints. As in Holland, current operational instructions were to remain in force in the event of emergency. Otherwise law and order was to be maintained in both areas and a firm but conciliatory attitude adopted.

Certain special arrangements were made for Norway. The C-in-C was authorised to issue such instructions as the situation might require to all three Services and to other organisations with the exception of the police. In addition SS-Brigadeführer [Major-General] Walter Schellenberg was entrusted with a special mission to the Swedish Government.[16]

The background to these measures was the so-called 'hostage theory'. Denmark and, even more important, Norway were regarded as valuable stakes with which to obtain more favourable conditions in negotiations with the Western Powers. In addition Dönitz had no notion how Field Marshal Montgomery would react or whether OKW and the government might not shortly be forced to look for a seat outside Schleswig-Holstein, from which to complete their task. With this in view Rear-Admiral Godt and Captain Hessler were despatched on a special mission to Norway.

To guarantee OKW and the Acting Reich Government 'freedom of movement and action', orders were issued for the defence of the Kiel Canal, Schleswig-Holstein was cleared of all superfluous personnel and troops not required for fighting were moved to Denmark. C-in-C North-West remained responsible for law and order in Schleswig-Holstein and the Reichsführer-SS in all other areas.

Naval Headquarters reiterated its basic order that ships of the line, cruisers, destroyers, new torpedo boats or E-boats, submarines and minor fighting ships were not to fall into enemy hands but 'if the situation necessitates were to be sunk or destroyed'. The Navy also ordered that by midday on 4 May all secret documents were to be destroyed by fire 'unless required for the most urgent current activity'.

Colonel-General Lindemann ordered: 'Any demand to lay down or hand over weapons is to be rejected. If force is used, it will be met by force of arms.'

Reports now began to arrive from the Admiral Commanding German Bight of increasing war-weariness among the troops and population; they were hoping, he said, that the example of Hamburg would be followed elsewhere and fighting against the Anglo-Americans would cease. This led to renewed fears of an untimely disintegration of the German forces. In order once more to make clear Dönitz' general concept, in a situation report of 4 May Naval Headquarters re-emphasised that his aim was 'to save the maximum number of Germans from the Bolshevist grip. Since the Western Powers support the Soviets, fighting against the Anglo-Americans will continue in accordance with the Grand Admiral's order. Purpose is to gain time and space for the leaders of the State to take measures in the political field.' If individual fortresses were ordered to surrender without a fight, the reason would be shortage of men or equipment. The conclusion should not be drawn that this presaged general capitulation. Premature destruction of weapons and ammunition or sinking of ships was forbidden. Signs of disintegration among the troops were to be countered by all possible means.

In the final days of the war, therefore, mutineers were still dealt with with the utmost severity, particularly in the Navy.[17] Today these sentences may seem senseless and savage. In the light of the situation at the time, however, they appeared to the military leadership essential. Only by iron discipline was the planned objective attainable. Whether the programme as such was practicable is another matter. In view of the general fear of the Soviets, however, Dönitz believed that he could not act otherwise.

Local Surrender in the North-West

The OKW delegation under Admiral von Friedeburg crossed the British lines on the morning of 3 May. They had been delayed by a traffic accident. Their first stop was at the Headquarters of British Second Army, where Major-General Wolz, Commandant of Hamburg, signed the city's surrender. Von Friedeburg then drove on to Field Marshal Montgomery's headquarters. The Commander-in-Chief of the British 21st Army Group was fully prepared for a visit by German delegates, since as early as 2 May General Blumentritt, commanding the army between the Baltic and the Weser, had expressed the intention of offering to surrender his troops to the British.[18] Montgomery had thereupon sought Eisenhower's instructions, which were to accept the offer as a tactical military measure but to do so nevertheless in the form of an unconditional surrender. Eisenhower even authorised acceptance of capitulation for Denmark, Friesland, the Frisian Islands and Holland in addition to the Schleswig-Holstein area. Other offers of surrender, for instance for Norway or troops on the Eastern Front, were to be handled by Allied Headquarters. Simultaneously Eisenhower informed the Soviet High Command of this instruction.[19]

The East-West alliance provided for the possibility of 'tactical surrenders in the field' in emergency. It did not call for prior consultation between Supreme Headquarters Allied Expeditionary Force (SHAEF) and the Soviet High Command. Should it appear that German formations wished to surrender, the appropriate commanders simply had to agree between themselves. Surrender of complete German armies, however, was not to be accepted unless a simultaneous offer had been made to the other allied front.

Eisenhower now made use of the tactical provision for far larger units of the German army – but he gave prior notification to the Soviets. Moreover on 12 April Churchill had stated in the Commons that piecemeal unconditional surrender was not impossible. On 25 April, in connection with Himmler's offer, he had written to Stalin that Himmler should be informed 'that German forces, either as individuals or in units, should everywhere surrender themselves to the Allied troops or representatives on the spot'.[20]

The German concept of a piecemeal surrender therefore ran parallel to certain ideas of the Western Allies; they had, however, assumed that the German formations on the western and eastern fronts would behave similarly. Accordingly when von Friedeburg proposed the surrender of German forces in the north-western area and withdrawal of Army Group Vistula to the western demarcation line, Montgomery told him tersely that he could accept no surrender from troops fighting on the Eastern Front.[21] Von Friedeburg interjected that no German soldier would willingly surrender to the Russians since he would assume that this would mean deportation to Siberia, but Montgomery cut him short with the remark that 'the Germans should have thought of all these things before they began the war, and particularly before they attacked the Russians in June 1941'. Montgomery refused to discuss the fate of refugees in the Mecklenburg area since this did not fall within his zone of responsibility; he gave it to be understood, however, that he was not 'a monster'. He refused to discuss further and asked the Admiral whether he was prepared to surrender all German troops on his western and northern flanks including those in Holland, Friesland with the Frisian Islands, Heligoland, Schleswig-Holstein and Denmark. In this case he would be prepared to consider it as a tactical battlefield surrender, including the reserves in Denmark.[22] The British commander reinforced his demands by showing von Friedeburg his situation map. Since von Friedeburg's authority did not extend to this, a protocol was drawn up in which Montgomery summarised his conditions:

1. All members of the German armed forces who come into the 21 Army Group front from the east desiring to surrender will be made prisoners of war. An acceptance by 21 Army Group of a complete German Army fighting the Russians is not possible.

2. No discussion about civilians possible.

3. Field Marshal Montgomery desires that all German forces in Holland, Friesland (including the islands and Heligoland), Schleswig-Holstein and Denmark lay down their arms and surrender unconditionally to him. He is prepared, when the

surrender has been agreed, to discuss the method of occupying the areas, dealing with civilians etc.

4. General-Admiral von Friedeburg is not at present empowered to give agreement to surrender as in para. 3. He will therefore send two officers (Rear-Admiral Wagner and Major Friedel) to the Oberkommando of the Wehrmacht to obtain and bring back the agreement. . . .[23]

Eventually von Friedeburg himself drove back to Flensburg with Major Friedel, Admiral Wagner remaining at British Headquarters. Arriving late that night, von Friedeburg gave a first informal report on his negotiations. The official conference did not take place until the next morning, 4 May, with Dönitz, von Krosigk, Keitel, Jodl, the latter's aide Lieutenant-Colonel Brudermüller, and Captain Lüdde-Neurath present. Basically all were agreed to accept the conditions; they appeared to allow continuance of fighting in the East and uninterrupted sea transport of refugees, an interpretation confirmed by von Friedeburg. Only Jodl was opposed to relinquishing the 'trump card' of Holland. A general debate took place on the demand, transmitted verbally by von Friedeburg, for the handing over of all weapons and ships undamaged; though not explicitly stated in the protocol, this was implicit in 'unconditional surrender'. The OKW representatives, still with their eye on the Wehrmacht's dignity, considered this unacceptable. They proposed immediate destruction of all weapons and were supported by Lüdde-Neurath, Dönitz' aide, who suggested that, since the agreement did not come into force until the morning of 5 May, fighting should continue until then and weapons be destroyed. Von Friedeburg opposed this idea, saying that it was contrary to the spirit of the agreement; he was supported by von Krosigk. Dönitz therefore had to decide between the traditional military outlook and the requirements of his new, and superior, position. He decided to disregard outmoded notions of honour and accept the conditions laid down by Montgomery. He assumed that prisoners of war would be decently treated and the hand-over of weapons take place in a dignified manner.[24] OKW was therefore instructed to issue orders for a dignified and disciplined hand-over of weapons. Accordingly on the same day a whole series of orders went out to Army, Navy, Luftwaffe and Waffen-SS units located in the area affected by the local surrender. Troops were told to remain where they were, with their weapons. Transport by sea was to continue but no demolitions or sinkings were to be undertaken.[25] The order was obeyed almost without exception, although the Navy found the ban on scuttling particularly hard. During the night 4/5 May, however, without Dönitz' knowledge or approval Lüdde-Neurath sent an order to all U-boats in North Sea or Baltic ports to scuttle themselves. Dönitz was taken by surprise, but no reprisals ensued from the Allied side.

Meanwhile von Friedeburg had flown back to Montgomery's headquarters. There a special tent had been erected for the signing ceremony, wired and with microphones; a press conference had been arranged. Montgomery read the instrument of surrender in English, adding that fighting would continue unless the German delegation signed at once and without argument. Having been authorised to sign by Dönitz, von Friedeburg did so.

The first two paragraphs of the Instrument[26] set out the areas in which German forces were to surrender unconditionally and the time at which this would come into force. There then followed a number of onerous conditions:

3. The relevant German headquarters to carry out at once, and without argument or comment, all further orders that will be issued by the Allied Powers on any subject.

4. Disobedience of orders, or failure to comply with them, will be regarded as a breach of these surrender terms and will be dealt with by the Allied Powers in accordance with the accepted laws and usages of war.

5. This instrument of surrender is independent of, without prejudice to, and will be superseded by any general instrument of surrender imposed by or on behalf of the Allied Powers and applicable to Germany and the German armed forces as a whole.

These provisions were in accordance with the directive issued by the Combined Chiefs of Staff in August 1944.

At 7.30 p.m. on 4 May von Friedeburg sent the following message to Dönitz: 'Conditions signed, including ships in adjacent zones. Ceasefire 8.0 a.m. 5 May.'

Twenty-five minutes later a second message followed: 'Since Dunkirk is in the area of his Army Group, Field Marshal Montgomery wishes that it be included in the armistice under similar conditions. Request decision whether such agreement may be signed by me. Leaving tomorrow by air for higher authority.'

The 'higher authority' was General Eisenhower. When authorising von Friedeburg to sign the local surrender in North-west Germany, Dönitz had commissioned him to fly on to the Supreme Commander and negotiate further local surrenders with the West. As proof of the 'goodwill' of the German Command he had already, on 4 May, ordered the release of the King of the Belgians, avoidance of incidents in Norway and the cessation of U-boat operations.[27]

On the same day Twelfth and Ninth German Armies on the Elbe ceased operations; Army Group Vistula had already surrendered on 2 May. As it withdrew Ninth Army under General Wenck was accompanied by long columns of refugees. There were heart-breaking scenes when the Commander of Ninth US Army refused to accept its surrender in view of his obligations to the Russians. Only individual deserters were allowed across the Elbe; passage was refused to the desperate refugees.

Throughout the Northern Zone, therefore, fighting had now died down or stopped. The only exceptions were Norway, the island of Rügen, which was evacuated on 5 May, East Prussia and Courland whither Lieutenant-Colonel de Maizière was despatched by air on 5 May to report to commanders and prepare the evacuation.

In all these areas compliance with the surrender terms began on 5 May.

Situation in the Southern Zone

Conditions in the south differed considerably from those in the north.

On 1 May arrived a long telegram from Ernst Kaltenbrunner, the Head of the RSHA, addressed to Hitler and transmitted to Dönitz, reporting on developments in Army Group Italy. He told of a regular rout of German troops following the American break-through, planned risings in all major cities and included details of the armistice conditions agreed with the Allies on 29 April. Kaltenbrunner also reported Mussolini's murder by partisans and concluded with the hope that, in spite of an extremely tense situation, the position might perhaps still be re-established 'with strong nerves and determined men'.[28]

Also on 2 May arrived a long telegram from Field Marshal Kesselring, Commander-in-Chief West. He reported that, without his knowledge or agreement, in the light of tactical and political developments in Italy the late C-in-C South-West had concluded an armistice effective at midday on 2 May. To prevent an overt revolt, he had felt compelled to lend his name to this procedure. He added that negotiations had taken place in the presence of two Soviet generals. Conditions included laying down of arms but retention of personal weapons by officers and security troops. Further discussions, at which the Soviet officers were not present, had revealed that the hand-over of territory would take some two months and that transport of prisoners was hardly possible owing to lack of shipping. Kesselring made no secret of the fact that this surrender constituted a severe blow to the entire German Front. 'I realise, however, that there is at least a possibility of extending this armistice on similar terms to other Army Groups in the West, whereas the struggle against Bolshevism need in no way be restricted, indeed would be reinforced.' Kesselring declared that he was prepared to answer with his life for this step, though taken without his knowledge; he proposed that the agreement concluded without the participation of the Soviets be extended to all troops under Cs-in-C West and South-East and, if possible, to all forces located in the West – he mentioned Holland and Denmark. By switching the forces located there, the Eastern Front could be reinforced. He asked for an immediate decision whether negotiations might be opened for the areas of Cs-in-C West and South-East.

Dönitz did not initially agree with this procedure. The unilateral action by Army Group Italy jeopardised the situation of Army Groups South-East, South and Centre. Moreover it had occurred just at the moment when authority had passed to him. If he passively accepted this, he would have to reckon on similar unilateral action by other military formations. As already described, local surrenders accorded with his general policy; if, however, he was to carry out his programme of withdrawal from the east, these local surrenders must be centrally co-ordinated by him on a proper timetable. During 2 May, however, there were signs that the situation in the north was also moving towards a local surrender and he had meanwhile obtained a clearer picture of the situation in Czechoslovakia;[29] at 1.05 p.m. on 4 May, therefore, he sent a telegram to Kesselring giving the necessary agreement and also authorising him 'to conclude an armistice with US Sixth

Army Group covering the troops on the Western Front between the Böhmer Wald and Upper Inn' (Army Group G, in other words). Kesselring, who was now C-in-C in the Southern Zone, was also commissioned to find out how far the Anglo-Americans intended to advance eastwards, so that negotiations might be initiated to rescue the Army Groups under Löhr, Rendulic and Schörner. These negotiations Dönitz intended to reserve to okw; they were one of the subjects of von Friedeburg's mission to Eisenhower's headquarters. The telegram to Kesselring also ordered Seventh Army to be placed under Schörner and the staff of okw South under General Winter to move to an area not affected by the armistice.

Dönitz did not at this stage authorise negotiations concerning Army Group South-East (Army Group E). Army Group C's capitulation in Italy had exposed it to the danger of a flank attack in north-west Croatia and the Ukraine, the collapse of the final German offensive at Lake Balaton in western Hungary and the loss of Vienna on 13 April having practically isolated it already.

In a telegram despatched on 2 May and received at 8.10 a.m. on 3 May the C-in-C of this Army Group, Colonel-General Löhr, the most senior Austrian officer in the Wehrmacht, had informed Dönitz of the situation in his area. The Army Group's plans were unchanged, he said; in other words he proposed to withdraw his troops as rapidly as possible to the Alps position along the old Reich frontier from Tervis to Radkersburg, in order to protect the southern flank of Army Group South. He did not anticipate more than partial success, since the Anglo-Americans were already operating in his rear. The majority of his troops were therefore likely to be annihilated by Tito's forces. He accordingly asked for immediate negotiations with the Western Powers, which he considered essential primarily on political grounds. Croatia was the only ally which remaining faithful to Germany and the Reich could not completely throw her to the wolves. Statements by the Tito Government indicated that 'a ghastly bloodbath' awaited the population of Zagreb and northern Croatia.

After Seventh and Fifth US Armies had met on the Brenner on 4 May all organised resistance in Austria ceased apart from isolated skirmishes. At 12.14 a.m. on the 5th Löhr sent another telegram to Dönitz: 'Maintenance of the Great German Reich no longer possible. Formation of an Austrian State by the enemy unavoidable. It is in the general German interest that this State should be as viable as possible and based on European moral principles.' Considerable parts of Austria, Löhr stated, were relatively undamaged and still unoccupied. His Army Group was on the defensive protecting the south-east frontier of the country and he had it firmly under control. He wished, Löhr said, to save his home country from Bolshevisation and therefore to offer his services to Field Marshal Alexander for the organisation of security forces. He was not seeking any preferential treatment for himself.

Löhr was given authority to negotiate that very day. The discussions with Eisenhower, however, soon removed its *raison d'être*.

Parts of Löhr's Army Group managed to escape westwards with Army Group South. He himself, however, was taken prisoner by the Yugoslavs and shot by an execution squad. Innumerable atrocities had been committed in Yugoslavia in the name of the Great German Reich. According to a Yugoslav statement, during the war as a whole 1,700,000 people had died either on the battlefield or in concentration camps.

Quite apart from the problems of Army Groups C, South-East and South in Italy, Yugoslavia and Austria, the position of Army Group Centre in Czechoslovakia presented Dönitz with particular difficulties. He knew nothing of Allied plans for this country. While Soviet troops were fighting their way through its eastern parts, by the end of April American forces under General Patton had crossed the western frontier and moved south-eastwards along the border. Simultaneously another column thrust eastwards to the line Carlsbad–Pilsen–Budweis.[30]

To obtain a clear picture of the situation Dönitz had ordered to Flensburg Karl Hermann Frank, Reich Protector of Bohemia and Moravia, Minister of State and SS-Gruppenführer, together with Lieutenant-General von Natzmer, Chief of Staff to Army Group Centre. A total of three meetings took place, on 2, 3 and 4 May.

Once more Dönitz' main concern was the rescue of the largest possible number of Germans. The idea of a possible 'bargaining pawn' and a move of the government to Prague were also discussed. Frank reported that Czechoslovakia was on the verge of revolution and could not be held for long either militarily or politically. He pointed out, as he had already done to Hitler,[31] that Czech bourgeois circles existed, with which he was in touch and which, from fear of Bolshevism, were working for occupation by Western forces. He proposed capitulation to the Americans with the assistance of Czech politicians. As we know, at the end of April Speer had favoured such a scheme. At this stage, however, von Krosigk and Dönitz did not think that the Allies would be persuaded to change their concerted plans at the last moment by a manœuvre of this sort. Frank was nevertheless authorised to sound out the ground. It was also decided to declare Prague an open city.

On the question whether Bohemia might serve as a suitable alternative location for the government in emergency, there were differing views. Keitel, Jodl and Himmler (who was taking part in the discussion) were for it, Dönitz against. He considered the political environment too uncertain and was also unwilling to see the German government functioning from a foreign country.

How right Dönitz was is proved by a comment in the *New York Times* of 4 May to the effect that, should the government continue to fight from foreign territory, it would lose its legitimacy and its members would be considered as bandits or pirates.

Discussion with General von Natzmer showed that Army Group Centre would only be able to defend itself for approximately another two weeks. Nevertheless the General was opposed to any withdrawal, arguing that the troops could be kept under better control in static operations. He was supported by Keitel, who pointed out the dangers of disorganisation during withdrawal and of a multiple break-through by Russian armour if the front gave way. Unwillingly Dönitz accepted the views of his military advisers. He regarded static defence by the Army Group as a mere short-term expedient, not a solution. Oddly enough the most pertinent comment came, not from the military experts but from von Krosigk; he pointed out the danger to the Army Group of a Russian flanking attack using forces liberated by the capture of Berlin and producing a last great encirclement.[32] Decision was postponed for the time being and in a radio message Jodl instructed Army Group Centre to 'organise their operations so as to gain time'. The front was to be held throughout its length and break-throughs dealt with at once. Should enemy superiority make the retention of Bohemia impossible, the troops were to withdraw south-westwards in order to escape from the Russian sphere of influence.

When on the evening of 4 May confirmation arrived from von Friedeburg that the local surrender on Montgomery's front had been signed, Dönitz issued an order to Army Groups Centre, South and South-East telling the soldiers that at this moment they were defending not only themselves 'but many millions of German men, women and children still to the east of the American zone'. Should they hear of individual armies in the north, west or south laying down their arms – he did not use the word capitulate – this would only be because the struggle against the western enemy had become purposeless and the only object of further fighting was 'to save the maximum number of Germans from Bolshevisation and enslavement'. This, Dönitz said, was their 'most sacred task' which they must fulfil 'as a legacy from our dead Führer and for the preservation of the German people'. All his political and military effort was devoted to safeguarding them and the population of Germany from annihilation. 'Anyone who selfishly thinks only of his own safety or that of his unit makes the rescue of the community impossible. He is a traitor to the German people and will be punished accordingly.

'Unquestioning obedience, iron discipline and general cohesion are more necessary than ever and are the indispensable conditions for the fulfilment of your great task.

'The German people will be grateful to you.'

CHAPTER SEVEN

General Capitulation

O N Montgomery's front, in Holland and in Denmark, therefore, the guns ceased firing; for the southern Army Groups, however, fighting continued. Meanwhile Admiral von Friedeburg journeyed to the headquarters of the Supreme Allied Commander. As already mentioned, to ease his task, on 4 May Dönitz had ordered U-boats to cease operations and return home. On 5 May, via Keitel, he despatched a radio message to General Kinzel, who had remained at Montgomery's headquarters, offering to include in the armistice the Channel and Biscay fortresses and the Channel Islands. Once again he stressed his desire to stop fighting in the West and that his aim was to work peacefully 'for the maintenance of the existence of Germans'.

Simultaneously over the naval radio Naval Headquarters West was informed, and a major operation against St. Malo-Granville, planned for 7 May, was called off.[1]

A message was also sent to the Commandant Eastern Aegean, authorising him, at his request, to 'get rid of' the disarmed Italians and conclude an armistice with the Western Powers. The message explicitly ordered continuance of fighting against the Russians and forbade any negotiations with them.

The reply from Major-General Wagner, the Commandant, is a copy-book example of National-Socialist jargon and one of the few instances in which Dönitz is referred to as 'Führer': 'With iron determination the entire garrison of the Aegean has vowed to you, as its new Führer in the struggle for the life and future of Germany, unconditional loyalty from the troops, faith and ineradicable acceptance of sacrifices. A battle may be lost, but faith never. A war may be lost, but a people's faith never. We shall hold on for as long as we are ordered. Where we stand, Germany stands. Heil to our Führer!'

Jodl's comments on this day, however, were blunt and unconventional. A message arrived with a protest from Montgomery about a 'silly broadcast' from Bremerhaven which did not assist co-operation; he demanded that only authorised texts be published.

Jodl commented: 'I do not know who is letting this nonsense through. I request him, however, to stop it.'[2]

General Eisenhower was told on 4 May of the imminent arrival of a German delegation. He at once informed the US Department of Defence and the Russian High Command; to the latter he suggested that the Germans be informed that 'their government should order all troops located on the Russian Front to surrender to the Russian High Command', whereas all forces on the Western Front including Norway should give themselves up to the Americans. By this Eisenhower hoped to obtain Russian agreement to a simultaneous armistice on both fronts at the earliest possible time.[3] The Supreme Commander also ordered General Susloparov and Lieutenant-Colonel Zenkovich to be invited to Supreme Headquarters before the arrival of the Germans. The background to this detailed briefing of Soviet officers was more than a mere Allied desire to meet their mutual obligations; the negotiations preceding the local capitulation in Italy had given rise to considerable anger on the part of the Soviets. Stalin had protested energetically to Roosevelt, describing them as a success for Hitler in his attempt to break up the alliance.[4] Although highly incensed by Stalin's letter, shortly before his death Roosevelt had described his accusations as misconceptions rather than indications of a general attitude of mind. In view, however, of Soviet susceptibilities and general lack of confidence in Allied good faith, special caution was exercised. On 26 April, for instance, Churchill had given Stalin further information and Soviet officers had thenceforth been present at the discussions. On 30 April Stalin had written Churchill that he had no objection to Field Marshal Alexander announcing the German surrender in Italy.

On the Allied side Supreme Headquarters' negotiators were General Bedell Smith, the Chief of Staff, and General Strong, the Head of Military Intelligence. Eisenhower instructed that there was to be no bargaining with the German delegation. He himself did not wish to see them before the instrument of surrender was ready for signature. His aversion to, indeed his hatred of, all Germans had deepened since 18 April, when he had himself seen the conditions in the concentration camps.[5]

Admiral von Friedeburg arrived in Reims at about 5.0 p.m. on 5 May, having been delayed by bad weather. General Eisenhower's terms were put to him forthwith by Bedell Smith. To demonstrate

their hopeless position to the Germans, maps were laid out showing the situation on the various fronts. As a precaution one or two
fictitious operations were shown on them, making a situation
which was difficult enough anyway seem entirely hopeless.[6]

Von Friedeburg's instructions were to arrange further local
surrenders in the west and, if possible, in the south, but Eisenhower's demand for general capitulation on all fronts faced him
with a problem outside his competence. Meanwhile a further
telegram arrived from Jodl asking him to discover the Western
Allies' intentions as regards Army Group E (South-East). If it
was not to be annihilated, the Anglo-Americans must be prevented from advancing north-eastwards from Upper Italy.
Friedeburg accordingly sought further instructions from Dönitz.
Having no code or agreed frequency with Flensburg, his message
was transmitted in code from SHAEF to 21st Army Group, de-
coded there and taken to Flensburg by General Kinzel. It ran
as follows:

1. Imminent and co-ordinated American and Soviet operations
   decisive for maintenance of Löhr's, Rendulic's and Schörner's
   present fronts. General Jodl's enquiry regarding Löhr therefore
   outdated.

2. Eisenhower's Chief of Staff proposes following alternatives:
   either order signature of unconditional and simultaneous surrender
   in all theatres,
   or despatch Chief of OKW and Cs-in-C Army, Navy and Luftwaffe
   to sign unconditional surrender.

3. Unconditional surrender includes following conditions:
   all troops to remain in present positions, ships not to be scuttled,
   neither ships nor aircraft to be damaged in any way;
   OKW to guarantee to transmit and carry out in all theatres all
   further orders issued by the Allied and Soviet High Commands.

4. The new government to carry the blame for any continuation of
   hostilities. 'Hela' and other plans imply continuance of hostilities
   on all fronts.

5. Active co-operation expected from German government in event
   critical food situation and any consequential chaos.

6. Decisions as in para. 2 of extreme urgency. Should I be authorised
   to act, written confirmation signed by Head of State to be
   forwarded to Field Marshal Montgomery's headquarters forthwith.

7. Final assurance regarding immediate cessation of hostilities will follow my signature. Subsequent official ratification necessary, however, by Cs-in-C as in para. 2.

This message is quoted *in extenso* because it includes one or two vital phrases which will be referred to later. It did not reach Dönitz until the morning of 6 May, and gave rise to heated discussion. Eisenhower's terms were regarded as unacceptable, since no one wished to see the eastern armies fall into the hands of the Soviets. Nevertheless, in view of the hopeless military situation and the danger of renewed bombing and ground attack in the west, it was essential to reach some accommodation with Eisenhower. Jodl was the most determined opponent of general capitulation. Dönitz therefore instructed him to fly to Reims and lay the German dilemma before Eisenhower. He was authorised to sign a surrender only with the West. Should this prove impossible, he might also sign a general capitulation, but only on condition that this was carried out in two stages. In the first stage, although hostilities would cease, the troops would still have freedom of movement. Movement would only cease in the second stage, which should be postponed as long as possible. During this period individual soldiers should be allowed to cross into the American-occupied zone. By this capitulation on a graduated time-scale, which he had discussed with von Krosigk, Dönitz hoped to enable the maximum number of people to find sanctuary in the Western Zone.[7] The minimum interval between the two stages was reckoned to be four days. Jodl was given written authorisation to sign a general capitulation, with the proviso that he was only to use it after obtaining telegraphic confirmation from Dönitz.

While the discussions on form and content of a capitulation agreement were in progress, news arrived of a rising in Prague. This made it clear that Frank's plan to obtain Western assistance through Czech bourgeois circles had failed.[8] Army Group Centre's withdrawal seemed even more problematical. The urgency of the situation was underlined by an enquiry from Headquarters Southern Zone regarding steps to rescue Army Groups E, South and Centre.

Meanwhile Field Marshal Kesselring had enquired of Eisenhower whether he might send an emissary to negotiate the surrender of the Army in the West. The reply was that this was

useless unless he could also offer the surrender of Army Groups
South and E together with all distant garrisons including those of
the islands still in German occupation; also that he must be
prepared simultaneously to offer the surrender to the Soviets of
all German forces facing them. The only 'local' surrender to
which Eisenhower was prepared to agree was that of forces facing
the US Sixth Army under General Devers, in other words Army
Group G in the Tyrol and Vorarlberg. This local surrender was
set in train straight away. An armistice was declared for midday
6 May and a reception area laid down for German troops. Allied
troops were to move in at midday 8 May.

Kesselring was ordered by Flensburg to operate with Army
Groups South-East, Ostmark and Centre in such a way that the
front facing the Soviets was withdrawn as quickly as possible into
the American Zone; his object was 'to be absorbed by the American
Front as in Mecklenburg'. No resistance was to be offered to the
eastward move of American troops in the Protectorate and
further south; Jodl, the message said, was on the way to Eisenhower as plenipotentiary. Kesselring was further ordered not to
initiate any separate negotiations.

So Colonel-General Alfred Jodl flew to Reims. He was
accompanied by General de Guingand, Montgomery's Chief of
Staff, who later recorded that it was a curious sensation to be
sitting in the same aircraft with a man who had worked in the
closest contact with Hitler for so long.[9] They arrived on the
evening of Sunday 6 May. After a short briefing from Admiral
von Friedeburg, discussions with Generals Bedell Smith and
Strong began. Jodl attempted to postpone signature of an
Instrument until Tuesday 8 May and to obtain an additional forty-
eight hours for the transmission of orders. When these proposals
were put to Eisenhower, however, they seemed to him merely to
confirm his view that the Germans would try to sow discord
between the Allies and play for time. He was not willing to
lose further time. His answer was therefore an ultimatum: If the
German delegation did not agree to sign the surrender terms
at once, he would break off the talks, close the Western Front to
German soldiers withdrawing from the east and restart bombing.
Capitulation must be signed that very day and whatever happened
would come into force at midnight 8/9 May. Jodl was given only
half an hour to think it over.

Jodl thereupon sent the following radio message to Field Marshal Keitel: 'Eisenhower insists that we sign today. If not, the Allied fronts will be closed to persons seeking to surrender individually, and all negotiations will be broken off. I see no alternative – chaos or signature. I ask you to confirm to me immediately by radio that I have full powers to sign capitulation. Capitulation will then come into effect. Hostilities will then cease on 9 May at 1.0 a.m. German summer time.'[10]

In Flensburg Eisenhower's terms were regarded as blackmail. In his Memoirs Dönitz says that Eisenhower may have been acting in accordance with political directives from Washington but that he clearly had 'no proper appreciation of the new turn of events in world affairs that had now taken place'.[11] Much has been written to show that at this time, not only Eisenhower, but also Roosevelt and the Combined Chiefs of Staff, were working on the principle of winning the war militarily and leaving the political consequences of their victory to take care of themselves.[12] In view of his own long-standing political connections, however, Dönitz' criticism seems out of place.

At 8.41 p.m. Jodl sent a further message: 'Orders required to all concerned to move in direction Frankenstrub as quickly and in as peaceful a manner as possible.' Frankenstrub was the codename for Berchtesgaden; this was therefore an undercover invitation to withdraw to the west the forces then on the Eastern Front. Obviously Jodl had succeeded in obtaining some conciliatory gesture from Bedell Smith, who was an old acquaintance from the time when he was in Berlin.

A two-hour discussion now took place in Flensburg as to whether Jodl should be authorised to sign. The fact that Jodl, of all people, had arrived at the conclusions he had, led everyone to suspect that there were additional weighty reasons. At 0.40 a.m. Keitel informed Jodl over the special radio link that he was empowered by Dönitz to sign.

Meanwhile in Reims all preparations had been made for a signing ceremony. Projectors, cameras and microphones had been installed in the Headquarters Map Room and the atmosphere resembled that of a Hollywood film studio.[13]

At 2.41 a.m. on 7 May Alfred Jodl signed the instrument of unconditional surrender in the presence of Generals Bedell Smith, Morgan, Bull, Sevez, Spaatz, Strong and Susloparov, Admiral

Burrough, Air Marshal Robb, Colonel Zenkovich and Lieutenant Chernayev.[14] General Smith then signed for the Supreme Allied Commander, General Susloparov for the Soviet High Command and General Sevez as witness for the French Army.

General Smith wrote of the ceremony: 'The Germans – Jodl and Admiral von Friedeburg – were militarily correct in their stone-like expressions. But I do not remember that any of the Allied officers around the table displayed elation at this ending of the long years of fighting. It was a moment of solemn gratitude.'[15]

After the signing Jodl rose and said: 'With this signature the German people and the German armed forces are, for better or worse, delivered into the victor's hands. In this war, which has lasted more than five years, both have achieved and suffered more than perhaps any other people in the world. In this hour I can only express the hope that the victor will treat them with generosity.'[16]

Jodl then had to sign a declaration guaranteeing formal signature before the Commanders-in-Chief of the Allied Forces and Soviet High Command. He was then taken to General Eisenhower, who asked him if all points in the document were clear. When Jodl replied 'Ja', Eisenhower added that he would be held personally responsible for any infractions of the agreement. With that the interview ended.[17]

Eisenhower's message to the Combined Chiefs of Staff was equally laconic: 'The mission of the Allied force was fulfilled at 0241 local time May 7 1945.'[18]

The Instrument of Capitulation was in five paragraphs:

Para. 1 stipulated simultaneous unconditional surrender of all German armed forces on land, on sea or in the air to Supreme Headquarters Allied Expeditionary Force and to the Soviet High Command.

Para. 2 laid down immediate issue of an order that at 23.01 central European time all hostilities were to cease and troops to remain in their positions. Ships were not to be sunk or aircraft destroyed.

Para. 3 laid upon OKW responsibility for issue of and compliance with the necessary orders.

Para. 4 stated that the surrender was not to be regarded as final but would be replaced by a general Instrument of Capitulation between the Allied Nations opposing Germany on the one side and the German armed forces on the other.

.Para. 5 threatened appropriate punitive measures should OKW or its subordinate forces fail to act in accordance with the terms.[19]

The origins of this document have given rise to suspicion and intrigue, in some cases going so far as to impute some sinister purpose to the failure to utilise the text drafted by the European Advisory Commission. Its history can be summarised as follows: By the end of February the Advisory Commission had drawn up the wording of a capitulation document which was approved by the American, British and Soviet Governments in March 1945. This document was very detailed, but it assumed that, at the time of capitulation, a political and military authority would exist in Germany. When, during the course of April, this assumption became questionable, the Allies discussed the possibility of issue of a proclamation containing the terms under which the capitulation of the Wehrmacht and the control of Germany would be accepted. Lord Strang, the British member of the Commission,[20] produced a draft, but it did not include the words 'unconditional surrender'. The USSR suspected some hidden motive behind this wording and gave it to be understood that they assumed that the change of wording indicated some change of policy towards Germany. Winant, the American member of the Commission, was thereupon informed by the State Department that Roosevelt did not wish to have any proposal or document not in consonance with unconditional surrender. These new difficulties concerning both the already agreed Instrument of Capitulation and the proclamation worried both the State and War Departments. On 19 April Winant was told that it was considered preferable to issue a short declaration containing the following basic ideas:

1. The demand for unconditional surrender and admission of Germany's total defeat.
2. A declaration of the assumption of control by the Four Powers.
3. The establishment of a Control Commission and the zoning of responsibilities.
4. The threat of punitive measures in the event of non-compliance with Allied orders.

5. Further resistance to the Allied Nations to be punished as illegal.

At the same time Winant was told that changes in the Instrument of Capitulation would be acceptable to the American Government, should these be thought desirable. The Commission was still busy with these changes and with the proclamation when the German negotiators appeared in Montgomery's and Eisenhower's headquarters.

The Advisory Commission's draft had apparently been transmitted to Bedell Smith. He had, however, quite simply forgotten its existence.[21] To make confusion worse confounded, there were two Advisory Commission drafts on capitulation, the first dated 25 July 1944 supposed to have been received by Bedell Smith shortly before D Day[22] (an obvious impossibility), and a second approved by the US, Britain and the USSR in March 1945, which Robert Murphy, Eisenhower's political adviser, is said to have handed to Smith. Whether Bedell Smith had forgotten both drafts or had only received and filed one, is unimportant. In any case he told Winant that he had neither received a copy of the Instrument of Capitulation nor had SHAEF been empowered by the four governments to sign such a document.[23] The last is the vital point. This was confirmed by Winant, who added that copies of the document were available for SHAEF. He had not, however, sent one to Bedell Smith, thinking that SHAEF preferred a short declaration to a long complicated text, which might have made more difficult the acceptance of unconditional surrender by the Germans.[24] In addition to these difficulties, moreover, from early May the document had become no longer valid. Although France had been a member of EAC since November 1944, she had only attained the status of a signatory power on 1 May 1945. As the result of a leak the French knew of the second draft but they had not participated in its production. It contained a paragraph on the dismemberment of Germany and Stalin had refused to answer all proposals regarding French membership of the Dismemberment Committee. Meanwhile he too had changed his views regarding the dismemberment of Germany, so that from all points of view the document was outdated. Winant therefore merely insisted on the inclusion of para 4 as an enabling clause for further terms as in the EAC instrument. For the rest Bedell Smith had used a draft produced some time before by McCloy, the Under-Secretary of the War Department, which was available in SHAEF files.

The Advisory Commission draft therefore seems to have been ignored, not through some machination or secret game between Eisenhower's staff and the State and War Departments, but simply from a combination of human error, the time factor and the current revision of the original Instrument of Capitulation. Finally on the Allied side it had been thought that the war would last some two to three months longer.

The fact that Eisenhower was at such pains not to ruffle Russo-American relations is a further argument against the existence of some backstairs intrigue. Moreover it seems improbable that Bedell Smith would have 'forgotten' the Instrument intentionally and been simply fooling Winant and Murphy. Though he was the only one to show some sympathy for Jodl's requests, he would certainly not have gone so far as to deceive his own people.

Bedell Smith maintains that the Russians raised no objection to the Instrument as submitted to them.[25] Murphy, on the other hand, says that shortly after he had got General Smith out of bed in order to ask him why the Advisory Commission document had not been used and had found the draft in Smith's personal safe, a telegram arrived from Washington reporting a protest from Moscow to the effect that the text as signed did not accord with the wording approved by the Russians.[26] In fact on 7 May Eisenhower did receive a telegram from General Antonov. It was in answer to his informatory message of 6 May, in which he had briefed Moscow on developments in Reims and at the same time enquired whether the Russians desired to amend the terms proposed by him, to repeat the signing ceremony before a Russian representative at a place to be designated by them and to participate in an official act of ratification.[27] Antonov's reply, though also dated 6 May, was not handed to General Deane, the Head of the American Military Mission in Moscow, until the morning of the 7th. It stressed that, in spite of his offer of an armistice, Dönitz was still issuing orders for fighting against the Russians to continue. The Russians therefore had the impression that a separate armistice with the West was being arranged. Antonov demanded the inclusion in the instrument to be submitted to the Germans of certain passages from the original document and a formal signature in Berlin, when Marshal Zhukov would represent the Red Army. He was opposed to any prior signature by General Susloparov.[28] Meanwhile, however, signature had taken place. Eisenhower replied at once: 'I am sure you will realise that we have adhered scrupulously to our obligation not to conclude a separate armistice on our front. When the enemy on our flanks began to surrender in large numbers, I attempted to drive on with my right centre in order to meet the Red Army. This movement was halted, however, when the Russian High Command informed me that large Russian forces would be operating in the area concerned and that confusion and complications would inevitably ensue. As a direct result we have refused to discuss a separate armistice with anyone and have acted entirely in accordance with Russian wishes as we understood them. . . .' Eisenhower added that, before the arrival of the Russian note, a short document had been signed in Reims but the German negotiators had been warned that a more formal signature would have to follow. Finally he declared himself ready to go to Berlin on 8 May at any time convenient to Marshal Zhukov. Should he be held up by bad weather, the Heads of the British and American Military Missions in Moscow could represent him. He concluded: 'My only wish is to complete everything quickly, correctly and in full co-operation with you.'[29]

The Russian protest about Dönitz' orders was no figment of the imagination. Shortly after Jodl had been authorised to sign, Keitel issued an order to C-in-C South, Field Marshal Kesselring, and Headquarters Southern Zone for transmission to Army Groups Centre and Ostmark and C-in-C South-East. It ran: 'Grand Admiral Dönitz orders

> On all fronts facing the Eastern enemy everything possible to be withdrawn westwards with the greatest urgency, fighting their way through the Russians if necessary.
> All hostilities against the Anglo-Americans to cease forthwith and surrender to them to be made.
> General capitulation will be signed today at Eisenhower's headquarters. Eisenhower has assured Jodl that hostilities will cease at 1.0 a.m. German summer time on 9 May 1945.

This order was the direct consequence of Jodl's second message from Reims. It should have been issued on 4 May at the latest but had been delayed because Dönitz had bowed to the views of his military advisers.[30] To compensate in some degree for this error, one of the most remarkable undertakings of these final days of war was initiated. On 7 May Colonel Meyer-Detring of the OKW Operations Staff flew from Flensburg to Pilsen in a British aircraft; there he was met by an American escort under Lieutenant-Colonel Pratt, Operations Officer of US V Corps, and conducted through the Czech resistance to the headquarters of Field Marshal Schörner, in order to brief him on the necessity for capitulation in the immediate future.[31] The Army Group had already been ordered to obey the capitulation terms, by telephone and radio on 7 May and verbally during an Army Commanders' conference on 8 May. The necessity for speed, however, made any orderly withdrawal impossible. Field Marshal Schörner offered to take personal responsibility for fulfilment of the capitulation terms on the Erz Gebirge front but emphasised that no order could compel the troops to leave their comrades in the lurch or surrender voluntarily to the Russians.[32]

Schörner's attitude and the confused situation in Czechoslovakia made it seem likely that strict adherence to the terms of capitulation was going to be difficult. Eisenhower had made OKW responsible, however, that the terms were carried out to the letter. A radio message from Schörner at 1.20 a.m. on 8 May is therefore to be regarded less as a situation report for Dönitz than advance justification for the continuance of operations after capitulation. Schörner said:

Difficulty in carrying out measures ordered since:

1. Partisans in the Protectorate continually damage the telephone network, capture couriers and render any regular transmission of orders impossible.

2. For some days partisan transmitters have been undermining the morale of the troops and issuing tendentious announcements contrary to the intentions of the supreme command.

Request immediate action with the Allies to cause partisans to cease their attacks and release occupied transmitter stations immediately, thus allowing me to carry out orders referred to.

Simultaneously an anguished message arrived from Kesselring indicating that 'in spite of the entry into force of the armistice at 0100 9 May whole formations are still on the march and fighting against the Soviets'.

Before hearing of the armistice agreement Schörner's intention had been to fight back across the Elbe and Moldau with his entire Army Group; Army Groups Ostmark and South-East, on the other hand, seemed largely prepared to accommodate themselves to the armistice conditions. C-in-C South accordingly proposed that Eisenhower be warned of the possibility that individual formations might continue to fight, so as to avoid any accusation of treaty-breaking. In addition he asked what view was taken of Schörner's plan.

On 8 May, therefore, Jodl despatched two radio messages to Kesselring. The first ('Flash' and 'Destroy when read') announced that Jodl had already on 6 May indicated to Eisenhower the possibility 'that individual soldiers and units might refuse to obey the order to surrender to the Soviets and might fight their way through to the Americans'. He had been assured that OKW would not be held responsible for this. Jodl then reiterated that all commanders must issue written orders for movement to cease at midnight 8/9 May and all weapons to be handed over to the first enemy forces to arrive. Finally he referred to Meyer-Detring's mission. The second message to Kesselring said: 'It is important, within the limits of orders already issued, to accelerate troop movements as far as possible and in addition to assist valuable elements of the German population. Compulsory evacuation and formation of civilian refugee columns should be avoided since they will hinder the main movement.'

Finally the following message was sent to General Eisenhower:

Fulfilment of capitulation terms seriously hampered by insurrectionary movement in the Protectorate.
Request pressure be brought to bear on the movement in order that:

(a) Damage to the telephone network may cease

(b) Couriers are not intercepted

(c) Transmitters now in the hands of partisans be liberated immediately for the transmission of orders.

At 7.03 p.m. on the same day arrived the following terse reply from Eisenhower: 'Your information of 12.50 8 May concerning revolutionary movements in the Protectorate received. We are initiating investigations. Eisenhower.'

The Supreme Commander had not, as originally intended, flown to Berlin on 8 May for signature of the formal capitulation.

Some of his staff, and also Churchill, had raised objections, pointing out first that capitulation had already been signed in Reims, and secondly that Marshal Zhukov, the Soviet C-in-C in Germany, was junior to him.[33] Air Chief Marshal Tedder was therefore sent. He was accompanied by Generals Spaatz and Strong, Admiral Burrough and General de Lattre de Tassigny for the French. The German delegation, also transported to Berlin in Allied aircraft, consisted of Field Marshal Keitel, Admiral von Friedeburg, Colonel-General Hans-Jürgen Stumpff, C-in-C Air Fleet 'Reich' representing Ritter von Greim who had been wounded, Vice-Admiral Bürkner and a number of junior officers.[34] In addition to Marshal Zhukov the Russians were represented by Vishinsky, Army General Sokolovsky, Colonel-General Serov and Colonel-General Malinin. Signature did not take place until after 11.0 p.m. (the exact time is in dispute – Germans say that it was after midnight, thus making 9 May the date of capitulation); from 4.0 p.m. onwards the Allies were haggling about who was authorised to sign.

General de Lattre had been instructed by General de Gaulle that, if Eisenhower signed, he was to sign as a witness; otherwise he was to insist on equal treatment with the British representative, unless the latter signed in place of Eisenhower. When de Lattre informed Tedder of his instructions, he was told that he and General Spaatz would sign as witnesses. Initially Zhukov apparently agreed to this arrangement. Then, however, Vishinsky appeared and declared that de Lattre could sign since he would thereby publicly register France's resurrection, but that there could be no question of Spaatz since Air Marshal Tedder was representing both the American and British forces. General Spaatz, however, insisted on signing if de Lattre did so; the latter declared that he could not go back without having signed the capitulation or he would be hung. After hours of argument it was agreed that Zhukov and Tedder should be the principal signatories with the names of the witnesses, Spaatz and de Lattre, lower down on the document.[35]

The Instrument itself differed only slightly from that signed in Reims. The 'High Command of the Soviet forces' appeared as 'High Command of the Red Army'. Para 2 was considerably expanded in that OKW was to order the German armed forces to 'disarm totally, handing over weapons and equipment to the local Allied commanders or to officers to be designated by the Allied Representatives'. The passage about damage and destruction was also expanded and a new para 6 was added laying down that both the English and Russian texts were authoritative.[36] Keitel attempted to obtain twenty-four hours' grace before entry into force of the punitive conditions in the event of non-compliance with the terms; he himself says that he was allowed twelve hours by the Russians.

Keitel's signature, given late at night on 8 May, finally brought to an end the war unleashed by Hitler on 1 September 1939. The Allies had achieved their military object. A formal declaration of their political object, the complete elimination of the National-Socialist State, was still to come.

Victory was celebrated on two different days by East and West. The Reims ceremony had prematurely become public knowledge through the Flensburg Radio broadcasts and the disregard by Ed Kennedy, the Associated Press correspondent, of the news ban imposed by SHAEF. Eisenhower had proposed that a simultaneous announcement of the surrender be made in all three capitals at 3.0 p.m. 8 May and that 9 May be celebrated as 'V-E Day'. Innumerable telephone calls and telegrams were exchanged between Washington, London and Moscow but no agreement was reached. The German capitulation was announced by the American and British governments as proposed by Eisenhower, but by Moscow only after the Berlin signature at 2.0 a.m. on 9 May.[37]

The Allied press gave the event fullest coverage. The *New York Times* wrote that the Germans had 'suffered the most resounding defeat ever administered to a major nation'. *Pravda* printed a proclamation from Stalin: 'Germany has been completely defeated. The German troops are capitulating. The Soviet Union rejoices in this victory, although she has never intended to dismember or destroy Germany. Fellow-countrymen! The Great Patriotic War has ended with total victory for us. The period of war in Europe is at an end. The period of peaceful development has begun.' *The Times* commented: 'Thus is put on record for history by the acknowledgement of the military authorities most qualified to speak, the fact of the total defeat by force of arms of every fighting organisation that Germany possessed. No room is left for propaganda to falsify the facts by fostering a legend that the German army was "stabbed in the back" by civilian cowardice or treachery.' *The Guardian*, while rejoicing in Germany's military defeat, demanded the completion of her political defeat: 'The Allies have to announce at once that they will accept no government linked, however tenuously, with the Nazi government or with the General Staff. If they do not, how can they treat war criminality justly? Secondly they must decide on the elimination or curative treatment of criminal elements in the German forces while they still hold these men in their power.' Similar sentiments were also to be heard from France. In *Le Parisien* Georges Duhamel wrote: 'Peace for men of goodwill and for them only; for the others begins the time of atonement.'

To the Germans their defeat was made public by the military orders for cessation of hostilities and laying down of arms.[38] As head of the newly-formed Acting Reich Government, Schwerin von Krosigk announced unconditional surrender as early as 7 May. He had prepared the draft of his speech and shown it to Dönitz on the 6th. The original and final drafts show that at the time there were one or two interesting and significant differences of opinion between Dönitz and his Foreign Minister. The two are therefore worth comparing.

In von Krosigk's draft he used the word 'armistice', but in his public speech he said: 'OKW has today declared unconditional surrender of all troops.' The amendment was undoubtedly made by Dönitz. Montgomery had already drawn attention to a similar instance; the Wehrmacht report of 5 May had referred only to a 'cessation of hostilities' in North-West Germany; Montgomery reacted at once and Dönitz sent him the following message: 'Regret the wording of first sentence of today's Wehrmacht report, issued without my knowledge. Will ensure clear and correct wording used in future.'

Von Krosigk's draft included the sentence: 'This is not the time to broach the question of responsibility for the immense national disaster which has befallen Germany.' This was dropped, presumably also on Dönitz' instructions. As Hitler's successor he could hardly disavow his 'predecessor', since he would then have been calling in question the legitimacy of his own appointment, quite apart from the fact that at this stage he was still convinced that 'The Führer' was a great historical figure.

Both versions stressed the German people's heroic struggle against a superior enemy over nearly six years. Whether as self-justification or insurance against a new stab-in-the-back legend, the government also emphasised its sense of responsibility to its own people, who had demanded an end to the struggle to avoid useless sacrifices. 'Responsibility to the nations which had allied their fate to that of Germany, and to Europe' is missing from the final version and is replaced by 'reverence' for the victims or casualties of the war and sympathy for the disabled and bereaved.

There then follows a passage about the hard times and sacrifices to be anticipated and a call loyally to fulfil obligations undertaken. This also includes certain amendments attributable to Dönitz.

Part 2 of the proclamation is devoted primarily to an attempt to rouse the German people from their mood of resignation. The final version is fuller than the draft and is based on a proposal from the government's Intelligence Service recommending a call to the people for determination to reconstruct the country and 'in view of our military defeat, an indication to them of the historical context of this occurrence'. Further to raise the spirit of the people it was recommended that 'they be reminded of the inner strength of the German character as shown in music, literature etc; this should be presented as indestructible and invincible'.

Von Krosigk then became almost lyrical, speaking of three stars shining through the 'darkness of the future', three stars which had 'always been the hallmarks of the Germans' – unity, legality and freedom. This passage seems to have been drafted by Dönitz and von Krosigk in concert. Unity had always been one of Dönitz' highest ideals and its achievement he regarded as the true merit of National-Socialism. The capitulation announcement therefore refers to the 'community of the people' [Volksgemeinschaft] and revives the old slogan of the Weimar Republic about the brotherhood of the trenches and the call not to relapse into class warfare.

The emphasis on legality as the foundation both of 'popular existence' and of international relationships can undoubtedly be ascribed to von Krosigk. Even before Hitler's death, when he thought that Himmler would be the successor, he had insisted on a proclamation of measures to demonstrate that previous methods were things of the past.[39]

Both Dönitz and von Krosigk obviously felt strongly about

freedom, particularly in the situation of May 1945. There followed a number of hopes or desires, for instance that the atmosphere of hatred now enveloping Germany would soon disappear. Worded slightly differently, these are to be found in von Krosigk's initial draft.

The next paragraph bears the marks of the Intelligence Service's thinking. It refers to 'the best traits of the German character . . . which have given the world imperishable works and values' – disregarding the fact that at this moment the world cared little for the spiritual longings of the Germans.

Emphasis was laid – undoubtedly by von Krosigk – on the fact that Germany belonged to Western Christian civilisation. The final sentence of his draft was included without alteration: 'May God not desert us in our misfortune and may he bless our heavy task.'

Dönitz himself announced the capitulation to the German people at 12.30 a.m. on 8 May over the Flensburg radio. He took as his starting-point his speech of 1 May but this time referred to the Führer's 'death'. In pursuance of his programme of saving German lives, he said, he had ordered the signature of capitulation. The soldiers now going into captivity were thereby offering 'the ultimate sacrifice for the lives of our women and children and the future of our people'. Then followed, as in the final draft of von Krosigk's speech, the standard formula about 'reverence' for the bravery and sacrifices of the war. The speech, moreover, was far more matter of fact and less full of pathos than was Dönitz' wont:

'I have promised the German people that, in the coming time of need, I will strive, so far as it lies in my power, to create tolerable conditions of life for our brave men, women and children. Whether, in these hard times, I can make some contribution, I do not know. We must look facts in the face. The foundations upon which the German Reich was constructed have been shattered. Unity of State and Party no longer exists. The Party has disappeared from the arena of its activity. With occupation authority lies in the hands of the occupying powers. Whether I and the government I have appointed can act or not, depends on them. If in my official position I can serve and help our Fatherland, I will remain in office, until the will of the German people can be expressed in the nomination of a new Head of State or until the occupying powers make the continued exercise of my office impossible. Only my love of Germany and my sense of duty keep me in this onerous office. Without regard for my own person, I will remain not a moment longer than I feel is required by the respect which I owe to the Reich, of which I am the highest representative. . . .'[40]

Comparison of these sentences with Dönitz' speeches and exhortations of March and April 1945 shows how far he had travelled in this short time. In its leading article of 8 May the *Flensburger Nachrichten* said: 'We are now a people which has put out of its thinking and its life all its more or less cherished illusions of the past.' Dönitz too had meanwhile lost his illusions and he acted accordingly.

There are a number of interesting reports on the German population's reaction to the announcement of capitulation; they must, however, be treated with caution since they apply only to the Northern Zone and originate from the Government's Intelligence Service. The people apparently received the leading occupation troops 'with curiosity rather than apprehension' and hardly regarded them as enemies. 'The background to this attitude seems to be that in the foreseeable future Germany and the Western Powers will make common cause against Bolshevism.' This belief was especially prevalent among officers and soldiers; the most circumstantial reports were of conversations with members of a fighter squadron which had operated on both the eastern and western fronts. 'Capitulation is regarded as a transitional stage only; political developments will soon be more favourable to Germany. As far as can be established, both officers and men are ready now to resume the struggle against Bolshevism.' It was admitted that few people were thinking deeply about the situation. The majority were fully occupied with problems of accommodation and nourishment, so that hardly anyone realised the full implications of the situation. There was general perplexity at the uncertainty of the future and the looming spectre of unemployment. 'The announcement of unconditional surrender *to the Soviets as well* has come as a complete surprise to a large proportion of the population. People cannot understand why fighting against the Soviets does not continue.' According to the Intelligence Service the morale of the people sank rapidly after the announcement of capitulation, particularly among the refugees from whom comments were to be heard such as: 'Now the last anchor to which we had clung, has vanished – that the Anglo-Americans would fight with us against the Soviets', or 'If, according to the capitulation terms, we are supposed to go back to our homes, as long as the Russians are there we would rather kill our children here', or 'The East is lost to us for ever'. There was also considerable criticism of the new government.

Detailed examination of the measures taken by Dönitz between the evening of 30 April and his authorisation to sign the general capitulations in Reims and Berlin leads to the following conclusions:

As Supreme Commander of the Wehrmacht and President of the Reich his freedom of action was limited by the following:
1. The shortage of ammunition, fuel and food supplies.
2. The war weariness of the troops and population.
3. The inexorable advance of the enemy both from East and West.

The most rapid possible termination of the war was therefore a military necessity, which only the spurious heroism legend of National-Socialism could deny. Although for years Dönitz had been preaching heroism, when he himself had to take the final decision he was not swayed by it.

At the time the following considerations argued against any immediate abandonment of the struggle:

1. Knowledge of the atrocities committed by Soviet troops as they advanced.
2. The desire to save as many Germans as possible from a similar fate.
3. The widespread hope of a reversal of alliances – though this hope was not shared by Dönitz himself.

The general situation and the positions of the opposing forces reduced to about ten days the time available for the planned 'rescue of Germans'. Comparing results achieved with the object sought, it seems that Dönitz was about 50% successful. He did not succeed in withdrawing all the troops in the East to the western demarcation line. Army Group Vistula and Twelfth Army did reach the western lines or were withdrawn by sea, as were the remnants of Ninth Army. Some 75,000 men of the Army of East Prussia were withdrawn from the Hela Peninsula and about 25,000 men of the Courland Army reached the West.

In the Southern Zone Army Group South withdrew to the West almost intact, but only fractions of Army Groups South-East and Centre;[41] many of those who reached the American lines were held by the Americans and handed over to the Russians. If one accepts OKW's estimate of 9 May which gave the total strength of the Eastern Front as 1,850,000 and prisoners as 780,622 plus 200,000 from Courland and East Prussia, the proportion is just about 50%. In addition there were the refugees, whose numbers could not be established. Sea movement continued even after capitulation; a document dated 18 May and entitled 'Baltic Situation' reports the shipment between 11 and 17 May of a total of 109,205 soldiers, 6,267 wounded and 5,379 refugees. A similar 'Baltic Situation' of 21 March gives further details of refugee ships; in all the total of soldiers and refugees transported by the Navy between 23 January and 8 May was reported as 2,022,602.

Total war losses (1 September 1939 to 1 May 1945) were given by OKW as approximately 2,007,000 killed and 2,610,000 wounded and missing[42] – 4,617,000 men in all.[43] Comparison of these figures with those of the preceding paragraph gives some indication of the achievement of these few days. Many a German, it may be thought, has cause to be grateful to Karl Dönitz. Imagine the situation, had he acted like Lindemann or Schörner and fought 'the last decent battle of this war'. Even Field Marshal Greim told Koller, his Chief of Staff, that he could not understand Dönitz; he (Greim) had promised to obey Hitler's successor only in military matters.

There is no indication that Dönitz' rescue programme had any motive other than the humanitarian. Up to the time of capitulation he harboured no illusions about an imminent break-up of the enemy coalition. Undoubtedly he hoped and wished that it would happen and so did not exclude the possibility. In any case, however, several hundred thousand soldiers in the West were to be preferred to an army of captives in the East. The one reason did not therefore preclude the other.

The ex-enemy countries, particularly the USSR, necessarily pass a different and more severe judgement on Dönitz. For them progressive capitulation implied a prolongation of the war with its additional human and material sacrifices.[44]

Dönitz' rescue programme was confined to his own people. As a military man after five and a half years of murderous struggle, it could hardly be expected that he would suddenly take account of his enemies. Exactly this, however, is what many leading German military expected from their western enemies – sympathy from Montgomery and Eisenhower for German soldiers and refugees.

Two trains of thought lay behind this attitude: first, that of the traditional soldier who after 'a valiant fight' thought himself entitled to 'an honourable defeat'; they did not stop to think that in this total war they had themselves been largely responsible for setting aside the 'rules of the game' and that the misdeeds of National-Socialism had extinguished any respect on the part of the enemy. Secondly, they were still convinced of the superiority of the German 'master race'; it could not be delivered over to the East. This was expressed in the oft-repeated phrase about rescuing 'the substance of the German people'; when, exceptionally, the word 'European' was used, this was only another way of indicating that the Slavs had no part nor lot in Europe.

CHAPTER EIGHT

Post-Capitulation

MPLEMENTATION of unconditional surrender in Germany
and the occupied territories was an immense task. The scattered
forces had to be assembled, accommodated in camps, registered
and released on a priority programme. Weapons, ammunition,
ships – all war material in short – had to be collected and handed
over. Organisationally the Germans were largely responsible for
implementation; the Allies merely supervised and controlled.

All German units which gave themselves up to the Russians
were assembled in camps and marched off into captivity, their
officers at their head. There was no further communication with
OKW or the Flensburg government. It is hardly possible therefore,
in this book, to deal with the implementation of capitulation in
Soviet-occupied Germany.

For the occupation of Germany Eisenhower had originally
prepared detailed orders to be handed on capitulation to the
Commanders-in-Chief of each Service. Shortly before capitulation
took place, however, he had realised that, owing to the division
into Northern and Southern Zones and the destruction of all
forms of communication, only Naval Headquarters in the north
still possessed an effective chain of command. Admiral von
Friedeburg was therefore the only Service Chief to receive a
ready-made order, handed to him by Admiral Burrough in Reims,
and the Navy was the only Service finally to surrender as a body.
General Jodl was merely told that the Army and Air Force
commanders on the Western Front, in Norway, the Channel
Islands and any other areas still occupied by German troops,
should hold themselves ready to receive detailed instructions
which would be passed on by the Allied commanders opposite
them. Simultaneously an exchange of liaison staffs between Reims
and Flensburg was agreed and the SHAEF representatives approved
Jodl's proposal to combine the OKW staffs North and South.
It was also agreed that, to maintain law and order, reliable
members and units of the Wehrmacht should remain armed.[1]

On 5 May OKW had already issued a first batch of orders for the

178

implementation of capitulation in the area covered by the agreement with Montgomery. Keitel sent a long teleprinter message to the Wehrmacht Commanders-in-Chief in Holland, Denmark and Norway, to the High Commands of the Navy and Luftwaffe and for information to the Reichsführer-SS, the Reich Labour Service Leader and Reich Minister Speer. Para 2, still in National-Socialist jargon, ran: 'Every soldier, and in particular every officer, must, by his proud manly bearing and dignity, help to ensure that even now, after nearly six years of heroic and honourable battle unparalleled in world history, the escutcheon of the German nation remains clean and unsullied. Only thus can we hold up our heads before the victims of this war and honour their memory. Only thus can we help our country in this grave hour and only thus can we expect from the enemy the respect to which every brave soldier has always been entitled.'

Keitel then ordered that 'on demand from the enemy' all weapons were to be collected and handed over 'in an orderly manner', all weapons, ammunition, fuel and food depots were to be guarded with special care and communications safeguarded. He made 'Commanders-in-Chief and commanders of all ranks personally responsible for the rapid and conscientious execution of this order'.

Dönitz meanwhile cancelled the orders for demolition and paralysation. The population in the western occupied areas was told 'to desist from any illegal warlike activity in Werwolf or other organisations'. On the same day an urgent teleprint from Keitel to Air Fleet 'Reich' said: 'It has been reported to me that parts of Air Fleet Reich are preparing for guerilla action. The situation *vis-à-vis* the Western Powers having changed fundamentally, any action of this nature is highly injurious to our general interests. I request that any activity against Anglo-American forces be stopped immediately and completely.'

The Naval High Command forbade sinking or destruction of merchant ships 'apart from those which cannot sail or be towed from ports due to fall into the hands of the Bolshevists'. All sea movement in the area covered by the surrender to Montgomery was stopped 'apart from personnel transports from the East and urgent coastal supply traffic'.[2]

On 7 May, as soon as Dönitz had approved signature of general capitulation, numerous further orders went out. The terms of capitulation were made known to all Commanders-in-Chief, the time being first given as 1.0 a.m. on 9 May and subsequently corrected. The announcement to Commanders-in-Chief stated explicitly: 'From 1.0 a.m. on 9 May all orders issued by Supreme Headquarters Allied Forces or the Soviet High Command to Commanders-in-Chief or commanders designated by Naval and Air Headquarters will be carried out. Should these authorities or their subordinate formations fail to act in accordance with the surrender terms, Supreme Headquarters Allied Forces and the Soviet High Command will take punitive measures or other steps outside the terms of capitulation.'

Naval Headquarters sent out the following radio message on all wavelengths: 'Having consented to unconditional surrender of all German maritime forces, scuttling of ships and demolitions will now cease. Any infraction implies serious contravention of Grand Admiral's explicit orders and will cause serious detriment to the German people.' A supplementary order from Keitel ordered ships at sea to proceed but no vessels to leave Danish ports unless sailing for German ports. Refugee transports from Norway ordered on 6 May might proceed but only up to 11.0 p.m. on the 8th.

At 8.0 p.m. on 8 May and in all subsequent bulletins the radio carried an OKW announcement of the time for cessation of hostilities and the general ban on destruction of weapons, aimed particularly at those who might not have received the necessary orders through military channels. In addition all radio traffic was ordered to be in clear.[3]

At 2.40 p.m. on 9 May Kesselring sent a repeat radio message to SS-Obergruppenführer Dietrich, C-in-C of 6 Panzer Army, reiterating 'the order of the Reich Government that the armistice terms are equally binding on Waffen-SS units'. This was necessitated by the fact that, even up to 11.0 p.m. on 9 May, members of Army Group South, and even more Army Group Centre, were still refusing to halt and surrender to the Russians. At 3.0 a.m. on 10 May SHAEF drew OKW's attention to this fact, demanding immediate steps to ensure that 'Commanders-in-Chief of the German Army Groups Centre and South conform soonest to the terms of capitulation'. The message demanded acknowledgement of receipt and a copy of orders issued to the two Army Groups.

The same day Jodl radioed back: 'Your radio of 0300 10 May

received. On 7 May Army Groups Centre and South received and acknowledged okw orders giving surrender terms. To ensure orders received, a further order was broadcast on 8 May. It is confirmed that Field Marshal Schörner has issued the strictest orders for scrupulous adherence to the surrender terms. Since no radio station in Army Groups Centre, South or South-East is presently on the air, we do not know whether some troops have disobeyed orders or whether the Czech resistance is hampering their execution. okw will again broadcast strict instructions to these Army Groups to obey orders. Texts of orders and broadcasts follow.'

On 12 May the 'Reich Radio Exchange' intercepted a further message from Eisenhower, drawing attention to and repeating Para 2 of the Berlin Instrument of Surrender. The message then continued:

> 2. You will observe that, according to this paragraph, all German units are to be completely disarmed. This does not affect the verbal agreement reached in Reims on 7 May between the Deputy Chief of Staff shaef and General Jodl, whereby reliable members and units of the Wehrmacht may be permitted by Allied commanders to retain their weapons for the maintenance of order and the protection of property.

On 13 May Keitel replied that German obligations were recognised; he referred to the various radio messages sent to and acknowledged by Commanders-in-Chief of Theatres, Army Groups and independent Armies. He drew attention to the orders broadcast over Radio Flensburg and two other stations which were still operative. 'Further orders could not be issued owing to the failure of communications, particularly to Field Marshal Schörner in Army Group Centre.'

Courland was another outpost to cause grave anxiety. On 2 May General Hilpert, the local C-in-C, had assured Dönitz of 'loyalty and discipline' in the name of all his forces. On 4 May Lieutenant-Colonel de Maizière was despatched to tell him of the new government's programme and initiate the necessary measures to rescue as many troops as possible. The plan was confirmed on 5 May after the local surrender in the north-west. That same day, however, the Military Governor radioed back (the message was signed by Brigadeführer [SS Major-General] Möller):

1. Population is ready to fight against Bolshevism to the last man shoulder to shoulder with the German Wehrmacht.

2. Proclamation of an independent Latvian state inevitable. Internally German interests will be safeguarded.

    (a) The Army Group will continue to fight as a free corps.
    (b) Guarantee of supplies essential.

At 9.35 that evening a further message was received from Courland, this time from Hilpert, passing on a report from the Admiral Eastern Baltic that the enemy was preparing to attack Bornholm and asking whether the situation still remained the same as far as Courland was concerned.

At 10.10 p.m. Jodl personally drafted the following to Army Group Courland: 'Enemy attack on Bornholm is silly gossip. Operate and evacuate as arranged with Maizière. No obstacles anticipated from British side.'

At 3.30 p.m. on 6 May a further message from Hilpert reported a new development, already foreshadowed by Möller and paralleling the attempts by Frank in Czechoslovakia and Löhr in Austria to form an anti-Soviet government. The Latvian National Committee, represented by Herr Anderson and SS-Standartenführer [Colonel] Osis had applied for recognition as a provisional independent government.

Chief Minister: Herr Osis
Programme: anti-Bolshevist
Immediate object: retention of the Courland area.

This last-minute attempt was overtaken by the Reims surrender. Keitel radioed back that, in view of the situation, he could see no possibility of recognising the Latvian National Committee as a provisional government. On the same day General Hilpert enquired of Jodl whether the 'cease-fire' also applied to Russia. He asked for freedom to negotiate with the local Russian commanders in order to avoid further casualties. He also wished to know whether the surrender terms permitted withdrawal of troops by sea. At 11.40 p.m. he was given authority to negotiate and told that, under the agreement, ships were allowed to sail up to midnight 8/9 May.

The last Wehrmacht report, dated 9 May, stated that only the wounded and fathers of large families could be moved. General Hilpert led the remainder into captivity. A senior officer who reached the West later told people in Mürwik that thousands of German soldiers were standing on the quay hoping for a place on board. No one shoved, cursed or swore; there were only shouts of 'Give our love to Germany' and many sang the national anthem.

Depressing news also came from East Prussia. In spite of the 9 May armistice the Russians had apparently attacked, using aircraft and mortars. The Army did not surrender until 14 May.

The Russian attack on Bornholm reported by Hilpert proved to be anything but 'silly gossip'. The island belonged to Denmark and OKW had assumed that, in accordance with the terms of surrender to Montgomery, it would be occupied by British troops. On 10 May, however, came a report from the Bornholm commander that Russian motor-boats had arrived and that he was being summoned to surrender. OKW immediately sent him the following instructions by radio:

> Bornholm is part of Denmark. As regards German troops in Denmark a clear agreement has been concluded with Field Marshal Montgomery. Any surrender agreement with the Russians concluded under Russian pressure will therefore be regarded by us as invalid. Take no further steps and await decision of Allied High Command which has been requested. In accordance with British demand for withdrawal of German troops from Denmark OKW still intends to move troops from the Danish island of Bornholm by sea to German ports as quickly as possible.

But OKW's calculation went awry. At 10.35 p.m. on 10 May arrived a message from Montgomery: 'Under Instrument of Surrender German commanders are obliged to act in accordance with instructions of SHAEF or the Red Army. OKW is, moreover, legally bound to observe the armistice. In spite of the above the German Commander Bornholm is still refusing to obey the orders of the local Russian commander.'

At 5.27 a.m. on 11 May on Jodl's instructions Major-General Dethleffsen sent the following message to General Gareis, Head of the Liaison Staff with Montgomery: 'OKW regards itself as legally bound by the armistice in respect of Bornholm. Commander Bornholm has been instructed accordingly. Instrument of Surrender clearly lays down that German forces in Denmark will surrender to Commander-in-Chief British 21st Army Group.' Dethleffsen asked for precise instructions 'whether the island of Bornholm was now to be surrendered to the Russians or whether we are to await the arrival of British troops for the surrender of the island'. Montgomery's decision was that, pending a subsequent settlement, the garrison of the island should initially surrender to the Soviet commander. This was transmitted to the Island Commander, Jodl noting in his diary: 'Montgomery's answer on Bornholm is unclear.' SHAEF, on the other hand, took the view that the island was covered both by the surrender to 21st Army Group and by the overall capitulation signed in Reims and Berlin.[4] In the event the Germans were taken prisoner by the Russians who remained in occupation until the spring of 1946.

In Denmark and Norway too there were difficulties. German troops there had not been defeated in battle and were both more numerous and better equipped than the Allied contingents despatched to receive the surrender; they expected more accommodating treatment. Complications also arose with the local resistance movements. Finally there were difficulties between the Western Allies and the Soviet authorities.[5]

In Denmark all went well at first. No sooner had General Lindemann and Dr. Best returned from the conference in Dönitz' headquarters[6] than they asked for his agreement to declare Copenhagen an open city, primarily because it contained 60,000 refugees and 15,000 wounded. At 11.30 p.m on 4 May agreement was given, should the city be attacked.

Meanwhile, however, at 8.0 p.m. the Danish radio had broadcast the news of the surrender to Montgomery. All over the country the population demonstrated, though there were only minor incidents. The Danish Freedom Movement sent armed patrols into all major cities, demanding to take over full authority and safeguard electricity and water works. Rail transport for Germans was suspended; bakeries, slaughterhouses and other installations supplying German troops went on strike. Isolated clashes occurred with the Freedom Movement. General Lindemann then received a letter from Goertz, the C-in-C of the Danish Army, requesting him, in view of recent developments and to avoid further unnecessary bloodshed, 'to order German troops and police in Denmark to cease all activities connected with the occupation and await further orders in their barracks'. Goertz also said that, pending definitive capitulation to the Allies, he was in a position to accept, 'in proper form' and in the name of the

Danish Army and Navy, the provisional surrender of all German armed forces and police.

Lindemann replied that he regarded the contents of this letter as overtaken by the cease-fire meanwhile agreed with Field Marshal Montgomery. According to the order he had received German troops were to stand fast, retaining their weapons and continuing their security duties. 'I have therefore ordered the troops not to leave barracks except on duty. For your part I would ask you to ensure that from the Danish side individual soldiers are not summoned to lay down their arms or leave their posts; also that supplies to the troops, the wounded and the refugees be assured in the same quantities as heretofore.' Lindemann copied both these communications to OKW, which confirmed that the cease-fire and subsequent surrender was valid only *vis-à-vis* British troops, not the Danish population or Freedom Movement. A correct, disciplined, unprovocative attitude was to be maintained; should the Danes resist, however, 'force was to be used as necessary'. OKW's message closed with the words: 'The reputation and dignity of the German soldier and German people will under all circumstances be maintained.'[7]

A little later that day C-in-C Denmark received an order from Field Marshal Montgomery demanding the withdrawal from Denmark of all German armed forces with the exception of the Navy. All Army, Luftwaffe and Waffen-SS units together with non-Wehrmacht organisations such as the Labour Service and Todt Organisation were to start movement forthwith into the area of Schleswig-Holstein between the Danish frontier and the Kiel Canal. The only personnel to remain temporarily in Denmark were members of the Navy, sick and wounded with their medical attendants, German refugees, non-German troops, auxiliaries, prisoners of war of all nationalities and foreign workers. Food and fuel were to be moved, as were serviceable trucks, ambulances and horse-drawn vehicles. A separate order was to follow regarding weapons, ammunition and war material.

On 5 May Major-General Richard H. Dewing, Head of the SHAEF Mission to Denmark, flew into Copenhagen and that evening held a discussion with Major-General Reinhardt, Lindemann's Chief of Staff, who handed over further details. Dewing pressed for rapid evacuation of the towns, particularly Copenhagen. Men were authorised to carry their personal weapons, whereas heavy weapons and equipment were to be assembled at points laid down. Transport allowed to the German forces was reduced to the strictest minimum necessary for the carriage of supplies 'required for bivouacking on the march'. Food was to be drawn from stocks, since the Danes were no longer willing to sell or provide without payment. Use of the railways was forbidden. Hungarians and Russians were to move with the troops.

The Wehrmacht C-in-C was also charged with the arrest of SD [Sicherheitsdienst – the SS Security Service] and Gestapo personnel. On 4 May Lindemann had already assumed command of the entire police force after difficulties had occurred with the uniformed Ordnungspolizei [Regular Police] in Copenhagen. Hitherto all police in Denmark had been under Pancke, the 'Senior SS and Police Commander', who was entirely independent of Lindemann and received his orders direct from the Reichsführer-SS. His had been the responsibility for maintenance of law and order and suppression of the Danish resistance movement and intelligence service. Under Pancke had been SS-Standartenführer Bovensiepen, the 'Commander of the Sicherheitspolizei [Security Police] and SD'. Their brutal methods had earned both of them the intense hatred of the Danish population. On the evening of 4 May Pancke and his Security Police disappeared from Copenhagen without trace; their whereabouts were unknown to the military authorities. Lindemann was told, that, should arrests have to be made, he was to apply to General Dewing's staff. This did not, however, apply to the Criminal Police or Regular Police.

Ships carrying refugees and troops from Courland and Hela were forbidden by General Dewing to call at Danish or Norwegian ports.[8]

As Head of the SHAEF Mission to Denmark General Dewing had available one Parachute Company for his personal protection, the Royals (1st Royal Dragoons) and one Parachute battalion. He could also call upon 6,000–9,000 men from the Danish police. On the other hand, as already mentioned, the German garrison amounted to 231,700 men and in addition there were 207,000 refugees. For the first three months the latter were to be cared for by the Danish Red Cross and then for a further three months by the Swedish Red Cross. In addition the Danes guaranteed deliveries to German troops up to the time of their departure from Danish territory. The official Danish authorities were therefore remarkably forthcoming to the highly unpopular occupation forces. The only incidents occurred when Danish resistance fighters attempted to disarm German troops.

Far more frequent clashes occurred with the British troops. In defiance of Dewing's assurances, isolated parties attempted to disarm German soldiers and took from them bicycles, vehicles, horses, wireless sets, field glasses, watches, and rings. General Lindemann at once protested to General Dewing, giving names of the British officers concerned and alleging that 'unconditional surrender' had been quoted as justification. 'Unconditional surrender', he said, 'implies that the German military authorities must obey the instructions of the Allied High Command. These are transmitted to me by you, General. It cannot, however, be the intention of the surrender terms that any local commander is empowered to issue instructions contrary to those of his own superior authorities.' Such goings-on, he continued, would undermine discipline and make it impossible to accelerate movement or control and supply the troops on the march. 'I declare formally that, should such conditions continue, I cannot assume responsibility for the smooth evacuation of Denmark, as is justifiably desired by all concerned.' Finally Lindemann referred to certain provisions of the Geneva Convention of 27 July 1929.

OKW supported Lindemann's protest and passed it on to Eisenhower. The result was that on 13 May, via Lieutenant-Colonel von Wedel of the Liaison Staff, Lindemann was informed by Allied Headquarters Denmark that German troops might not take bicycles out of Denmark, that in individual cases the relevant commanders would decide on the number of bicycles necessary. The letter stated that personal possessions such as wrist-watches, fountain pens and money, would not be removed from German troops as they left Denmark, but that they might carry only personal weapons, in other words rifles, revolvers and sub-machine guns. Since the Germans apparently thought that they could impose conditions even after capitulation, General Dewing's reply was categorical: 'General Lindemann should realise that the treatment meted out by the Allies to the Germans in Denmark after their unconditional surrender is incomparably better than that accorded by Germans to Allied troops in German captivity. Many Allied soldiers now in Denmark have themselves seen or experienced what our prisoners have had to suffer. Nevertheless the discipline of Allied troops will ensure that the German withdrawal from Denmark is controlled in the spirit of the instructions issued by me.'

Comment in the War Diary of Headquarters North: 'Colonel-General Lindemann's protest against the instructions of the British Major-General Fewing [*sic*] was loyally answered by the latter' (!)

Evacuation of Denmark by the German Wehrmacht then proceeded apace. In the first week after surrender some 43,000 men had left, a figure almost doubled in the second week. Early in June General Dewing decided that he no longer required the services of General Lindemann and had him arrested. By this time there were only a few German troops remaining.[9]

The evacuation of Norway proved far more complicated. The German garrison, together with the Todt Organisation, numbered over 400,000 and in addition there were 90,000 Russian prisoners of war or labourers and 30,000 foreign workers, all scattered throughout the country. As for Denmark, evacuation was the responsibility of a SHAEF Mission. Its Head was General Andrew Thorne, who had been C-in-C Scottish Command from 1941 and had been nominated Commander Allied Land Forces Norway in 1944. Ever since autumn 1943 he had been preparing detailed plans for the event of a German withdrawal from Norway, a German collapse or a German surrender. When signing in Reims Jodl had been told to despatch representatives of the Wehrmacht to Edinburgh to prepare for the surrender of German troops in Norway. The early arrival in Oslo of General Thorne's deputy was forecast.[10]

Keitel informed General Böhme, the Wehrmacht C-in-C Norway, that General Thorne's deputy would arrive late in the afternoon of 7 May or early 8th. He referred once more to the surrender terms and stressed that there should be no move of German armed forces to Sweden,[11] since this would constitute a breach of the agreement. Up to midnight 8/9 May, however, incriminated persons need not be prevented from crossing the frontier.

General Böhme had already refused to contact the Swedish Government via the German Minister in Stockholm or to negotiate for the internment of German troops in Sweden. On 6 May

OKW had confirmed his operational instructions and to these he adhered pending further orders. Equally he refused an offer from the Swedish Red Cross to provide nurses for prisoners of war in Norway, since he did not wish to become 'dependent on Sweden'. Instead he urged that released prisoners from the more inhospitable parts of Norway be transferred to Sweden and OKW gave agreement to this proposal on 7 May.

In an Order of the Day Böhme showed what he thought of surrender: 'I know that this message is a severe blow for us. In Norway we stand undefeated and as strong as ever. No foe has dared to attack us and yet, for the good of the German community, we must now bow to the enemy's *diktat*. In doing so we trust that we shall be dealing with men who respect the dignity of the soldier. In their attitude to German soldiers we expect the Norwegians to give proof of discipline similar to that which we have always shown to them. As far as you are concerned, my comrades, I expect you to behave in a similarly exemplary fashion which even the enemy is bound to respect. Grit your teeth, maintain discipline and good order, obey your superiors and remain what you have always been – German soldiers who love their people and their country more than anything else in the world.'

General Thorne's representatives arrived in Norway on 8 May. During the next three days further Allied forces flew in, British destroyers anchored in the ports and early in June American reinforcements arrived. Even so the Allies numbered only 40,000, whereas there were over 400,000 Germans to be evacuated.[12]

The surrender terms, covering 50 typed pages, seemed to General Böhme 'intolerably severe'. He declared that the troops were 'shattered' and that any further demands would have serious repercussions. He reported to OKW that the terms included: Disarming all existing agencies, formations and branches of the Party and SS; arrest of all members of the SD, military offices, Section VII of the RSHA, Field Security Police, headquarters of anti-guerilla formations, Security Police, General SS, Ordnungspolizei officers, Hitler Youth, Party functionaries from office or district head upwards and all heads of section in the Reich Commissariat. This, Böhme said, was regarded by the soldiers as 'dishonourable'. Additional conditions mentioned were the immediate evacuation of towns, and coastal battery positions. He was particularly incensed by the stipulation that only existing petrol stocks might be used for evacuation, pointing out that the troops would as a result be immobile and would have to be 'set going' by march route as a 'mass of men' without even the scantiest provisions for supply. After being disarmed, therefore, half a million Germans would be 'defenceless outlaws'. The final insult in Böhme's eyes was the preferential treatment accorded to Russian prisoners of war. His message closed with the words: 'Woe to the vanquished.'

In the case of Norway too OKW sent a protest to Eisenhower, pointing out that the surrender applied exclusively to the Wehrmacht. Disarmament and arrest of members of the Party, SS or Gestapo or of German political personalities in Norway should not, therefore, be carried out by the troops, particularly since they lacked the necessary evidence. If such procedure were insisted on, fulfilment of the surrender terms would be questionable. General Böhme was informed of this *démarche* and instructed 'to protest on the spot, emphasising that, as far as his headquarters were concerned, such orders would not be carried out by the troops, would lead to loss of discipline and chaos and would make fulfilment of the surrender terms questionable.'

Headquarters North War Diary noted on 12 May that Böhme had protested against the troops 'being required to arrest Germans. As far as their basic attitude and discipline *vis-à-vis* their superiors is concerned, there is no difference between the members of these organisations (which were being subjected to degrading discriminatory treatment) and the troops in general.'

Meanwhile, however, additional Allied forces had arrived, so that the problem of the arrest of Party and SS leaders by the Wehrmacht no longer arose. In any case Terboven, the Reich Commissar, and Rediess, the Police General, had committed suicide on 10 May by blowing themselves up in their bunker.

In general the evacuation proceeded smoothly and discipline was maintained by the German troops. There were only isolated incidents, for instance when Allied soldiers attempted to disarm Germans on their own initiative, appropriated personal possessions or indulged in petty pilfering. In addition there were some instances of Russian prisoners breaking into German supply depots, occasionally assisted by Allied soldiers.

The SHAEF Mission had every cause to be satisfied with the way things went. On the other hand there was considerable friction with the Russians, partly over the repatriation of Germans to the Russian-occupied zone and partly owing to the refusal of many Russians and Yugoslav 'displaced persons' to return home.[13]

In the Channel Islands and the 'Western fortresses' the surrender proceeded according to plan. In some garrisons the news produced demonstrations of loyalty to Germany. On the morning of 10 May, for instance, Lieutenant-General Junck, the Fortress Commandant of St. Nazaire, announced that he would surrender next day and ended his message with the words: 'We have faith in Germany.' General Fahrmbacher, the Fortress Commandant of Lorient, also announced his surrender for 10 May and radioed: 'I take my leave with my steadfast undefeated garrison. Our thoughts are for our sorely tried country. Long live Germany.'

In the Northern and Southern Zones surrender was implemented through the regional commanders, as Eisenhower had laid down in Reims. Overall responsibility for the Southern Zone rested initially with Field Marshal Kesselring, after his arrest by the Americans[14] with Colonel-General Dessloch for a time, and finally with General Westphal. Apart from this, following an OKW proposal, C-in-C West, now in Alm thirty miles south of Salzburg, dealt with 12th US Army Group through General Obstfelder, late Commander VII Corps; for Army Group G General Schulz, now in Saalfelden thirty miles south-west of Salzburg, dealt with 6th US Army Group and Colonel-General von Vietinghoff (C-in-C South-West in Bolanzo) with 15th US Army Group.

In the Northern Zone Field Marshal Busch, located in Lang-wedel, was generally responsible, although he had had a violent altercation with Keitel about the local surrender and in theory had been dismissed. Under Busch was a central or co-ordinating staff through which Armies, Corps and divisions were linked to the relevant authorities; also subordinate to him were Blumen-tritt's Army Group in the area between the Baltic and the Weser, the troops in Schleswig-Holstein, Lindemann's army and Twenty-fifth Army under General Blaskowitz in Holland. Headquarters Staff A under General Kinzel was made available to him as a liaison staff to Montgomery; it consisted of twenty-two officers and forty-seven NCOs and men and became known as the

'German Military Mission to British Headquarters'. Its responsibilities extended beyond the purely military; in addition to normal supply to the troops, the quartermaster sections had to provide for the civil population and deal with traffic, postal and currency problems. A special representative was therefore attached to C-in-C North-West as adviser on civil affairs and the local Government Representative [Regierungspräsident] together with detachments from certain ministries were incorporated into his staff. These detachments were under the Deputy Chief of Staff (Supply) but received technical instructions from their ministries. A large Luftwaffe staff under Major-General Übe was also attached to Busch; the Navy, on the other hand, was represented only by a liaison officer, Captain Conradi, since, as already mentioned, contrary to the other two Services it was located in its entirety in the Northern Zone. Finally General Jäckel, the most senior medical officer available, was included in the Liaison Staff to deal with civil health problems.

As agreed with Jodl in Reims, Field Marshal Montgomery had authorised the constitution of security troops from reliable men, who were permitted to retain their personal weapons and in some cases even machine-guns. Probably misled by the relatively extensive powers accorded to him under the surrender terms, and under the illusion that the British would treat him as a potential ally against the Russians, on 11 May Field Marshal Busch issued an order which gave rise to a storm of indignation, particularly in England. He said: 'In accordance with the Grand Admiral's orders and in agreement with the British occupation authorities I have assumed command in Schleswig-Holstein and the area to be occupied by Field Marshal Montgomery's forces. I have been charged with the maintenance of law, order and discipline, supply of the troops and the civil population in all sectors of public life. To carry out this task all military and civilian authorities in my area have been subordinated to me. They will receive directives from me or from the military and civil authorities represented in the Supply Section North. Executive instructions will be issued separately. I expect unquestioning obedience and devotion to duty in respect of all orders, and willing collaboration on the part of every individual in fulfilment of the tasks laid upon me.'

This announcement was broadcast over Radio Flensburg

which at the time was still in the hands of the German Government. Already on several occasions Montgomery had been vexed by objections to or tardy compliance with his orders and he now summoned Field Marshal Busch and dressed him down. He said that he 'was making use of Busch and his headquarters so long as the job of implementing the surrender could be more efficiently carried out by that method. If he did not carry out his orders promptly and efficiently, I would remove him from his command and find some other senior German officer to do the job. In the last resort the British Army would do the job themselves; but this method would result in delay, which could only cause further hardship to the German civil population, and this I was anxious to avoid. He was to understand that the German Army had been utterly defeated in the field and must now accept the consequences of that defeat.'[15]

On the same day as Busch issued his arrogant order and was put in his place by Montgomery Dönitz produced two orders about the attitude to be adopted by German soldiers and their behaviour to the occupying power. He told them to remain where they were and await further orders. Demobilisation from the Wehrmacht depended on the occupying power. 'Until then it is the bounden duty of every German soldier to show himself worthy of his uniform by his manner and bearing, and to obey his superiors as hitherto. By his manner he must show firm determination to continue to serve our people and his own family as a useful member of society. His bearing should be military and saluting discipline will be maintained.'

Regarding behaviour to the occupying power his instruction ran: 'In contacts with our Anglo-American ex-enemies we should behave with dignity and pride. We have nothing to be ashamed of. Over these six years the achievements of the German Wehrmacht in battle and the endurance of the German people have been unique in history and in the world. Never has there been such heroism. We soldiers stand without a stain on our honour. It would therefore be undignified now to go rushing to our ex-enemies. It is right that we should wait for them to come to us, but then meet them with propriety and courtesy.'

This summons to an attitude of proud reserve sprang from deep personal conviction on the part of Karl Dönitz. In spite of the ban on fraternisation far too many Germans were trying to be friendly and gain contact with members of the occupying forces, and to this he wished to put a stop. 'The arrogance and aggressiveness of Germans when in a position of strength have often been commented on; this went hand in hand with an equal submissiveness in defeat'[16] – this has often been cited as a German characteristic. In fact the attitude of the Germans in the immediate post-war period made an unpleasant impression on many British soldiers. From the outset the government's information service in its 'Points for the public guidance media' had issued repeated appeals that people should maintain a dignified attitude.

After his dressing down by Montgomery and Dönitz' orders an Order of the Day of 15 May from Busch to Lindemann's army struck a very discreet note. He said that the German Wehrmacht had been 'finally and completely defeated', that the Army, Navy and Luftwaffe would be disbanded and called upon every soldier for 'calm, order and discipline'.

Field Marshal Kesselring's Chief of Staff issued a similar order to troops in the Southern Zone. All commanders were enjoined to remain with their troops; 'moreover absolute calm and reserve is essential to preserve the dignity of the German soldier. . . . There can be no doubt that *all* soldiers are now prisoners of war. As a result no demands of any sort can be made.'

The Liaison Staffs

In Reims it had been agreed that an OKW Liaison Staff should be attached to Eisenhower's headquarters and on 8 May this was called forward to arrive on the 9th. Air transport was provided by British 21st Army Group, while a road echelon travelled separately. The strength indicated was fourteen officers with the necessary ancillary personnel. The staff was to consist of a Commander, two Army General Staff officers, two Air Staff officers, one officer for questions of overall strategy and technical naval questions, one submarine specialist, three quartermaster section officers, two officers for questions of Wehrmacht organisation and two officers to deal with postal problems and Service communications of all sorts including ciphers. The composition of the subordinate staff was to be such that the group could function completely independently, in other words it had to include typists, interpreters, orderlies, drivers and signals personnel. SHAEF proposed to provide only petrol and food. After some delay owing to non-arrival of the British aircraft, the staff eventually arrived. It was headed by General Fangohr and its final composition was twenty officers, fifty-nine NCOs and men, ten cars and four trucks.

A Liaison Staff was also formed for Marshal Zhukov's headquarters in Berlin, following an agreement made by Keitel immediately after signature of the capitulation. In an initial conversation with Colonel-General Serov about 1.0 a.m. on 9 May Keitel had promised only to despatch a staff officer with maps showing the layout of German forces in the East. About 6.0 a.m., however, shortly before his departure, he had a further talk with Colonel-General Malinin, Zhukov's Chief of Staff, who pressed for the immediate provision of a map – even if only a rough sketch – showing movements of German troops and commanders in the East.

Keitel refused to produce anything on the spot; he promised, however, to despatch a courier (a General if possible!) during the afternoon with maps showing all army formations; he then turned the conversation to the question of a liaison staff. Colonel-General Malinin had no instructions on this subject, but after checking with Zhukov it was agreed that an OKW Liaison Staff would arrive in Berlin on 10 May.[17] As agreed, a General Staff officer, Lieutenant-Colonel Scheibe, arrived with the maps but Zhukov was apparently furious because they only showed army formations instead of the Wehrmacht as a whole, in other words omitted naval and air units. According to an entry in Jodl's diary Zhukov also demanded detailed situations maps for Army Groups Centre and Courland, copies of all orders issued by OKW for the cease-fire and surrender and the necessary data to establish direct radio communications with the two Army Groups. Zhukov ordered the OKW Liaison Staff to remain in Flensburg for the present and Lieutenant-Colonel Scheibe to return with the information demanded.

It was thought better that Scheibe should remain in Flensburg since he had been a member of the Intelligence Section 'Foreign Armies East'. On 12 May, therefore, Lieutenant-Colonel de Maizière flew to Berlin with the information required. In detail he produced: a map showing the situation in Courland and East Prussia; a map showing positions of Army Groups Centre, Ostmark and South-East; a map showing naval forces (including shore establishments) in the eastern and central Baltic; a map showing the lay-out of the German Air Force on the Eastern Front; a map of army supply depots; charts showing the organisation of the German army in the East; a summary of the orders issued by okw in announcing and implementing the surrender; W/T data for communication between Marshal Zhukov's headquarters and okw.

De Maizière returned on 16 May. He reported that he had been well received; accommodation and food had been excellent and he had been well looked after; Russian newspapers, books and cigarettes had been provided without question; the only request refused had been one for a wireless set. The majority of the questions put to him concerned the information which he had brought. To his own questions, however, he had received no reply. His radio messages to okw had not been despatched.

Although Zhukov was apparently satisfied with the information provided, he said nothing on the subject of the despatch of a Liaison Staff. The group, consisting of nine officers, nine NCOs and men and three interpreters under General Matzky, waited in vain for a summons.

Reorganisation of OKW and the Seat of Government Problem

There was much to do, however, apart from forming liaison staffs for the Allies. On 10 May okw itself was reorganised. Implementing Hitler's order of 24/25 April,[18] the okw Operations Staff and the General Staff of the Army were combined. The Deputy Chief of the okw Operations Staff dealt with all business arising from the surrender for all three Services, using the Demobilisation Section for negotiations with the Allies, communications to the Reich Government and the general direction of demobilisation. For the Army implementation of surrender was dealt with by the Chief of the Army Operations Staff. This was Major-General Dethleffsen, who had been Chief of the Operations Group in okh [Army High Command] from 23 March to 24 April and the last Chief of Staff of Army Group Vistula under von Tippelskirch, the successor to Colonel-General Heinrici, dismissed by Keitel.[19] For the Northern Zone General Dethleffsen double-banked this appointment with that of Deputy Chief of the okw Operations Staff; in the Southern Zone General Winter acted in this capacity. To avoid confusion, from 14 May

Headquarters Staff B was entitled 'okw Detachment South'.

The reorganisation of okw in fact meant little in practice, since it presupposed combination of okw North and South. Though this had been agreed in Reims and many proposals for combination of the staffs or elimination of unnecessary personnel were made, okw remained divided.

Concentration of okw was directly connected to the question of the 'seat of government', since obviously the headquarters and the government should be in the same place. As already mentioned the desirability or necessity of moving Dönitz' headquarters had been discussed during the conference on Norway and even more exhaustively during that on Czechoslovakia and the Southern Zone. Keitel had argued for Prague and Jodl for Berchtesgaden, leading one of the senior officers present to enquire sarcastically whether Germany therefore still had air superiority. Dönitz had decided to remain in Schleswig-Holstein for the present, provided the Allies permitted him to retain the necessary area.[20]

This idea had first made its appearance in a letter which von Ribbentrop, the ex-Reich Foreign Minister, had sent to Dönitz on 2 May – probably to show that he was the sole surviving expert on such questions. After outlining the hopelessness of the military situation, Ribbentrop had recommended that, in the North, everything be concentrated in the Schleswig-Holstein area. This, he thought, was feasible since 'the British would refuse Russian assistance in the conquest of this area'. He estimated that it could be defended for a long time, if not permanently. Politically he recommended efforts to ensure that 'Schleswig-Holstein, or at least part thereof, was not occupied, so that the Reich Government would have a chance to rule from free German territory'.[21]

Though there is no certainty, it must be assumed that Dönitz and von Krosigk read this letter. Be that as it may, the question of a special area for the government and okw was discussed in connection with the despatch of Admiral von Friedeburg to Montgomery, on which occasion General Dethleffsen threw in the idea of an 'enclave'. Though by no means expressing the government's real intention, the term gained currency and in two radio messages early on 5 May General Kinzel informed Jodl: 1. that an officer would be bringing an answer on the enclave question; 2. that it was intended to deal with the 'enclave problem' during 'an interview with higher authority next day'. On the second message Keitel noted: 'If this does not succeed, Supreme Military Headquarters must either capitulate here or move south. Leave by air evening 5th.'

In fact Supreme Headquarters did capitulate and remained in Schleswig-Holstein. In the light of Jodl's subsequent proposals it may be assumed that he had discussed the question in Reims but that it had been temporarily shelved. In his Berlin talk with Keitel on 9 May Colonel-General Serov also seems to have shown some interest in Dönitz' location and to have said that 'the Grand Admiral with his military headquarters must "legalise" himself, for which a location in Flensburg was not well suited'. Serov apparently also suggested that the question of a move to central Germany should be examined 'to establish communications and subsequently gain contact with the Allies'. Keitel agreed.[22]

In practice the matter was settled on 12 May between Admiral Bürkner, the Head of the 'Foreign' section, and Brigadier Churcher, commanding the British Infantry Brigade stationed in Flensburg, minor alterations being made to the boundaries of the 'Special OKW Area' originally proposed.

The Allied Control Party

During this discussion Brigadier Churcher demanded that a building be made available for the Control Party from Eisenhower's headquarters, the arrival of which was announced for that very day, 12 May. The *Patria*, a ship proposed for the purpose, did not seem to him to have adequate communications facilities. Admiral Bürkner asked that this decision be left to the Party itself and it eventually decided to remain in the *Patria*.

On 12 May the 'SHAEF Control Party of OKW' duly arrived. It consisted of fourteen Americans headed by Major-General Lowell W. Rooks and eleven British under Brigadier Foord.

The opening discussion between a representative of OKW and the Anglo-American Mission took place from 8.25 to 8.45 p.m. on 12 May. It began inauspiciously since the OKW representative, Colonel Meyer-Detring,[23] was late, having been delayed by a car accident, and was reprimanded by the Chairman, Brigadier Foord. In addition to Brigadier Foord there were present on the Allied side Brigadier-General Lewis (US), a naval captain, an

RAF staff officer, two other officers and an interpreter. Meyer-Detring was ordered to produce by 10.0 a.m. next day the following:

The organisation of OKW, the Navy and the Luftwaffe in the Northern and Southern Zones together with all their affiliated agencies;

A nominal roll of all senior officers, in particular Generals and Admirals on the active list;

A location plan for the Flensburg area showing OKW, Navy and Luftwaffe offices;

An organisation chart of OKH – Meyer-Detring interposed that this had now been absorbed in OKW.

In addition, though without a time limit, Brigadier Foord demanded a list of all government personalities present in the Flensburg area and of persons arrested by the government. The possible arrest of Himmler was the subject of a special enquiry.

This information, amounting to a complete 'stocktaking', was compiled by OKW and handed over on time. On Jodl's instructions Meyer-Detring emphasised that, particularly in respect of the Southern Zone, details were fragmentary owing to the inadequacy of communications. By this means Jodl hoped to force the two staffs together and perhaps obtain agreement to a move to an area more central to the Allied forces. In addition, on several occasions proposals were made that Field Marshal Kesselring and General Winter be ordered to Flensburg-Mürwik.

The discussion with Meyer-Detring was no more than a *prise de contact*. The real work began with an interview at midday on 13 May when Grand Admiral Dönitz was summoned to present himself to Major-General Rooks in the *Patria*. From the German side the meeting is recorded in an office minute. Through an interpreter General Rooks announced himself as General Eisenhower's plenipotentiary 'to work in future direct with the Grand Admiral and OKW'. He had summoned the Grand Admiral to tell him on behalf of the Supreme Commander that Field Marshal Keitel was to be relieved of his post forthwith and regarded as a prisoner of war. On Eisenhower's instructions Jodl was to be installed as temporary successor. He had summoned Dönitz in order to tell him this – which he regarded as a courtesy! Further, so the minute continues, Rooks said that he would do his best to work with OKW for their mutual advantage and that he himself was a representative of the military, not civilian, agencies. Dönitz took up this remark to point out that he was both Head of State and Supreme Commander of the Wehrmacht and that the OKW staff was necessary to him for the execution of his orders. He also seized the opportunity to refer to the most pressing problems of the time – those of food, finance and communications. He stressed that if the food supply could not be assured forthwith, starvation, disease and chaos would be the inevitable results. It is interesting that on the previous day Dönitz had emphasised that the points to plug were: hunger, disease, communism and a firm organisation for collaboration with the Allies. His further aim was centralised direction. To all these problems he referred at his first interview with Rooks. He said that it was vital that there should be *'one* central agency through which everything would be settled; it was no longer possible to deal with matters in isolation'. According to the German minute Rooks was of the same opinion and forecast a solution on these lines. The imminent arrival of a Russian delegation pointed in the same direction. In conclusion Rooks recognised the validity both of Dönitz' views and his measures.

The American description of the interview[24] says that Rooks brushed the 'central agency' aside and stated that the Western Powers intended to exercise their functions through Allied Military government. So unequivocal a statement at this time seems impossible since the Allied attitude to a central German authority had not yet been determined at this stage.[25]

In the immediate post-war period American tactics were characterised by caution and camouflage, as instanced by their procedure for arrests. Except in Keitel's case, arrests were not announced publicly but the victims were summoned to Eisenhower's headquarters 'for discussions'. This occurred, for instance, in Kesselring's case; he was summoned on 15 May together with Backe and Dorpmüller. It seems more probable, therefore, that in discussion with Dönitz Rooks merely made polite noises about existing arrangements and that on the German side these were taken as agreement.

No reason was given for Keitel's arrest, Rooks merely told him that he had a bare two hours before departure, saying that he himself had only just been informed.[26] This does not, however, accord with the official account which states that General Rooks acted quickly in order to emphasise SHAEF's authority.[27] It is conceivable that Keitel was arrested following an order issued by Eisenhower after the Berlin capitulation. This had closed the western lines to fugitives from Army Groups Centre and South-East, laying down that officers and men were to be handed over to the Red Army for contravening the surrender terms. Simultaneously the immediate arrest of senior officers – Keitel, Kesselring, Jodl and Warlimont – was ordered. This order was in response to General Antonov's strictures about non-observance of the terms of capitulation by German soldiers in the Southern Zone. After some delay, due probably to considerations of expediency, Keitel and Kesselring were arrested on 13 and 15 May respectively. Jodl was still essential and was only arrested later with the government and the rest of OKW.

To Rooks' question whether he wished to make any statement, Keitel replied that he had nothing to say 'since he had himself signed unconditional surrender and was fully aware of the consequences thereof'.

Jodl assumed that Keitel had been arrested because he had issued Hitler's order for the liquidation of escaping British officer prisoners; in his diary he noted that Dönitz was glad that 'despite pressure from various quarters he had not jettisoned the Chief of OKW'. In fact Dönitz had discussed the matter with Jodl on the previous day, saying that he was under continuous pressure from the Army to get rid of Keitel and asking whether a change would not be advisable. Jodl opposed this once more, saying that 'the animosity against the Chief of OKW stemmed from the earliest days of the Third Reich and was shown mostly by older officers'. His conclusion in his diary was: 'Chief OKW must now remain.'[28]

On Keitel's arrest Dönitz charged Jodl with all OKW business. At the same time he requested Eisenhower 'to order Field Marshal Kesselring to Mürwik so that he may take over the duties of Chief of OKW in place of Field Marshal Keitel'. This he did because, as he now says, he thought Jodl's workload as both Chief of OKW and Head of the OKW Operations Staff to be too great. It was therefore no reflection on Jodl's capabilities – on 10 May, with effect from 6 May, Dönitz had awarded him the Knight's Cross with Oakleaves. Dönitz also ordered General Winter to report at the same time as Kesselring. This must therefore be regarded as one more attempt to get the staffs together.

Shortly after Keitel's departure Jodl was also summoned to the *Patria*: Rooks demanded a copy of all OKW orders within four hours; all written and signals traffic to Eisenhower's headquarters was to be routed through him, the German Liaison Staff SHAEF being intended only to keep the Supreme Commander informed.[29] Jodl agreed and seized the opportunity to turn the conversation on to 'Plan Eclipse' and the Allied precautions to prevent a repetition of the events of 1918. He emphasised that 'present circumstances were not to be compared with those of 1918 and that no authoritative person in the German Wehrmacht was so stupid as to repeat the practices of that time'. His own obligations Jodl outlined as follows: 'I shall invariably come to you and ask you to countermand anything likely further to increase the misfortunes of the German people. I shall invariably come to you if the honour of German troops and the German people is being trampled in the dust by local commanders' orders. I repeat that I regard it as my sole duty to assist the German people by carrying out such orders as you may give for this purpose to the best of my knowledge and ability.'[30]

Among other things Rooks also demanded the right for all members of the Control Party to enter all OKW offices at will. Shortly afterwards Brigadier Foord appeared to inspect them but his visit was cut short by a little ruse; in one of the rooms lay a female staff assistant 'in an elegant posture'; the escorting Colonel announced 'Female personnel resting after night duty'. The British Brigadier retired hastily and then had a discussion with Jodl during which he asked whether OKW still saw virtue in concentrating the staffs of North and South; Jodl of course replied in the affirmative. Foord seemed very worried over the German food situation, having recently discussed the matter with German experts.[31] Jodl backed up with a message from General Winter in the South, showing that bread supply was sufficient only for another two to three weeks and asking for urgent assistance. He rejected complaints regarding difficulties in disarming the troops, saying that initially perhaps there had been fears of guerilla warfare by the SS; Obergruppenführer Jüttner had, however, now been ordered to assemble them all in a camp. Inevitably therefore the conversation turned to Himmler. The previous day Rooks had asked Dönitz where the Reichsführer was. Jodl replied that he had last seen him shortly before his departure for Reims; Himmler had asked what he should do and he had advised him to fly to the Southern Zone in a night fighter and join the main body of SS troops. Whether Himmler had followed this advice he did not know. No one knew the whereabouts of the Reichsführer-SS.

From the provisional government's point of view it would have been better had they been able to arrest Himmler rather than allow him to vanish. Later, when he knew of conditions in the concentration camps, Dönitz regretted having missed the opportunity. In the atmosphere of the time, however, it was hardly surprising that it did not happen. Only a fortnight before Himmler had been generally regarded as the most powerful man in the State. The anxiety shown by General Rooks and Brigadier Foord over his disappearance proves how greatly he was feared. It was suspected that he would be secretly organising resistance somewhere. No one knew that of all his might nothing remained but a piteous shell, a miserable vagabond.

On 17 May the Russian Control Party arrived. It was headed by General Truskov[32] with an aide, Major Vassiliev, a Major-General with aide for air and air defence questions, three officers for army questions, two naval captains, a Colonel and Lieutenant-Colonel for political questions, Colonel Smirnov and Major Siomontchuk for scientific questions, one signals officer and three interpreters.

Jodl's first interview with the head of the Russian delegation took place in the *Patria* on 18 May. Discussion turned primarily on the Western Powers' instructions regarding the German fleet and air force, details of demobilisation, OKW's situation and the whereabouts of records. Jodl referred to the division between Northern and Southern Zones with 55 % of capacity in the North and 45% in the South; most of the operational branches were in the North but vital demobilisation sections in the South. For greater efficiency, therefore, he had applied to General Rooks to concentrate both staffs in central Germany; he indicated the area Erfurt–Kassel–Fulda; Berlin might even be considered. Jodl adroitly took up the remark made to Keitel by Colonel Serov in Berlin on 9 May and was obviously attempting to enlist Soviet support for his plan to concentrate and strengthen OKW. He promised to give Truskov all information on the same footing as the British and Americans and said that the Russians naturally had permission to look at all files – as if this depended on OKW! Jodl also tried to turn the conversation towards Allied political intentions regarding Germany and received the answer: 'You know Stalin's intentions from both radio and press. We have no plan to starve or exterminate the German people. We shall endeavour to do everything to assist the people.'

This declaration by the Russian in no way ran counter to Jodl's own activity in the cause of Germany. Obviously he was working on the principle followed by von Hammerstein, Schleicher and even Groener in 1919: 'They need us; they will always need us; we are a sovereign power since the army is the cement of the Reich.' In fact he was a 'super-Prussian', for whom the salvation of the country and that of the Wehrmacht were one and the same thing.

Jodl was indefatigable. There were a number of briefing conferences daily: a short section conference at 9.30, Chief of OKW Operations Staff conference at 12.0 and the Deputy Chief of Staff's conference at 6.0 p.m. He issued instructions on how to treat the late enemy and in particular the Allied Commission. It was to be flooded with regulations and proposals and kept busy on organisational questions.

A good idea of the variety of problems dealt with by OKW can be gleaned from a summary of 14 May, supplemented on 16 May, by Major-General Dethleffsen, the Deputy Chief of the OKW Operations Staff, together with a whole series of other available records. Many of its problems were organisational: accommodation for OKW, movement of staff from the Southern Zone, signals communications, spheres of authority, co-operation with Allied authorities, implementation of capitulation including collecting points for stragglers, transit camps, rationing points, appointment of road commandants, use of troops etc. In addition there were numerous questions concerning release from the Wehrmacht. Then came another whole series concerning the urgency of the food and financial situation, traffic problems, in particular the repair and reactivation of the railways and postal services.[33] Emphasis was continually to be laid on the fact that 'in the long run the break-up of the family will leave the Germans without roots and will lead to a pronounced communist tendency.'

On 14 May application was made for the use of Radio Flensburg and two mobile transmitters to broadcast instructions on the maintenance of law and order, but this was refused by General Rooks on 15 May.

Newspapers for the troops were not allowed to be printed by Germans. Orders were published in a news sheet controlled by the occupying powers. This was in accordance with a regulation forbidding the appearance of German newspapers apart from the occupation authorities' news sheets. Even foreign newspapers were withheld from the population.

A further problem was the hand-over of chemical warfare and research establishments. For this General von Blücher was responsible. OKW also had to deal with the military law problem, a British order having forbidden Müller's military court to impose sentences of death or corporal punishment. On 22 May, the day before members of the government and OKW were arrested, the Demobilisation Section filed a request on the subject, pointing out that even the severest disciplinary punishments were not always sufficient to maintain discipline and asking that serious offences be judged, as before, by Wehrmacht courts according to the rules of war. In the last days before capitulation use of military law may have been unnecessarily severe but in certain cases it was probably justified; this could no longer possibly be the case, however, twelve days after the surrender.

Military Status Symbols

An inordinate proportion of OKW's activity was devoted to questions of national and military symbolism, such as flags, decorations, badges of rank and the rules for military saluting. Obviously admission of defeat came very hard and, by clinging to the old status symbols, people were trying to conceal from themselves the extent of the catastrophe. Characteristic of this refusal to look facts in the face was the repeated use of the term 'armistice' instead of 'surrender'.

The first case in point was that of the Hitler salute. On more than one occasion this had been explicitly forbidden by the British occupation forces and on 8 May the normal military salute was reintroduced, in spite of the fact that, together with Göring, Dönitz had been responsible for prescribing the Hitler salute for the Wehrmacht.[34] The Government's Information Service reported that this order was considered unfortunate by the younger officers and men – 'voluntary abandonment of the German salute before the enemy has ordered it, is considered an undignified spectacle'. General Böhme, the Wehrmacht C-in-C Norway, wished to retain the Hitler salute but was answered by the following telegram from Jodl: 'Decision on the use of the German salute by the military: The Grand Admiral has ordered reintroduction of the military salute for the entire German Wehrmacht. From the disciplinary point of view it is essential that in all theatres of war the Wehrmacht preserves its uniformity in this particular matter and is not disrupted by local orders from the occupying powers. While appreciating the special conditions prevailing in Norway, the request to retain the German salute cannot therefore be approved.'

This and similar criticisms may have been the reason for Dönitz' particularly intransigent attitude over the question of removal of decorations and insignia as demanded by British troops on several occasions immediately after the surrender. As early as 10 May Keitel enquired of the German delegation to Eisenhower's headquarters whether a similar demand, applicable to the Wehrmacht as a whole, was to be anticipated or whether this was simply unauthorised individual initiative. Jodl raised the question at his first interview with General Rooks, pointing out that all war decorations and all insignia carried the swastika; he assumed, however, that 'out of respect for the achievements of the German Wehrmacht the Allied High Command would recognise and respect these distinctions'. General Rooks replied that so far no decision on the subject was known and that, until it was, local commanders would act according to the relevant instructions.

When Dönitz read the record of this meeting, he demanded clarification. Decorations and insignia, he noted, were protected by international law and he would never agree to their removal.

On 15 May Dönitz despatched to all commanders and agencies an order to the effect that decorations and insignia were protected by Article Five of the Prisoners of War Convention of 27 July 1929 and were not to be removed. His stand on this matter was all the more remarkable in that on the same day he ordered the removal from all rooms liable to be visited by members of the

Allied Commission of pictures of 'leading political personalities of the Third Reich'. At the same time guards and sentries were ordered to salute Allied officers.[35]

Reports continued to multiply, however, of British troops tearing off badges of rank and rumours began to circulate that the Allies would shortly issue a general order on the subject. On 17 May, therefore, Field Marshal Busch enquired whether it would not be better for OKW to issue an order of their own free will. 'Although decorations and insignia are protected by the 27 July Convention on Prisoners of War, the ruling will inevitably be made applicable to the Iron Cross and Oak Leaves Clasp; the swastika is regarded as a symbol of defeated National-Socialism and therefore any decoration on which it appears in a conspicuous place is intolerable to members of the occupying forces.' The Demobilisation Section under Colonel Poleck thereupon drafted a note on the removal of insignia. The legal position was examined and it was established that a soldier's uniform and its individual components were protected by international law and that prisoners of war were allowed to retain them even in the event of unconditional surrender. The actions of Allied commanders were therefore described as contrary to international law. In the political appreciation of the problem the proposal to remove insignia in order to avoid incidents was rejected as 'politically inexpedient':

1. The enemy's tactics are to turn the screw on us gradually until he meets resistance. The earlier this resistance shows itself, the better the prospect for the maintenance of some residual German rights. Should the enemy insist on removal of insignia despite our protest, then OKW would have acted under compulsion and so saved its face.

2. It will not be easy for the enemy to insist, since he would then be in contravention of international law, for the re-establishment of which he maintains he went to war. From the German point of view there is no reason for OKW to relieve him of the painful necessity to act illegally by itself issuing an order to remove insignia.

3. By ordering removal of insignia OKW would seek to sever its political connections with the past. By so doing, however, it would in fact be accepting the enemy thesis that the war against Germany was not war in the normal sense but police action to destroy a criminal disturber of the peace, to whom the normal rules of war did not apply. . . .

4. Finally the judgement of history must be taken into consideration. During the present time of crisis every individual measure taken by high-level agencies of the Reich will be highlighted. In such times every act, however unimportant and even if explicable to contemporary opinion by considerations of expediency, takes on a symbolic character. An order to remove insignia will be regarded by posterity as voluntary renunciation of the sign under which millions of soldiers, and men and women in the home country, have died for their Fatherland in six years of war.

The note ended with the suggestion that the Allies be requested to desist from attempts to cause German soldiers to remove their insignia.

More than most, this document sheds a significant light on the view of history current at the time. Nationally the arguments used were primarily self-justificatory; National-Socialist and German interests were equated – as we have already seen, both Dönitz and Jodl did so. Fear of being stigmatised later as traitors to the nation led people to defend national status symbols with particular vehemence.

On 20 May Field Marshal Busch passed on a detailed order issued by Field Marshal Montgomery on the insignia question and Jodl at once protested to the Head of the Control Party. 21st Army Group had ordered that no insignia, cockades, badges or decorations of National-Socialist origin might henceforth be worn. The only exceptions were medals or decorations for merit or long service, with the proviso, however, that the swastika was removed from them. The German Cross in Gold or Silver might no longer be worn. Compliance was to be reported by 31 May.

In Dönitz' name Jodl asked Rooks for suspension of this order pending agreement on a uniform ruling. The swastika, he said, was admittedly a National-Socialist symbol but the German eagle was not. He pointed out that the German Wehrmacht were prisoners of war and that under Article Three of the Prisoner of War Convention prisoners were entitled to respect for their persons and dignity; under Article Six personal papers, badges of rank, medals and valuables might not be removed from them. No German prisoner had been so treated in Russia nor any Allied prisoner in Germany. In 1918, moreover, no one had attempted to remove the imperial insignia.

General Rooks replied that the order had presumably been issued by SHAEF. Moreover, he continued, the Geneva Prisoner

of War Convention was applicable to States at war but not to a
force which had surrendered and so brought the war to an end.
He would give an answer shortly.[36]

This reply obviously infuriated Jodl. In his pencilled minutes
of the meeting he recorded his answer as follows: 'Had no wish
to start a legalistic argument; must, however, emphasise that
"there would be a revolt" if decorations won in battle by German
front-line soldiers were removed from them and that the present
smooth progress of surrender would be seriously jeopardised.'
Rooks' answer to this Jodl noted as follows: it was Allied policy
'to do away with everything National-Socialist' and this was the
background to Montgomery's order. Regarding the possibility of
revolt 'the Germans must be clear that the Allies would suppress
anything of the sort with all the force at their disposal'.

Jodl now evidently realised that his threat had been a tactical
error and said that revolt would not, of course, be instigated from
above. Nevertheless no German officer existed who would not be
ashamed to issue an order for the removal of war decorations. If
the Allies insisted, it could only be done by force – and that
OKW could not prevent.

The comment that the Russians had not removed decorations
was another error of Jodl's. Like similar remarks by Dönitz
about the good behaviour of the Russian occupation forces and
the misdeeds of the Anglo-Americans,[37] it must have sounded to
Rooks like confirmation of the warning contained in Plan
Eclipse that the German object would be to sow discord among
the Allies. The frequent references to international law, moreover,
must have been unpleasantly reminiscent of the reproaches
voiced during the Weimar Republic days and avidly revived by
the National-Socialists about non-observance by the Allies of the
1918 terms of surrender.

Naval Headquarters drew up a comparison between the Franco-
German Armistice agreement of 22 June 1940 and the unconditional surrender of 8 May, also showing the similarity between
present developments and those of 1918. It included this:

> The basic psychological reason for the failure to create a peaceful
> world after the First War was that the German people felt that they
> had been unjustly treated by the Allies. We cannot stress too soon or
> repeat too often that, if our western enemies behave as in 1918 and
> merely make use of the great ideals of justice and right to camouflage

their plans for annihilation, the British- and American-occupied portion of Germany, if not the whole country, will be heading for lawlessness and chaos in the foreseeable future.

After receiving Jodl's report of his interview with Rooks and checking with Field Marshal Busch, which brought to light further alarming rumours, on 21 May Dönitz issued an order for the removal of insignia and of the German Cross; on 11 May he had already ordered that the Golden Party Badge might no longer be worn.

As a result of General Rooks' remark that the provisions of the Hague Land Warfare Convention did not apply to Germany since she had capitulated and therefore brought the war to an end, OKW submitted an *aide-mémoire* to the Control Party. It was based largely upon a legal interpretation, drafted by Naval Headquarters, of the 1929 Geneva Convention on Prisoners of War and Wounded and the 1907 Hague Convention on Land Warfare. In the view of German military headquarters the scope, the wording and the sense of the 8 May capitulation showed clearly that it applied only to the German Wehrmacht and was therefore a military surrender in the sense of Article Twenty-Five of the Hague Convention. The war had therefore been brought to an end *de facto* but not *de jure*; for the latter a peace treaty was necessary. OKW continued that in the unanimous view of all professors of the subject capitulation was an act under international law and therefore 'in default of other specific provisions' its declaration 'did not affect other existing international agreements'. The provisions of the Hague Land Warfare and Geneva Prisoners of War Conventions therefore remained in force. Article Twenty-three of the Hague Convention was quoted to prove the point – 'an enemy who, for better or worse [a clear reference to Jodl's statement in Reims], surrenders unconditionally, does not lose the right to prisoner of war treatment in accordance with the Hague Convention'.

OKW was probably only too well aware that in invoking international law it was treading on thin ice. An indication that this was so is the fact that Jodl's final draft carefully omitted to mention the Preamble to the Hague Convention which refers to 'usages established among civilised peoples', although the Naval Headquarters *aide-mémoire* had drawn attention to this passage. At a briefing conference on 15 May, moreover, Jodl admitted:

'We broke the law – not indeed until the enemy had first done so – but we did not act within the law. We should have achieved far more by doing so than by force.'

OKW's memorandum also stressed the continued existence of the German Reich as an entity under international law, even in the temporary absence of any German government. Finally reference was made to Article Thirty-five of the Hague Convention which lays down that 'even in the event of a surrender the requirements of military dignity should be respected'.

Consideration for military dignity, however, was noticeably absent. Contempt for the ex-enemy was clearly shown over the saluting problem. There was no general rule, though a 21st Army Group instruction, confirmed by General Rooks, laid down that British and American officers on duty were to be saluted but that in general courtesies would not be exchanged. The Russian occupation forces showed themselves more forthcoming. Here the rule was that German guards and sentries would salute Russian officers and Germans would salute officers of senior or equivalent rank. These differing rules led to ludicrous situations. When General Truskov paid an initial call on Admiral Dönitz – in contrast to General Rooks who had summoned him to the *Patria* – the sentries presented arms. When a senior General Staff officer visited the Russian Control Party the British sentries did not present, whereas Soviet staff officers waited to be saluted. General Truskov shook hands with German officers and offered them vodka and cigarettes. An ex-member of OKW says: 'We can only be thankful that the Soviets did not make use of the opportunities offered them during the weeks immediately following the surrender.'

On 19 May Rooks passed on a directive from Eisenhower dated 13 May setting out 'Rules governing military courtesies to be observed by Germans in occupied Germany'. Jodl noted in his diary that they were 'worse than anything conceivable'.

After a general introduction about the importance of military courtesies and the division of the Germans into two categories: 1. Prisoners of war and disarmed military, 2. civilians, including police and fire brigades, this document laid down detailed instructions for military saluting. 'The military salute is a form of greeting or sign of recognition between members of recognised standing armies; alternatively it is a sign of respect for authority.

Between members of the German Wehrmacht and military personnel of the Allied Nations there will be no exchange of courtesies *in the form of a greeting or sign of recognition*'. Instead of saluting German military personnel were to stand to attention when an Allied officer entered a room or remain still if sitting; in the open they were to stand to attention when the national anthems of any of the Allied nations were played, they were to remove their headgear when passing an Allied flag, on hearing a roll of drums or as a personal salute. Courtesy calls were not to be made. In short it was a complete handbook of denigration, in line with the instructions issued to American soldiers and drafted by the émigré German Emil Ludwig: 'You are entering Germany not as a liberator but as a victor. Do not keep smiling. Never offer a cigarette to a visitor whom you do not know well, nor offer him your hand. . . . Forget the American habit of meeting everyone in an open way. Distrust everybody who has given you no proof of his honesty. . . . The only way to get along with the Germans is to make them respect you, to make them feel the hand of the master.'[38]

Two things are striking about the period of implementation of the surrender:
  1. The emergence of Jodl as a personality;
  2. The assumption by okw of tasks outside its true sphere of responsibility.
The Provisional Government now having been set up in the administrative buildings of the Mürwik Cadet School, Dönitz found himself barely able to cope with his flood of problems and visitors. He accordingly issued an instruction setting up a 'military channel' to Jodl and a civil channel to Schwerin von Krosigk, thus relieving himself of work and avoiding having to deal with every detail. Hitler's 'strategic assistants' had, after all, been taken on because of their mastery of the technical and military machine. Even after the surrender, however, deluded by the mass of problems to be solved, Jodl was full of hope for Germany's future political role and his own position. This stands out clearly from his remarks at the briefing conferences. On 12 May, for instance, the government's Intelligence organisation commented that, even in complete defeat, Germany was already

again a factor in Europe; this was entirely in line with Jodl's
thinking and he said: 'The moment will come when we shall
play off the Russians against the Anglo-Americans.' On several
occasions he advised a wait-and-see attitude: 'We must sit on the
fence and be neutral.'

Colour was lent to this idea by the contrast between the
forthcoming attitude of the Russians and the stiff, if not actually
humiliating, treatment meted out by the Anglo-Americans. Jodl's
original sympathies were with the West; it is not impossible,
however, that, had okw continued to exist, he would not have
swung over to the Russians, somewhat after the manner of
Seeckt. He might even have come to terms with communism,
particularly seeing that, like so many others at the time, he was
convinced that no return to a bourgeois way of life was possible.
If Russia had offered Germany a chance, he would certainly have
seized it. Politically he was a weathercock, an opportunist. Many
of his May 1945 statements, moreover, show what had drawn
him to Hitler. In their basically militant attitude he and the
dictator were largely alike. Gerhard Ritter has said that the
hallmarks of the militarist are blinkered technical military
thinking and a basic attitude of bellicosity. The description applies
to Jodl and, in extreme form, to Hitler. Moreover both were
exaggerated nationalists and highly ambitious. The differences
between them were of degree rather than kind. Jodl, brought
up on strict standards, strove to keep within the bounds of
convention and law; he felt that excesses must be tolerated as
revolutionary aberrations or temporary measures in the interests
of Germany; the amoral Hitler, on the other hand, recognised
no restrictions of a legal or humanitarian nature. Jodl simply did
not perceive Hitler's total lack of inhibition; his undoing was
that he thought he was serving a man of firm moral principles
who had only the advancement of his people at heart. Nevertheless many of his utterances of that time bore the stamp of racial
prejudice, and even later he was capable of such grotesque
remarks as 'The Allied Control Commission must be used as a
buffer between us and our Jewish enemy' who was only waiting
to rob and humiliate the Germans. He equally indulged in the
well-worn clichés about the death of German nationhood and its
extermination by the Slavs. His mood swung from lofty hopes
('I feel myself called upon to master the greatest problems') to

realistic appreciation ('We are entering a month- or year-long period of misery. What awaits us in the future will be more depressing than ever').

His views on the duties and prospects of OKW led him, whenever possible, to refer to Dönitz at briefing conferences as Commander-in-Chief of the Wehrmacht rather than Head of State; he spoke out against any tendency to regard the Wehrmacht as a mere executive organ of the Reich Government.

This was the view of widespread General Staff circles; its background was a desire for effective representation of the German case rather than an attempt to perpetuate the Wehrmacht organisations. This emerges clearly from a note for the file by the Deputy Chief of the OKW Operations Staff:

> 1. It is not yet possible to say whether the Ministers now in office will be recognised, or indeed tolerated, by the Allied Powers either collectively as a Reich government or individually as ministerial experts. No official statements on this subject have been made. The majority of the enemy press indicates that the life of the present government will be short. Its task is regarded primarily as the implementation of capitulation. Then it can go.
> At any time, therefore, the present government may disappear and its place be taken by some unified central administrative organisation.
> *Then either:*
> OKW will become responsible for all questions of food, economics, finance, communications and administration,
> *or:*
> everything will be run by an Allied Military Government, later by an Allied Civil Administration.
> This government will then temporarily be the sole representative of German interests and as its counterpart, representing Germany as a whole, will remain only OKW with its liaison staffs.

Since the supply divisions of OKW had nothing like adequate experience of civil administration, General Dethleffsen proposed that civilian advisers be incorporated into this section, as had been done in the case of the Liaison Staff to British Headquarters. To avoid the impression that this was an undercover step towards a central government, to which the Allies were opposed, these advisers, Dethleffsen said, should be incorporated at once; they should not be well-known figures but come from the 'second level'.

A similar development was planned for the Southern Zone.

There the Wehrmacht was initially intended to deal with all economic and supply questions for the civil population, while the civil administration remained in the background. The Reich Ministers nominated plenipotentiaries subordinate to the Generals concerned. On 19 May Jodl applied to the Head of the Control Party for approval of this arrangement.

To some extent the planned incorporation of civilian experts was effected. The simultaneous arrest of the Government and OKW on 23 May, however, put an end to all attempts to provide some responsible German contribution to the solution of these problems.

CHAPTER NINE

Government Business

MOST of the conversations leading to the formation of this government of Nazified experts took place between 3 and 5 May. They were not yet complete when the first crisis appeared on the horizon.

On 5 May Speer notified the Chief Minister in writing that he would carry on the business of his Ministry (which had not yet been disbanded at this point) and of the Ministry of Economics 'only in the area not yet occupied by the enemy' – the remainder of Germany, Bohemia and Moravia, Norway, Denmark, the remainder of Holland and Italy; there he would 'issue the necessary legal regulations to ensure maximum uninterrupted maintenance of the economy and of production on the basis of the old legal status'. He refused to exercise his functions in the occupied areas and was prepared to make himself available, if desired, only for a winding-up operation. As soon as surrender was complete, he wished to resign from the government.

On 7 May, as soon as Jodl had signed the surrender in Reims, Speer sent Dönitz the draft of a letter of dismissal. From this it emerged that the Minister for Armaments and War Production did not regard the surrender as a military one only: 'With the completion of capitulation on . . (day) . . at . . (hour) . . the sovereign rights of a German government have ceased to exist. Simultaneously the task handed down by the Führer has been fulfilled. . . .' Speer wished to leave it to Dönitz whether to approach the Allies regarding transfer of affairs to them.

On 8 May Speer drafted a proclamation to the German people and a letter for Dönitz to send to Field Marshal Montgomery. This too emphasised that the Berlin signature was *'the last signature* in the name of the present Reich government. . . . After this decision a Reich government possessing freedom of action no longer exists. Henceforth *the future fate of the German people* will be decided *exclusively* by the enemy.'[1] Both the proclamation and the letter contained an offer of co-operation during the transitional period in order to ease the German people's situation. In

216

addition Speer stressed that 'despite our co-operation the enemy will hold us responsible for our actions exactly as they do all other responsible personalities of the National-Socialist State'.

It is not clear whether Speer drafted this on Dönitz' instructions but at least its contents were in line with the Grand Admiral's views. As already mentioned, Dönitz regarded his appointment as a commission to bring the war to an end. Once this was done, he wished to withdraw. He considered that at the most the Allies would make use of German experts' know-how without allowing them much freedom of action. Moreover he was well aware that the majority of Germans were not worrying their heads over the problem of the State leadership but were occupied almost exclusively with the anxieties of daily existence.

This was no more than a sober appreciation of the facts. In any case Dönitz considered that continuance in his present offices was incompatible with his personal dignity and that of the Reich.

Not so Schwerin von Krosigk. He countered by arguing the continuity and sovereignty of the Reich. He insisted on the necessity for some central German authority to deal with the difficult problems of food supply, assistance to the bereaved, etc. The presence of the Grand Admiral he regarded as an essential guarantee for the maintenance of security and good order and as moral support. The Allies too, he said, might require a German government as a factor in the maintenance of order, perhaps to evade responsibility for future developments or even because they would need a strong 'rump of Germany'. It will be noted that these ideas were not dissimilar to those of the Reichsführer-SS.

It was finally agreed in Flensburg to observe and analyse political developments with care, so that the government might announce its resignation 'at the right time whatever might happen'. On 8 May, therefore, Dönitz issued his proclamation previously agreed with von Krosigk.[2]

Since the new cabinet regarded itself merely as a government of experts one would have expected a series of well-informed treatises on problems in the various fields. Administratively, however, the government's activity was extremely limited. Some departments did indeed follow Jodl's advice and flood the Control Party with proposals and memoranda; some papers, statistics and information were produced, but in general, in the short time

available and with inadequate information, the problems could
only be indicated broadly and in outline. Many of the documents
seem to have been compiled in great haste and hardly even
checked. This at least seems to have been the case with a government paper of 10 May entitled '*Aide-mémorie* on urgent supra-
regional questions' and described by Speer as a 'note verbale'
for the cabinet.

This document consisted of five main sections dealing with
food, supplies to industry, finance and currency problems, labour
and social security, general administration. Every department
being involved, it was practically a government manifesto, yet its
main characteristic was its lack both of form and substance. The
first section on the food situation, for instance, did no more than
list eight immediate requirements pending clarification of the
question whether the agricultural areas of Eastern Germany
could be considered as available for the supply of the West.
Requirements were set out under four headings:

(a) Release of all Wehrmacht equipment and supplies and all fishing
vessels.

(b) Maintenance of existing food organisations, primarily the
National-Socialist creations such as the Reich Food Front and
Economic Associations, but also the military supply organisation.
Existing marketing arrangements and control of commodities in
short supply to be continued.

(c) Immediate reconstruction of communications and food industries.

(d) Supply to agriculture and food industries of coal, fuel, power,
artificial fertilisers, etc.

In view of the widespread destruction, the dispersal of authorities and the almost total stoppage of traffic, the government was
of course in no position to carry out any precise stocktaking
under the individual headings. Considering, however, that
Ministers had been versed in their subjects for years, it is difficult
to see why the lists drawn up should consist entirely of statements
such as the following:

(a) 2 lbs of nitrogen produces 30 lbs of grain, so nitrogen works
must be reactivated rapidly:

(b) one horse requires as much corn as 10–15 men. The more
tractors used in agriculture, the greater the saving of horses.
Use of tractors, however, is dependent upon the quantity of fuel

available. Therefore rapid resumption of oil production refineries and hydrogenation plants.

One wonders whether they thought that the occupying powers came from a non-industrial society, for on 11 May this disquisition was forwarded to Eisenhower with the request that it be transmitted to the British, French and Soviet High Commands.

Typical of the text is the following sentence: 'Until next harvest there will in any case be an import requirement, particularly cereals, potatoes and fats. This import requirement will arise under all circumstances.' The section ends with the comment that all these measures are similarly applicable to the forestry industry.

Supplies to industry were dealt with in three short paragraphs. Requirements were stated to be: strict control of management, prices and distribution, central supra-regional direction and reconstruction on 'general national economic principles'.

The next passage, dealing with technical financial problems, is the only well thought-out section of the paper. It gives well supported arguments showing the lack of means of payment, leading to a demand for a centralised solution; it also raises important questions such as the recognition of the Reich as a debtor and creditor.

The section on 'Labour and Social Security' – the only contribution to anything apparently made by Seldte's department – lays down that all important questions must be settled on a uniform basis under centralised arrangements. Requirements were said to be: guarantee of the continuance of labour exchanges and security of employment. Social insurance was described as 'of the utmost importance'.

After these profound thoughts the final and longest section of this great work consists of a real hodge-podge of requirements of the most varying nature and magnitude: refugee problems, reunion of families, youth welfare, control of accommodation, re-establishment of communications, reactivation of water, gas and electricity works, coal supply, non-local compensation, maintenance of law and order, telecommunications, official journeys, administrative expenses, central financial settlement, resumption of education in schools, publication of newspapers, use of radio stations – a complete reference list in fact, assembled higgledy-piggledy. In fact this first government memorandum is typical of the government itself – makeshift and purposeless.

A few notes on the activities of individual departments, the result of prolonged research, serve only to reinforce this impression. In some cases memoranda and proposals from OKW are included since, as he said to Rooks, Dönitz used OKW for certain civilian tasks, which OKW was only too glad to accept since it was reckoning upon the possible disappearance of the government. Co-ordination was effected through a daily ministerial conference under von Krosigk, at which Major-General von Trotha was present as OKW Liaison Officer.

Food

The opening discussions on this subject between representatives of the occupying powers and members of the Provisional Government took place on 12, 13 and 14 May. The German case was presented by Backe, the Minister, and Riecke, his State Secretary; the Allied team varied. The first move was a talk between Backe and British officers on the evening of the 12th. Surprisingly Backe reported that the British had declared themselves in favour of a central Ministry of Food and maintenance of existing organisations. This would have been entirely in line with the German ideas, since in all their negotiations Backe's and Riecke's tactics were simple: they drew attention to difficulties and grievances and, to deal with them, recommended central direction and the earliest resumption of contact with all organisations still in existence. They stressed that, should the long-term food situation remain bad, there would be serious consequences such as food riots, epidemics and moral degeneration.

On most subjects the starting-point was the 'excision of the surplus-producing agricultural area east of the Elbe'. 'East of the Elbe' and 'West of the Elbe' were current phrases. To a note on a discussion with Anglo-American representatives on 13 May Backe attached a table showing 'Implications on the food position of non-availability of the areas east of the Elbe'. East of the river were thirty million Germans compared with fifty-five million west of it. The bread cereals harvest from the West, however, produced only 41 % of the total and the potato harvest 42%. The 65% of the population in the West possessed only 58% of the cattle (56% milking cows) and 53% of the pigs.

As an initial measure of assistance Backe therefore demanded the import before next harvest of 400,000 tons of bread cereals

and 500,000 tons of potatoes. He also requested the 'Interallied
Military Government' to issue instructions that, apart from certain regulations to be explicitly cancelled, all food legislation
remained valid. He proposed increased penalties for black-market-
ing. Further decrees were to lay down that 'the entire food organisation at provincial, district and community level, including the
economic associations' was to resume activity forthwith. He also
pointed out that all data must be assembled afresh since, as a
result of the war, none of the overall figures were now valid.
Justified though this was, it looked like a manœuvre to ensure
the continuance of a German administration.

Backe also maintained that distribution could only be carried
out through administrative channels, but this must be regarded as
another tactical manœuvre. He pleaded for the retention of a
uniform ration card system on existing lines. To solve immediate
difficulties he proposed measures already suggested in the *aide-
mémorie*: release of all Wehrmacht stocks and equipment,
particularly horses, vehicles and agricultural equipment; release of
all soldiers previously employed in agriculture or the food industry; reactivation of communications and food factories; provision
of coal, power, fertilisers and fuel.

On 14 May Riecke had a 'private' interview with General
Lewis, Rooks' deputy. Why this emphasis on its 'private' nature
is not clear – perhaps Lewis thought that Riecke would talk more
frankly. The latter, however, merely insisted on the rapid reconstruction of the food industry organisation, maintenance of
market control and rationing, the requirement for an early assembly of the necessary data and 'the absolute necessity for central
direction of the food industry'. He also asked for resumption of
contact between the Ministry and subordinate authorities and
greater freedom of movement for senior officials. At Lewis'
request the government sent in an official application for all this
on the very same day (signed by Kritzinger); it merely repeated
the old arguments, adding a reference to possible bread riots and
the danger of the spread of epidemics.

Stuckart, the State Secretary in charge of the Ministry of the
Interior, also took a hand in the food problem when a ministerial
conference revealed the fact that the standard ration was to be
reduced by half. He called in General Handloser, the Head of the
Wehrmacht Medical Services, to provide detailed figures of

calories required to maintain health and insist on the dreadful consequences of undernourishment:

1. Reduction of capacity for work ending in complete physical exhaustion.
2. Reduction of the physical powers of resistance to infection leading to grave danger of epidemics.
3. Bread rioting and moral degeneration.

Stuckart seized upon this, specifying the most dangerous diseases as typhus, dysentery and spotted fever and adding increased infant and old-age mortality, increase of venereal disease and of all forms of radicalism.

Jodl too manifested anxiety over the nourishment of the German people, recalling OKW's numerous proposals for the release of German prisoners of war as labour;[3] he was prepared to make nitrogen stocks available for agriculture. An excellent method of relieving the German food position seemed to him to be the rapid repatriation of ex-prisoners of the 'United Nations'. He drew attention to the delay in the return of Polish, Yugoslav and Rumanian prisoners. Acceleration of their return, he said, would 'constitute a considerable alleviation of Germany's food position' and be 'a valuable contribution to the aversion of the threatened food catastrophe'.

Jodl was not the only one to wish to be rid of useless mouths. A memorandum from the Flensburg Chamber of Commerce, for instance, drew attention to the large number of refugees in Schleswig-Holstein; they were divisible into three categories: those from western areas, those from the area between Elbe and Oder, those east of the Oder. They should be moved as quickly as possible in that order of priority. Against the last category some rather more perspicacious person had written in the margin: 'Where to?' The sheer egoism of people who had been largely shielded from the horrors of war also showed itself in the suggestion that non-functioning industries be reactivated but new establishments forbidden.

This is only one illustration of what people were really interested in at the time. The majority thought only of themselves and their material well-being; the Reich 'was to them Hecuba', as Schwerin von Krosigk had put it.

There seem to have been no further concrete proposals and no assembly of detailed data on the overall food position. On 15 May Backe flew to Eisenhower's headquarters for discussions and was there arrested. In his absence Riecke carried on the business of the Food Department and had several discussions with the Control Party. Even later, when a prisoner in Oberursel in the Taunus, he was still being asked for papers and memoranda. Apart, however, from these sporadic discussions the Acting Government did little of real value on the food front.

Transport

Dönitz says[4] that Speer and Dorpmüller thought that the communications and transport system could be restored in the short period of six weeks. No concrete plan seems to have been worked out by the Flensburg government, however. This is hardly surprising since Dorpmüller and Ganzenmüller, his State Secretary, who, as already mentioned, were located in Malente, did not accede to the Control Party's summons to discussions until 19 May. On 20 May Dorpmüller had a talk with representatives of the Russian Commission about reconstruction of the communications network in eastern Germany. Shortly thereafter he flew to Eisenhower's headquarters. Apparently for a short time he was placed in charge of reorganising the German transport system but a little later he died.

The only documents discoverable on this subject originate from OKW. In both layout and content they adhere closely to the standard government formula. The final sentences, for instance, of a 'Study of reactivation of the transport system – necessary initial measures' dated 16 May and drafted by the Head of Transport in the OKW Demobilisation Section, read as follows:

> V. *Without* a rapid restoration of all forms of transport it will not be possible to feed the civil population, German prisoners of war on German territory or the armies of occupation, or to reactivate industry or industrial life in the over-populated area west of the Elbe.
> *The absence or inadequacy of a solution* to this burning question *must lead to the most serious consequences in all sectors* (starvation, disease, riots).
> These questions cannot be settled *locally*; they must be dealt with *supra-regionally,* i.e. for the entire country. The structure of the country requires a settlement covering almost all sectors and this can only be done by means of transport of all types.

Like the Government's 'note verbale' the study does no more than list and emphasise the urgency of the civil and military problems upon the solution of which the reactivation of transport depended. It set out eighteen 'Immediate measures' which in effect amounted merely to retention or reinstatement of existing arrangements and inclusion of Wehrmacht specialists to do the work.

More concrete data, though concerning only the area north of the Kiel Canal, are to be found in a report by the Transport Minister's Representative attached to the Wehrmacht Head of Transport. This showed that on certain stretches of line in the west a maximum of one train each way per day was running, whereas on the remaining lines traffic had been completely suspended since 11 May on the orders of a British Colonel. The order was hardly surprising considering that at the time out of 1,600 miles of railway in the British Zone only some 600 miles were usable, 3,000 out of 7,500 passenger cars were out of action and most of the remainder damaged and less than half of the normally available locomotives serviceable.[5] These figures were not, however, available in Flensburg at the time.

The Transport Ministry representative therefore merely pointed out that the board of the Reichsbahn possessed general data of all sorts and imparted a few further useful details.

The existence of the OKW study is further proof that General Dethleffsen had had some success with his proposal to incorporate a 'second level of government' into OKW.

No further efforts about transport seem to have been made since in mid-May the occupying powers took over the Reichsbahn. It was months before rail traffic was running again, even spasmodically and on an improvised basis.

Finance

As a result of the general collapse, the Reich's financial position had deteriorated even further. Lack of liquid assets was such that it seemed impossible to meet even the most urgent requirements of the population. Owing to the breakdown of communications it was impossible to provide the Northern Zone with adequate means of payment. The Reichsbank had made every effort to get money through but could no longer meet current demand. Early in May its Flensburg branch had something over one million marks in notes and three-four million in treasury bills available for circulation after cancellation. Under normal circumstances this would have been enough to meet demand in the Flensburg area. With the demands of the Wehrmacht, however,[6] of the agencies now located there and the mass of refugees, funds seemed likely to be exhausted in eight to ten days.

On 5 May members of the Provisional Government under the chairmanship of Ohlendorf met representatives of the local banks and discussed the question of a possible emergency issue. All were unanimous that a local currency must be avoided and that any emergency issue must have more than regional validity. Some provincial institution, however, must appear as house of issue, since the Reich could only issue currency having nation-wide validity.

The government's moves for a single issue of emergency money, were, however, frustrated by the Government Representative [Regierungspräsident] of Lübeck. Hamburg produced a plan for the issue of emergency money through the *Land* Bank and in Schleswig-Holstein there was a proposal to do so through individual parishes [Gemeinde].

The government was determined to prevent the further inflationary pressure to which the issue of local currencies would have given rise. They proposed that the *Land* Banks issue money as similar in appearance as possible. Payments should be cleared through Reichsbank branches where they would be covered by Reichsmark assets, in other words issues should not exceed assets available in the Reichsbank. The Finance and Economics Department of the government therefore worked out regulations empowering *Land* Banks, Savings Banks and clearing-houses to issue emergency money in denominations of one, two, five, ten, twenty, and fifty marks.

All these measures, however, required approval from the occupation authorities. To restrict cash circulation they laid down that notes of 100 marks and upwards might no longer be presented in payment.

The financial position forced the government to consider cancellation of the Reich's current or lump-sum indebtedness. Reduction of salaries, particularly for senior officials, was also considered, together with employees' and workers' wages and pensions. All were agreed that reduction of social security and welfare payments, including those of the disabled, was unavoidable, though special consideration was to be given to the needy, particularly women with several children. Nevertheless, up to and including June 1945, the government contrived to pay in full the salaries of their own officials and employees.

The Finance and Economics Department also had to deal with the Wehrmacht's indebtedness. On 7 May OKW raised this question with the government and referred to payments on account, cancellation of debts and moratoria. They clearly thought it both inexpedient and intolerable to attempt to meet their debts in full. The Economics Department, however, took the view that in the interests of the economy and of economic reconstruction the principle of full settlement of debts must be adhered to, though as far as possible settlement in cash should be avoided. The first step, they considered, was to draw up a balance sheet showing assets and liabilities but even this had to be negotiated with the Allies since under their Law No 52 all Reich assets were frozen.

In short, here again all government activity was dependent upon the occupying powers. Ohlendorf accordingly drafted a memorandum entitled 'General monetary and financial problems of the Reich' drawing attention to the most important questions. As in the government's 'note verbale', the starting-point was the necessity for central direction and solution. Ohlendorf also pointed to the inevitable consequences if the occupying powers set up regional administrative authorities and forecast a breakdown of the economy.

On the day before the government's arrest the Economics Department drew up a list of 'Immediate measures in the field of finance and economics'; in effect this suggested re-negotiation and freezing of salaries, wages and incomes, revaluation of the credit notes in the hands of industry and the necessity for encouragement of saving, if necessary by tax relief.

The Provisional Government could hardly do more than make suggestions. The majority of their discussions with the Control Party dealt with organisational questions; at least they gave the Allies some insight into the various problems before they finally assumed responsibility for government in Germany.[7]

External Affairs

No functioning organisation was available to the new Reich Foreign Minister to deal with external affairs. As early as mid-March the majority of Foreign Ministry personnel had been sent on indefinite leave and the last officials and employees had left Berlin for Bavaria in mid-April. Only von Steengracht with a small staff had returned to the North.

The new Foreign Minister's first official act took place on 4 May, when he requested German missions abroad to inform their host governments that 'On 1 May 1945 Adolf Hitler, the Führer of the Great German Reich, has died a hero's death. In accordance with German constitutional law Herr Karl Dönitz has succeeded him'. Both the 'hero's death' and the inaccurate date eventually became generally accepted. Dörnberg, a Foreign Ministry official, passed a precisely similar message to the Head of foreign Missions in the Southern Zone. A diplomatic exodus thereupon began: all senior Italian officials departed (Anfuso, the Ambassador, had left Germany on 26 April); Oshima, the Japanese Ambassador, followed suit and the Danish representative departed owing to 'lack of communication with the Reich Government'. At this time Germany was at war with fifty-five states and the few neutrals with whom she still had diplomatic relations now broke them off: Portugal on 6 May, Sweden on 7 May, Switzerland on 8 May and, after capitulation, even Spain and Ireland.

Prior to the break in relations with Sweden and Denmark, however, the Acting Government took certain action.

Von Krosigk, now the Foreign Minister, had been pressing for months for a more active foreign policy and had made no secret of his disapproval of his predecessor's methods. He had proposed that prominent German personalities should gain contact with the West via neutral countries. He was likely, therefore, to take some initiative. His first appointments as Foreign Minister were those of Dr. Walter Best, late Reich Plenipotentiary in Denmark, and Walter Schellenberg, Head of the RSHA Foreign Intelligence Service, both of whom were nominated 'Envoys' – hardly the happiest of choices.

Best's appointment had no practical consequences. He had been a Ministerial Counsellor [Ministerialrat] and Head of Sections

I and III (Personnel, Organisation and Legal including counter-espionage) in the RSHA; he had been involved in the 'Final Solution of the Jewish Question' in France and Denmark but had later apparently turned against the SD terror policy.[8] He was now commissioned by von Krosigk to hold talks with the new Danish government nominated by the King and turn himself into the *de facto* Head of a German diplomatic mission. In view of the situation Best thought it better to place himself at the disposal of the Danish Government. Officially he was interned but, initially at any rate, he was free to move about in Copenhagen and telephone other German authorities in Denmark. He narrowly escaped being shot by the Wehrmacht C-in-C Denmark who heard that the Legation building was being guarded by members of the Danish resistance movement and wrongly assumed that Best had placed himself under their protection.[9]

SS-Brigadeführer Walter Schellenberg had been authorised by Himmler, after his interview with Count Bernadotte, to negotiate with the latter for the withdrawal of the German occupation forces in Norway and their internment in Sweden until the end of the war. He was to act as Germany's special representative in Scandinavia to negotiate a peaceful settlement there. At the end of April Schellenberg flew to Sweden and contacted the Swedish Government via Thomsen, the German Minister. The Swedes said that they required explicit proposals from the German Government for ending the occupation of Norway. They had been pressed by the Norwegian government-in-exile in London to make some demonstration, including the use of force if necessary, to bring about the surrender of German troops in Norway, but were afraid of becoming involved in hostilities at the eleventh hour. They considered that, if they acted, they would meet bitter resistance from the Germans and the result would be widespread destruction in Norway. Sweden therefore attempted to reach a solution by negotiation.

On 1 May Schellenberg[10] left Copenhagen, where he had briefed Best, and reached Himmler's new headquarters near Lübeck. There he learnt of Hitler's death and the surprising news of the succession. Himmler wished Schellenberg to tell both Dönitz and von Krosigk immediately of his negotiations and they both drove over to Plön. There Schellenberg reported to Dönitz as Head of State and Supreme Commander of the Wehrmacht, also to

Keitel and Jodl, and finally to von Krosigk. When the latter told him that Norway was still a 'pawn in the game', Schellenberg decided so to inform his Swedish opposite numbers. On Himmler's instructions, however, he first prepared a draft on future co-operation with the new Foreign Minister, in which he apparently suggested dissolution of the NSDAP, the Gestapo and the SD.[11]

After giving the Swedish representative in Copenhagen a short account of all this, Schellenberg moved to the new seat of government in Mürwik, where he had further discussions with von Krosigk and Dönitz. The latter was opposed to the internment of German troops in Sweden since he feared that they might later be handed over to the Russians, as in fact happened with the refugee troops from Courland. Urged by von Krosigk, however, who thought that an early evacuation would be a sort of 'goodwill act' in Allied eyes, Dönitz eventually agreed that Schellenberg should probe further but without power to conclude any agreement. A warrant, signed by Dönitz and dated 4 May, was prepared in the name of 'Envoy Walter Schellenberg' authorising him to negotiate with the Swedish Government for the end of the German occupation of Norway and 'to conclude agreements subject to any necessary ratification in accordance with current legal regulations'. This form of words was chosen to give Schellenberg's mission greater standing in the eyes of the Swedes; in fact, however, he was told to make no agreement without further approval from the government.[12] Von Krosigk sent a letter to Thomsen in Stockholm asking him to give Schellenberg 'maximum support in every way during his stay in Stockholm and provide him with such technical and financial resources as he might require to carry out his duties'. The letter also referred to certain special responsibilities with which Schellenberg was charged and of which he would tell the Minister verbally. These seem to have been details concerning the surrender and Germany's relations with Sweden.

Count Bernadotte also mentions a request, transmitted by Schellenberg, for a meeting with Eisenhower.[13] Von Krosigk remembers nothing of this, from which it may be assumed that Schellenberg was either acting on his own initiative or on behalf of Himmler.

By the time Schellenberg resumed his discussions with the

Swedes, the local surrender in the North had taken place. The Swedes therefore proposed to discuss the matter with the Western Powers' representatives in Stockholm. In addition General Böhme in Norway had to be informed of the situation. At 11.0 a.m. on 6 May a discussion took place on the Norwegian-Swedish frontier between Thomsen and a representative of Böhme. Thomsen produced Schellenberg's authority and explained his mission; speaking for his commander, however, Böhme's representative said that the operational task in Norway had been re-confirmed by the Chief of the OKW Operations Staff on 6 May and so the Wehrmacht C-in-C was not empowered to enter into communication with the Allies directly or indirectly. For this he would need a new and explicit order from OKW.

Schellenberg informed the Acting Government of this development. When he called again on 8 May von Krosigk told him that general capitulation had been signed the previous night and that he should therefore take no further official action.[14] A further letter informed Thomsen that the German Government now had no further possibility of negotiating with the Swedes for the withdrawal of German troops from Norway. The Reich Commissar in Norway had been relieved of all his functions on 7 May and all questions concerning German forces would be settled direct between the Wehrmacht C-in-C and a British Liaison Staff.

General capitulation put an end to diplomatic contact between the Third Reich and Sweden. On 13 May von Krosigk once more approached Bernadotte direct, asking that the Swedish Red Cross take charge of passengers in the *Drottingholm*, due in Gothenburg. They consisted of German repatriates from Turkey and South America, including members of diplomatic and consular missions. Von Krosigk asked to be informed of their proposed disposal and sent them his warmest thanks and heartfelt greetings. He seems to have had no reply; nevertheless the Swedish Red Cross did take care of the travellers.

One final piece of diplomacy took place between the German Reich and Japan.

In a personal telegram to Dönitz on 5 May Admiral Wennecker, the German Naval Attaché in Tokyo, advised that, in view of the latest developments and anticipated difficulties, Otto Stahmer, the Ambassador, be replaced by Wohltat, the Head of the Far East Economic Mission. Wennecker also said that considerable Japanese military circles would not be opposed to surrender, even on severe terms provided they were honourable. On the same day von Krosigk sent Stahmer a coded radio message via the Naval Attaché asking him to transmit his warmest greetings to the Japanese Foreign Minister and inform him as follows:

'Up to the last minute the Führer believed that, through a military success in the decisive battle for Berlin, he could bring about the turning-point in this war. For these beliefs he gave his life and died a hero's death in battle. After the adverse outcome of the battle for Berlin, the war must be considered militarily lost. Considering the complete exhaustion of the German power of resistance, it has become impossible to carry on the war and thereby continue to fulfil the obligations of our alliance with Japan. To avoid further useless sacrifices and maintain the substance of the German people, the German High Command considers itself compelled to enter into discussions – not yet concluded – with the Western Allies for an armistice. The Reich Government also desires a cessation of hostilities against the Soviet Union, but can only do this after exhausting every possibility of saving millions of Germans from annihilation by Bolshevism.' Von Krosigk then emphasised to the Japanese Foreign Minister how much he regretted that his first official act should be to transmit such news to his Japanese friends and allies; he expressed the hope that 'in the interests of world peace and the welfare of all peoples, the just demand of the German and Japanese peoples for an honourable and assured future will eventually meet with success'.[15]

Next day von Krosigk was forced to send another telegram to Tokyo. The BBC reported that, over the Japanese radio, Togo, the Japanese Foreign Minister, had accused Germany of failing to inform her ally of Himmler's surrender offer or of the peace negotiations. Moreover the German intention to conclude peace with the West but continue to fight against Soviet Russia was contrary to Japanese war aims. Japan therefore reserved the right to withdraw from the Tripartite Pact and all other agreements with Germany. Von Krosigk thereupon requested the German Ambassador to inform Togo that there was no question of peace negotiations. Dramatic developments on all fronts had led to a cessation of hostilities in widely separated sectors; an approach to the Western High Command by the German High Command had become indispensable. Discussions were still in progress and von Krosigk stressed that these negotiations were on a military level only and in no sense peace talks. Technical difficulties had made it impossible to inform the Japanese sooner. There was no question of a violation of the Tripartite Pact and the German Government would be most distressed, should the slightest doubt as to its loyalty arise.

On 8 May von Krosigk seized his last opportunity to communicate with a mission abroad as an independent agent. He thanked Stahmer for his work and expressed the hope that from the ruins of collapse a Reich would arise, in the reconstruction of which the Ambassador and his staff could play their part.

On 10 May two coded telegrams arrived from the Ambassador in Tokyo in reply. Stahmer reported on his conversations with Togo from which he had gained the impression that Japan wished to withdraw from the Tripartite Pact of 11 December 1941 but to lay the blame for so doing on Germany. The press of the last few days reinforced this impression. Many people in Japan likened the present German regime to the Badoglio government. Stahmer said that, as instructed, he had stressed the pressure of the military situation and the intention to open armistice negotiations with Soviet Russia also. For the future he recommended that emphasis be laid on the impossibility of continuing the struggle and that decision on any dissolution of the Tripartite Pact be left to the Japanese Government.

The second telegram reported another interview with Togo which in essence had confirmed the BBC report. Both the Foreign Minister and the Ambassador had reiterated their arguments. Togo enquired whether the Nazi Party had been dissolved, quoting a speech by Dönitz, unknown to the Ambassador. Stahmer ended his message with the comment that it was his impression that Togo wished to recover Japan's freedom of action, probably by breaking off diplomatic relations with Germany; he was, however, now in some embarrassment since the German Government still recognised the alliance and he did not wish to be solely responsible – probably because the Japanese Cabinet was not unanimous on the subject.

And so things remained. The Tripartite Pact was never officially dissolved, although in his memoirs Togo says that he was
determined to cancel all agreements with Germany and had taken
the necessary steps to that end.

On 10 May Kosak, the Croat Minister, arrived in Mürwik to
visit the Foreign Minister. He had been charged by the 'Poglav-
nik' (the anti-Pavlovich leader in Croatia) on 3 May to go to von
Krosigk and ensure that no final decision would be taken during
the surrender negotiations without prior consultation with the
Croat Government. His journey had been quite an odyssey
– through Copenhagen already occupied by British troops and
thence by German naval vessels; he did not arrive until his mission
had long since been overtaken by events. Kosak reported contacts between the Croat Government and Mihailovich, leader of
the Serb nationalist 'Chetniks', with a view to the formation of a
common front against Bolshevism; he attempted to obtain the
support of the German Government for Anglo-American action
to assist his country. Von Krosigk, however, told him that 'in
her present situation it was essential for Germany to avoid giving
the impression that she was banking on differences between the
Western Allies and the Soviet Union'; he said that Croatia could
not now avoid surrendering.

After several fruitless attempts to obtain an interview with
Brigadier Churcher and, after its arrival, with a member of the
Control Party, Kosak and his deputy asked to be allowed to return
to the South.

Nothing is known of any further initiative by the Reich
Government in the foreign policy field. After the surrender a
number of neutral governments withdrew recognition from
German diplomatic missions and consulates, but no protest
seems to have been made, although in a memorandum of 16
May OKW recommended this procedure and on 18 May described
the behaviour of the neutrals as arbitrary. In particular Naval
Headquarters called for a protest against the action of the Swiss
Legation in Washington which had made over to the State
Department all German diplomatic property in the United States,
including blocked German funds.[16]

The increasing violence of the Allied press campaign against
the existence of the Acting Government, however, made any
protest seem both inopportune and futile.

Part Three

IDEAS AND TRENDS

CHAPTER TEN

Internal Politics

Dönitz' period in office produced no fully-fledged plans for the future Reich's internal political structure. There are only random remarks and memoranda drafted by experts, from which the intentions of the Grand Admiral and his associates can be deduced. The reasons for such a lack of material are obvious.

Since their purpose was to bring the war to an end, first militarily and then on the civilian front, Dönitz and the Acting Government regarded 'their task as limited in time and circumscribed in scope'. They were prepared to conduct the business of the State only until the German people could once more voice their opinion concerning the form of State, the choice of a Head of State and the election of a new government. How the will of the people was to be expressed remained obscure. In view of the general uncertainty over the immediate future and Germany's utter defeat no time scale could be foreseen. The government aimed no higher than a smooth transition. As far as its business was concerned, it was intended to be purely professional – a 'non-political' cabinet.

It must be remembered that Dönitz was unprepared for governmental office and the task of guiding the political and military destinies of the country came to him as an unwelcome honour. Tempting though it may be, therefore, comparison with the detailed plans of the resistance, worked out through years of labour, is hardly applicable. As a professional officer Dönitz was a stranger to politics; he was no expert in governmental organisation or constitutional questions. His ideas on State structure were therefore only indicated in outline.

Faithful to the ideals of his younger days, Dönitz would have undoubtedly preferred to place the fate of Germany in the hands of some monarch.[1] In May 1945, however, any such notion was mere irresponsible wishful thinking. Talking to Lüdde-Neurath shortly before receipt of the first radio message from Berlin, Dönitz had said that 'the authoritarian principle, which he fully

237

supported in the military field', was not entirely suited to top-level government, 'because the success of the principle was over-dependent on the personality of the man who wielded power in the State'. Division of authority between a Chancellor dealing with current business and a President holding the balance seemed to him the best solution. Other passing remarks show that, though opposed to the one-party system, he did not wish to see revived the multiplicity of parties characteristic of the Weimar period. Goerdeler expressed similar ideas, but he was an experienced politician and had worked out detailed proposals; with him parliamentary control was a matter of course, whereas the idea finds no place in Dönitz' statements. Dönitz maintains, however, that he weighed the idea of a second chamber assembling 'epoch-making brains',[2] somewhat on the lines of Standartenführer Franke-Grieksch's 'Council of Estates'[3] or Goerdeler's Upper House of fifty 'Germans of repute'.

Though intellectually and politically the two men were poles apart, the comparison with Goerdeler is not fortuitous. The ideas of both bore the stamp of the right-wing bourgeoisie. There was an anti-liberal restorationist element in Goerdeler's political ideas for the reconstitution of Germany, and in Beck's too. Whereas Goerdeler, however, taught by the experience of recent years, argued for self-government, decentralisation and federalism, Dönitz was always stressing the necessity for central direction. His constitutional ideas were governed by his ideal of an authoritarian or semi-authoritarian state. For him an important additional issue was the preservation of the 'popular community' created by National-Socialism. 'We must be jealous guardians of the best and finest legacy of National-Socialism, the solidarity of our popular community. In spite of today's total military collapse, our people presents a different face from that of 1918. It has not yet been divided. We may ourselves abolish many of the trappings of National-Socialism; others may be abolished by the enemy; but the best aspect of National-Socialism, the community of our people, must under all circumstances be preserved'. He expressed similar sentiments in a farewell message found in his desk on his arrest.[4]

Here is highlighted once more Dönitz' misconception of the true nature of National-Socialism. He failed to distinguish between his objectives of a united Germany and the Nazi method of creating a monolithic bloc solely for the naked pursuit of power. This misinterpretation was the reason why Dönitz only cut loose from the Nazi institutions and symbols hesitantly, slowly and surreptitiously. He never ordered the official disbandment of the NSDAP, preferring to leave it to Rosenberg, who, however, could not bring himself to do so.

In his speech of 8 May Dönitz declared that the unity of Party and State no longer existed, but this was after signs of voluntary dissolution had appeared in several places. Removal of pictures of leading Nazis was ordered only for rooms liable to be entered by members of the Allied Control Commission. The flag problem was handled in a dilatory fashion, flags being taken down only at the explicit demand of the local occupation commander. The war flag in front of Dönitz' office in Flensberg was only hauled down on 10 May as the result of a direct order. In the spirit of the Demobilisation Section's memorandum, he was unwilling to 'sever his political connections with the past'.[5]

Apart from his personal commitment to National-Socialism, the reason for his hesitancy lay in his conviction that wide sections of the population were still identifying themselves with the Party. He therefore preferred to leave to the occupying power measures which he thought would be unpopular. Almost all his speeches, ordinances and instructions indicate a desire to justify himself before the nation and a fear of falling victim to a new stab-in-the-back legend.

Such being the climate of opinion, democratic ideas were hardly likely to flourish. From the outset, moreover, the cause of democracy had two millstones hung round its neck: the failure of the Weimar Republic and Allied pro-democracy propaganda. Dönitz referred to the 'way of life imposed on us by the enemy'.[6] It never entered the head either of Dönitz, von Krosigk or any other member of the government to call in ex-members of parliament or even trade-unionists. In his letter to Dönitz Ribbentrop had mentioned the possibility of 'a Brüning government with the Democrats and Communists or a Thälmann [Communist] government with the Catholics, Democrats, etc.', but only as an Allied instrument in the event of the complete occupation of Germany and the internment of the Reich Government.[7] The proposed composition of this government betrays complete ignorance and this was not confined to the ex-Foreign Minister.

Many German democrats were rebuffed by the Acting Government, some because they had played an active part in the Weimar Republic and were therefore regarded by the Nazis as out of date and reactionary, but even more because they had been émigrés, an argument which, as we know, has not yet lost its force with many Germans today. 'Emigrés who have not borne the burdens of the front or the air war or even shared the experiences of social partnership with the people cannot provide the impulse for a new start or control the pro-radical forces' – thus the draft of a memorandum probably originating from the government's Intelligence Service.

The composition of the Acting Government shows that there was no true tendency towards democracy. There was no real political brain to lead the way, no clear call to sever ties with the past.

Speer was the only Minister to realise that a break with the past was an absolute necessity for any future development in Germany. In a letter to von Krosigk of 15 May he stated that it was essential to construct a government in which the Allies could have confidence. He himself, he said, could not be included because of his political past. In any case he considered that he had no qualifications whatsoever for the post of Minister of Economics, since he had no knowledge of finance, credit or currency problems. He went so far as to say that to entrust an artist and architect with the problem of debt liquidation would be as unprofitable a procedure as the recent experiment of 'handing the Reich Foreign Ministry over to a champagne merchant'.

The only tasks which Speer was prepared to undertake, and that for a limited transitional period, were the reconstruction of production and the revival of the building industry, since he had gained some knowledge of these over the course of the last three years. His primary responsibility, however, Speer considered to be the protection of his staff – 'shielding them from any accusation which may be made by the enemy, in so far as they were acting in accordance with my instructions'. This, be it noted, was an internal document, written therefore not with an eye to publicity nor intended, as some have insinuated, to curry favour for its author with the Allies. It is therefore all the more remarkable that Speer should have admitted that the former top-level leaders were collectively responsible for the fate of the German people:

'The previous leaders of the German people carry a collective responsibility for the fate which our people now faces. Every individual involved in the leadership must carry his part of this collective guilt, so that the burden which might otherwise fall on the German people will be largely transferred to the shoulders of individuals.'

Speer therefore considered reconstruction of the Cabinet to be essential and demanded that it be formed by men 'who can contribute more to the German people and the idea of a unified Reich than I am in a position to do at the present time'. Accordingly he asked once more to be released from his offices.

Unhappily neither the new Head of State nor his Chief Minister were prepared to make a similar admission. As von Krosigk says in his memoirs, so convinced were they of the propriety 'of their behaviour under Hitler, seeing that it had been dictated solely by good will', that the idea of the Allies refusing to accept the Dönitz Government and backing some other regime as a strait-jacket for the Reich never entered their heads. As a result no attempt was made to appeal to prominent representatives of the German parliamentarians to participate in the government.

The only reference by von Krosigk to possible political reform was in an interview which he gave to Edward Ward, the BBC correspondent, on 11 May. He stressed that after capitulation he had explicitly proclaimed a state based on the rule of law, 'as a transitional phase between the dictator state and a constitutional state'; the next day Dönitz had declared the unity of State and Party to be at an end. 'In the space of a few days, therefore, epoch-making measures have been taken which should be regarded as the basis for our intended further development. I need hardly emphasise that the solemn proclamation of the legality state implies a fundamental renunciation of methods which have given rise to much criticism both internally and externally.' Since for years von Krosigk had served a state in which law meant nothing, this statement was not altogether convincing, any more than was his reference to the freedom and dignity of man in his speech of 2 May. The *New York Times* of 7 May[8] commented that so complete a reversal of German policy would be received by the Allies with scepticism. It should also be remembered that von Krosigk had visualised the necessity for similar declarations in the case of a Himmler government.[9]

The declamatory nature of these statements is clear when they are compared to Beck's call to the German people which referred to the 'majesty of the law' and offered to atone for the persecution of the Jews and the crimes committed in the occupied territories. On these subjects Dönitz' Chief Minister said not a word – and no wonder since several members of the government, himself included, though not actual perpetrators of crime, had participated directly or indirectly in administrative measures discriminating against the Jews, excluding them from public life or deporting them. Now, however, through American newspapers brought by von Friedeburg from Montgomery's headquarters, details about the concentration camps became known in Flensburg and on 9 May the Port Captain reported ghastly conditions on a ship moving concentration camp prisoners; Dönitz and von Krosigk felt compelled to do something. The Chief Minister reported to Dönitz by letter stating that 'if things have occurred in concentration camps or in connection with arrests which are repugnant to the generally accepted rules of law and morality or the feelings of decent people, only very few in Germany knew anything about them'. This fact must be made clear, he said, but a mere statement was not enough. The German people would wish 'to do its own house-cleaning'. Von Krosigk proposed that the Reich Court be given exclusive jurisdiction in this field.

The same letter demanded a 'clean-up of public life' in another sector also. In recent years, von Krosigk said, contrary to all moral and legal principles a few people had shamelessly lined their pockets. A special commission should be formed to investigate these abuses.

The fact that in the same breath von Krosigk could mention both punishment of 'crimes against humanity' and offences such as illegal personal peculation betrays a hopeless 'confusion on the most elementary questions of morality'.[10]

A letter to Eisenhower proposing that the Reich Court be made responsible for the punishment of those involved includes the following: 'Unanimously and indignantly the German people repudiates the abuses and atrocities reported by the Allies; they are incompatible with the principles of its way of life and with its moral sense. To satisfy the German people's real and undiminished sense of legality, the crimes committed should be punished forthwith and with all severity.'

From one who had been Finance Minister of the Third Reich for so long the reference to 'undiminished sense of legality' may sound peculiar; the proposal that these crimes be judged by German courts and according to German principles of law, however, was unassailable – even Goerdeler and the Kreisau Circle had regarded this as a basic principle, though the latter had gone further and demanded the establishment of international legal standards. What is lacking, however, is any admission of shame or shock such as any normal man should suffer on hearing of such bestialities. Lest this judgement be thought harsh, compare von Krosigk's letter with Goerdeler's declaration on the December 1942 Atlantic Charter, which included this:

> The rule of law and decency must be re-established in Germany. All those who have committed crimes or offences will, without exception, be called to account by the German people in accordance with the precepts of the law. Unhappily, for much that has happened no atonement can be made. The German people has been kept in ignorance. When it learns of it all, it will regard it as a natural duty to alleviate suffering. It will have to carry through history the anguish of having its name for ever linked to fearful events and to the violation of all decent feeling.

The lack of feeling shown by Dönitz and his Chief Minister stemmed from a number of views and convictions current at the time:

1. The reports were considered to refer to isolated instances – this is clearly established by a letter from Dönitz to von Krosigk. Such cases, it was thought, should be judged in accordance with existing legal regulations.

2. Concentration camp inmates were regarded as 'seriously incriminated persons and morally depraved elements', as 'criminals and deserters'; for such 'anti-socials' Dönitz considered confinement in camps to be justified, though he was utterly opposed to inhuman conditions. In fact he drafted an announcement to the Wehrmacht in this sense but its publication was forbidden by General Rooks.[11] It was somewhat similar to one issued by the C-in-C of the Navy which said that the Navy had had nothing to do with these camps, that the 'detention of professional criminals in wartime' was right but that abuses and excesses, 'which had apparently occurred', were to be most severely condemned. General Vietinghoff, the C-in-C South-West, and Colonel-General

Dessloch, acting C-in-C West, also issued statements repudiating the atrocities reported in the press and denying all knowledge of them.

3. A *tu quoque* defence was often employed. Jodl, for instance, based on an *aide-mémorie* from the new Foreign Minister, argued as follows: 'If the concentration camp question is raised and we Germans are condemned because of some Niemöller or other murdered cleric, then ask: "Why do you Allies not get excited about Russia where 12,000 patriarchs were murdered in short order?"' No comment on the indefensibility of such views is necessary.

4. The majority of the reports were considered to be enemy propaganda, a parallel to the atrocity stories about German soldiers spread during the First World War. The government's Information Service fostered this preconceived notion; its daily report of 9 May, for instance, contained a section on 'atrocity propaganda': 'Propaganda about atrocities under the Nazi regime *is increasing*: it is clearly intended as an accompaniment to and a factor in the public discussion about the future of Germany. A notable example is a report by eighteen American newspaper publishers and editors who apparently had material available which staggers the imagination. This report will presumably be the subject of American leading articles for a long time to come. It satisfies the American predilection for sensational novelties, panders to American humanitarianism and so will be good business for the press. Increased vilification of "Nazism" is therefore to be anticipated in the next few days; we must also expect that use will be made of this to damage the reputation of the present Reich Government.'

This report in fact puts its finger on the main object of the Acting Government's activities. No further efforts were made to establish the 'state based on the rule of law' proclaimed by von Krosigk; there was nothing resembling the law prepared by Popitz on 'Re-establishment of ordered conditions in the governmental and legal spheres' which had hinted at 'denazification'. In fact stress was invariably laid on the necessity to maintain the indispensable experts in their previous posts.

In the economic, financial and socio-political fields too no really basic planning was done. Government memoranda dealt only with the immediate emergency and their only recommendation was for central direction.[12] Clearly the intention was that everything should continue as before; in his speech of 2 May, for instance, von Krosigk praised Nazi achievements in dealing with unemployment and crises, even when the economic situation and living conditions for the workers were at their most difficult; Ohlendorf described 'Economic Groups' as the best agencies to assume responsibility for self-administration and reactivation of the economy. He also proposed that, via the Chambers of Commerce in each Gau, government influence should be brought to bear on individual firms.

There is not the smallest indication of any plan to revive the trade unions. The 'socialist veneer' which his period in England had left on von Krosigk's conservatism had long since worn off.

The only decipherable tendency – and it is a very pronounced one – in the government's plans for the future social and economic order is its abhorrence of communism, both as a social system and an ideological and governmental principle. The jeremiads about the threatened Bolshevisation of Europe sound like anticipatory cold-war cries; they stemmed, however, from the anti-Russian streak in German nationalism, reinforced by racial prejudice. 'A Bolshevised Europe is the first landmark on the well-planned road to world revolution which the Soviets have been pursuing for twenty-five years. Either the attainment of this goal or the third world war is the inevitable result. The world can only be at peace if the Bolshevist wave does not flood over Europe. In a unique heroic struggle lasting four years Germany, acting as the bulwark of Europe and therefore the world in stemming the Red flood, has expended her last reserves of strength. She could have defended Europe against Bolshevism, had she not been attacked in the rear.' The quotation is from von Krosigk's speech of 2 May 1945.

The reference to the salvation of Europe is no more than a throw-back to Goebbels' propaganda line that Germany was fighting for European culture. It was a call to the Western Allies to join this 'Kulturkampf', conveniently overlooking the fact that the Soviet advance into Europe was only the direct result of German aggression. Moreover before the German attack on the USSR von Krosigk had argued very differently.[13]

In his speech of 2 May von Krosigk also used the phrase 'iron curtain' coined by Goebbels and always wrongly attributed to Churchill.

This fear of communism was not peculiar to Dönitz. Its background was primarily emotional but it was also a factor in foreign policy tactics as is shown by Dönitz' favourite trilogy – hunger, disease, communism.

In conclusion, their paucity is once again the most striking feature of the Flensburg Government's initiatives in the internal political field. In vain do we look for a renunciation of the past and a revival of the moral forces. The few steps taken by the Chief Minister towards the establishment of his 'legality state' make a colourless unconvincing impression. They bear the stamp of pure pragmatism and are devoid of any moral or spiritual element.

CHAPTER ELEVEN

External Affairs

Poverty of ideas was the Acting Government's most striking characteristic in the foreign policy field also. To a certain extent this was inherent in the situation but it was also proof of inability to cut loose from the past. Both from the personal and material points of view the past was too close for new solutions.

The only major external question was the choice between East and West, but no clear expression of opinion was ever made. In view of the Reich's catastrophic situation all thought and discussion understandably revolved solely round the possibility of finding some method of ensuring Germany's continued existence. A recurring theme was that no account should be taken of ideological arguments and that the sole basis for any action was a sober dispassionate appreciation of the situation. This did not necessarily imply any real change of heart, however. Under Hitler ideology had merely served as a pretext to cover national and racial ambitions born of centuries-old emotional trends. National-Socialism's propaganda in praise of the fight or struggle in fact now became a handicap, since it gave the Allies an excuse to check the suitability of every German for future employment in an official capacity.

As already described, Dönitz' appreciation of the situation was a sombre one and up to the time of capitulation he had had little hope that Germany's fortunes might change as the result of a split in the enemy alliance. During his short period as President of the Reich and Supreme Commander of the Wehrmacht, however, various developments and indications, together with the influence of his immediate advisers, led him to include a split in his list of possible developments, though he was still under no illusions as to his own personal fate. Various factors contributed to the slow rise of this hope. In the first place, even after signature of the Reims and Berlin capitulations, the British 21st Army Group still tacitly respected the 'enclave'. In his letter, already quoted, Ribbentrop had pointed out that some accommodation with the British and Americans over Denmark and Norway combined with non-occupation of Schleswig-Holstein might constitute a first and important step in undermining the terms of unconditional surrender. Dönitz, Lüdde-Neurath and von Krosigk all mentioned a visit as early as 6 May by a British Lieutenant-Colonel to advise acceleration of the withdrawal of Schörner's Army Group. This and Lieutenant-Colonel Meyer-Detring's journey through Czechoslovakia under American protection were taken as the first signs of growing understanding for the German case. When, therefore, in a broadcast speech of 8 May[1] Churchill referred to Dönitz as the 'designated Head of the German State' and, at his first interview, Rooks did not explicitly reject his allusions to the necessity for central direction, Dönitz must have felt that the prospects for a reversal of alliances were not quite so illusory. Numerous individual reports of growing disagreement between the major allies reinforced the tendency to optimism.[2] In addition the Intelligence Service reported that considerable sections of the population and also of the troops were counting on support from the Western Allies for resumption of the struggle against Bolshevism in the foreseeable future.

For Dönitz the only possible allies were the British and Americans. Signs now began to multiply, however, of an increasingly pro-Eastern attitude among the younger officers, particularly in the Navy; having operated primarily against England, it regarded her as the main enemy, nor had it experienced the severity of the fighting in Russia; a similar tendency was noticeable both in working-class and intellectual circles. All this caused Dönitz to think that a more active foreign policy, as recommended by von Krosigk, was necessary.

Numerous reports of this period prove that Dönitz' fears about the 'Bolshevisation' of Germany were based, not upon instinctive reaction, but on actual information. The value of such reports was undoubtedly overestimated and they were taken as welcome confirmation of his own fears.

A communist propaganda news-sheet from the Hamburg assembly camp was circulating in all the Flensburg offices, both military and civilian; it attracted considerable attention and gave rise to lively discussion. Its appeal was clever. First it brought the soldiers face to face with the hopelessness of their situation

– wartime disturbance, loss of all material possessions, the uncertainty of the future. The war had been lost, it said, not by the soldiers or the home front but 'simply and solely by the leadership'. Not only Europe but the West as a whole had gone under. Bourgeois notions and ideals had lost all meaning.

National-Socialism's great error, the pamphlet continued, had been its compromise with capitalism, imperialism and the bourgeoisie, resulting in a 'fictitious socialism'. Workers' benefits had stemmed solely from the armaments industry. 'Had Germany been led by a true popular government, a workers' government of marxist type, she would never have come into conflict with Soviet Russia; instead she would have embarked upon a highly profitable economic and political partnership, for which all the necessary natural conditions were present, and indeed inviting.'

The pamphlet pointed out that in defeated Germany no existing group of people could lay any valid claim to the leadership. The bourgeoisie was described as 'worn out and outmoded', the officer corps as 'stupid, mentally rigid and unproductive'; because of the past both should be deprived of any right to a say in affairs. It was a barely concealed attack on the new government.

The soldiers were urged not to cling to non-existent middle-class ideals but to turn to the future. 'Do not let yourselves be frightened by the words "communism" and "bolshevism"; in thousands of newspaper articles, broadcasts and speeches the Nazis deliberately turned them into bogeys, distorting their true meaning and content in the process. Only one concept can guide us aright for the present and the future, can point the way for us into the future – "communism". As a result of the Nazi terror we have no opposition; the German people in their millions are now leaderless, like a scattered flock of sheep. There can be only one way – strict adherence to the Bolshevist system of government. Be ready. The call will come to you soon.'

A single incident will show that such inflammatory material combined with the Russian broadcasts gave rise, not merely to academic discussion, but to serious debates. One evening Captain (Navy) Assmann of the OKW Operations Staff appeared with an urgent request for Major-General Dethleffsen, the Deputy Chief, to go to the torpedo-boat depot-ship anchored in the roadstead; a large number of young torpedo-boat commanders returning from Courland had collected there. They were discussing whether to put to sea again and place themselves at the disposal of the Soviets in Swinemünde. So disillusioned were they with the West that Dethleffsen, Assmann and Admiral Rogge, who had also arrived, had all they could do to dissuade them.

This and similar incidents were reported to Dönitz by a member of the Intelligence Service on 16 May. The argument most frequently used was: 'In view of our humiliating treatment by the Western Powers, we must fight our way through to the East as a body.' Stalin's pronouncement against any dismemberment of Germany proved a powerful factor in this increasing pro-Eastern trend. The younger generation was impressed by the East's apparently greater potential in terms of power and by the possibility of better career prospects. In an analysis of the political situation drawn up on the same day Dr. Stellrecht of Dönitz' civil Private Office reached some highly pessimistic conclusions. He too considered a return to the bourgeois way of life impossible. 'In addition our youth has always had a highly developed national consciousness and in recent times we have succeeded in rousing similar sentiments among the workers. The nationally minded youth and that section of the working class which is nationally conscious, will find the dismemberment of the Reich intolerable; the worse, therefore, they are treated by the Western Powers, the greater will be the urge to turn to the East and adhere thereto. This may quite easily happen with the working class and among the young intelligentsia it is much more likely to occur than after the First World War. Even then the situation in the German High Schools was serious enough. Today many young officers are saying to themselves that Soviet Russia can offer them their daily bread and a future as officers. At the same time, even if only in self-justification, a case for some move in this direction can be made, since it holds out some hope of preserving the unity of the Reich and the German people. With his pronouncement that the unity of the German people must be maintained, Stalin has produced one of his most dangerous themes.' Stellrecht reached similar conclusions in regard to the attitude of the German peasantry.

Such analyses and reports called for some reaction from Dönitz. The danger of communism, hitherto trumpeted as an exhortatory phrase, now seemed to have turned into a tangible threat. The

Navy still remembered the 1918 mutiny with mortification. Now it was threatening to repeat itself on a far larger scale and end in revolution worse than that of 1918/19. Equally disturbing reports came from the Army. After a tour of inspection in the Oldenburg–Neustadt area Colonel Meyer-Detring reported signs of a slackening of discipline as a result of Russian radio propaganda. In a report on visits to Blumentritt's Army Group, the headquarters of Wehrkreis [Military District] X and Commander-in-Chief North's area, Lieutenant-Colonel de Maizière expressed serious anxieties about the morale of the troops. He reported civilians beginning to trek back to the Russian zone, the appearance of soldiers' councils and the distribution of Russian leaflets.

As these reports came piling in Dönitz felt that he must do something. Apart from Stuckart, who seems to have adopted a somewhat more lenient attitude towards these pro-eastern tendencies,[3] the majority of the government was solidly pro-western, Dönitz more than them all.

Dönitz therefore ordered the preparation of memoranda analysing the problem of an eastern or western orientation for Germany. Of these there have survived two papers by Dr. Stellrecht (formerly Staff Officer in Rosenberg's Office in Berlin), a memorandum probably originating in Intelligence Office circles, a personal note from the Ministry of Economics and a draft found on Speer's desk on the day of his arrest. The Stellrecht papers are clearly only working-level documents. Neither Dönitz nor von Krosigk can now remember Stellrecht but the papers should, nevertheless, not be written off as unimportant. They show an astonishing uniformity of thinking and argumentation and contain ideas which undoubtedly originate from Dönitz and Krosigk themselves. It must be assumed that Wegener[4] passed the proposals on, combining them with those of other desk officers. At least some of these papers must have been read by Dönitz. Echoes of them are to be found in his conversation with Rooks and Foord, as also in the government manifesto of 20 May. Finally the document found on Speer's desk was clearly a précis of all these various ideas, embellished with one or two new thoughts; it was obviously intended for the Allied Control Commission, but whether Speer was its author is not certain.

In view of the lack of concrete plans from the government these papers are worth dealing with since they shed light on the prevailing intellectual and political climate of opinion; moreover among their outdated ideas are to be found certain thoughts still valid today. Though little more than political castles in the air, they do indicate what the possible developments were.

Stellrecht's memorandum of 16 May entitled 'On the political situation' opens with a general historical disquisition, in many ways reminiscent of the Hitlerian historical distortions. A favourite illustration in those days was comparison with the Thirty Years' War; even Speer had used it in his speech on 16 April when referring to the widespread destruction. Stellrecht employed it to show that whereas, after the Thirty Years War, two ideologies had been accepted, the situation of May 1945 was very different. 'There can be no question of everybody living happily ever after according to his own lights. Both ideologically and materially communism is still advancing victoriously; in the Anglo-Saxon countries capitalism, though laying less emphasis on ideology, has scored enormous material successes. The National-Socialist ideology, together with fascism, has officially disappeared from the scene. The other two ideologies remain.'

The outcome of the French elections was cited as proof of continuing inter-allied disagreement. The Socialist Party had emerged as the strongest party but with the communists second. 'American material superiority was able to liberate France but cannot prevent her turning ideologically towards communism.'

Faithful to official Party doctrine, the author then described National-Socialism as the only ideology capable of withstanding communism and asked himself how, after its disappearance, a trend similar to that in France would work out in Germany. Here again appeared the argument that a bourgeois way of life was no longer possible since it presupposed the existence of property and this had been 'eaten away by the war'. Western ideas, moreover, were no more attractive to Germans than was the communist doctrine.

'Against this, however, there are millions in Germany who say to themselves that only with the help of the Western Powers can they recover their lost homes, and are ready to fight for them. But they would be equally prepared to co-operate with the East if they were offered more tolerable living conditions.'

From this analysis of the situation Stellrecht concluded that, if they wished to have Germany on their side, the Western Powers would be crazy not to leave the German people to work out their own ideas and the institutions resulting therefrom. Peace was a long way off – 'We are not at the end of a great war but in the middle of it.'

From Jodl came similar views – 'Undoubtedly there can be no question of an end to the war until the three great powers are agreed among themselves.'

The government's Intelligence Service reported that the thoughts of the population were moving on similar lines. This continuous barrage of information and advice cannot have been without its effect on the formation of Dönitz' views. There is little doubt that he regarded National-Socialism as the ideology and form of government best suited to the German character and, in a more lenient 'high-class National-Socialist' form, would have preferred it to the Western-type democracy.

The memorandum already referred to, probably originating from Intelligence Service circles, may be taken as a preliminary draft of some government pronouncement. It repeats many of the well-worn themes: 'Law, order and reconstruction are the focal points around which everybody's thoughts revolve.' The measures, threats of punishment and radio announcements of the occupying powers, however, were forcing people to turn their minds to political matters. In particular propaganda issuing from the Soviet-controlled radio gave the impression that life might perhaps be better in the eastern half of the country. 'We are most disturbed to note the development of a situation which may lead to surprising results. If, in the near future, people start to draw a comparison between the obviously hopeless situation in the west and the theoretical possibility of better prospects of life in the eastern zone, their thinking may quickly become politically coloured and this may lead to incalculable consequences.' In the margin of this passage is the manuscript comment: 'Too weak. Situation has deteriorated already.'

The draft gave a lengthy analysis of western policy – 'purely negative', an attempt to turn the wheel of history back to 1918 and, compared to the more favourable prospects in the east, lacking 'the impulse of an idea'. The Dönitz Government, in effect prisoners of war, could not make their voices heard or exert any positive influence. No mention was made of the government's aims; if they were to be achieved, however, it was stated, a whole series of concessions, such as travel and communications facilities, were necessary; these were required purely for administrative purposes and did not imply any political activity. Though somewhat fuller, the paper bears a strong resemblance to the government memorandum of 19 May.

The paper also included the demand for continuity of personnel. Recent years, it said, had given rise to such a complicated system of rationing, quotas and licensing that it was impossible to do without the experience of the people who had operated it. Only the inefficient should be dismissed. 'It would not be useful to upset the management of public affairs by introducing another brand of politics or removing all National-Socialists' – an obvious attempt to reintroduce National-Socialism by the back door, while officially describing it as dead.

The theme recurs once more that time was working for the East and its potential was continuously increasing. In a properly constituted Germany, therefore, and 'in further development of the German community concept lies the sole guarantee against the radicalisation and subjugation of all Europe – that Europe which constitutes the strongest economic partner of all other continents, and above all of the United States, and which, as a family of free peoples, is called upon to contribute further to the well-being and culture of mankind . . .' – phrases reminiscent of the Goebbels-type hymns of praise for 'cultural achievements'.

A further section of the memorandum deals with the question of the reckoning with National-Socialism. This part is unpolished, nebulous and full of vague nationalist and very elementary trains of thought. It culminates with the sentence: 'If the occupying powers leave the German people to administer themselves in regard to the necessities of life (food, social security, employment, transport, reconstruction), then they must allow them to work out solutions which accord with their own character and disposition. If they interfere in these matters, if, for instance, they object to the arrangements for local self-administration, public assistance, labour service etc, then they assume full responsibility for what happens.'

The trend is clear. Outwardly the government presented itself as a purely administrative regime; it tried, however, to gather all the reins into its hand and, once firmly in the saddle, would have imposed its specifically German solution – in other words National-Socialism. Should the Nazi experts not be left in their posts, the Allies were threatened with responsibility for any incidents which might occur. OKW had acted similarly when it refused all responsibility for the future behaviour of SS troops after the arrest of Obergruppenführer Jüttner. [5]

The second and longer paper by Dr. Stellrecht, entitled 'On the question of an eastern or western orientation', is both more informative and more comprehensive. Owing to her central position between East and West, it says, only on rare occasions and thanks to the ability of a Bismarck has Germany been able to hold the balance between the two sides. Recent experience had made it abundantly clear that the idea of a strong central Europe was impracticable. In the long run it was possible to exist only with the support of one side or the other.

Stellrecht forecast as follows: 'If the present position continues, not only are we threatened with a long-term territorial division of the area of the Reich into two halves, but the German people may be divided in their outlook into Eastern-orientated and Western-orientated parties.'

One method of preventing this division, he went on, would be 'if the government could succeed in making Berlin the seat of government. The unity of the Reich would be emphasised and the establishment of a separate regime under the Russians avoided.'

Here Stellrecht was obviously referring to the discussion, already mentioned, about a move of the seat of government. In various quarters Berlin had been mentioned as a possibility but the Acting Government had been unable to decide to make any official move in this direction. Right up to the time of their arrest they were not really agreed as to what to do. The only area referred to as suitable was central Germany, without specifying further. They did not wish to queer their pitch either with the Anglo-Americans or the Russians. For the same reason from the outset they adopted a forthcoming attitude to the Russian Control Commission and, without being officially requested, issued orders that 'all important requests, applications or proposals despatched to the Control Commission of Allied Supreme Headquarters' should also be passed to the Russians.

The government's main interest, according to Stellrecht, was the avoidance of partition of the Reich. Pursuing the argument of the necessity of adherence either to East or West if such a policy was to be successful, he then analysed the advantages and disadvantages of an eastern or western orientation.

'For the Germans the first inclination would be to join the West. The Anglo-Saxon powers are felt to be basically Germanic and therefore kinsmen. They have won and have lost a battle for leadership of the Germanic race. As a result, not only is it necessary but the Germans are prepared to recognise this fact and to take second place in a new power structure. This might perhaps go so far as acceptance of a place in the British Commonwealth, provided this could be done with dignity and with a guarantee of the necessary basis for existence.'

In *Mein Kampf*[6] and in his 'Second Book'[7] Hitler had referred to England, as well as Italy, as a desirable ally. Later, in the so-called 'German Monroe Doctrine', he had proposed to keep the continent as a preserve for Germany and her satellites. Now, in May 1945, people in Flensburg were discussing no more than Germany's entry into the British Commonwealth as a junior partner.

Both Dönitz and von Krosigk toyed with such ideas. Who was the moving spirit it is impossible to say. Independently of each other both have stated[8] that they considered such possibilities and Dönitz maintains that he gave agreement to the drafting of a proposal on these lines. Apart from the reference in Stellrecht's paper, however, no document has so far been discovered dealing with the question in any greater detail. Dönitz may perhaps have mentioned such possibilities in conversation in the same way as he outlined his ideas on possible State and governmental structures. His views may have been passed on via Wegener and taken up by Stellrecht in his memorandum. These days preference for the West is hailed as proof of democratic leanings and used in self-justification. Stellrecht's reasoning, however, shows clearly that the basis of all these ideas was racial and biological rather that cultural and political. The historical arguments cited in support of these ideas all bear the stamp of old-fashioned Germanic imperialism. Stellrecht, for instance, refers to the struggle of the Saxons against the Franks and to the Germanic mass in Europe wherein Germany must take the place due to her potential and importance. He doubts, however, whether England, as

opposed to Germany, was yet ready to unite with the other
Germanics. Churchill is paid the doubtful compliment of being
classed as the only 'possible partner in a great new political
concept'. His attitude being still unknown, however, Stellrecht
thinks it better to keep to the traditional British 'balance of
power' system and examine the question of the place which
Germany might occupy therein. Since he calculates on an early
withdrawal by America – the other Germanic power – England,
he considers, has no choice but 'to ensure that Europe acquires a
realistic balance of power within itself. This can only be done by
the European powers themselves and they cannot do it without
Germany. Within limits, therefore, England must wish for a
revival of German power but will at the same time endeavour to
ensure that that power is dependent upon her own policy.'

Politically this was sound thinking. The writer had overlooked
the fact, however, that for the Western Allies in general and
America in particular such ideas were unrealistic unless and until
their declared aim of a change in German morality had been
achieved. Like all those hoping for a reversal of alliances, he
underestimated the emotional element in Allied policy and
overemphasised considerations of *realpolitik*.

Stellrecht's train of thought about the maintenance of a German
fighting potential (which in his view must be in England's
interest) shows similar gross misconception of Anglo-Saxon
mentality and Anglo-Saxon aims, interspersed with a number
of sound ideas.

His basic assumption was that in her further pursuit of power
England could not but need a strong Germany fighting at her
side. Though starting from a false premise, this led Stellrecht to
the entirely correct conclusion that: 'Had not National-Socialism
embarked on the course it did, Germany would not have been
able to fight the recent war'; he therefore argues that, for this
reason, England must allow National-Socialism to continue in
Germany. Obsessed with the idea that every state must strive
solely for the expansion of its power and that wars are therefore
inevitable, it was inconceivable to him that anyone could base
his thinking on anything other than continuous readiness for
battle and could therefore wish permanently to do away with
something which seemed to him indispensable for the ideological
and political struggle. In their desire to eliminate the German war

machine for all time, however, nothing was further from Allied thoughts than the necessity to defend Germany in what might for them be a mortal struggle.

The reason was that the true political purpose of the war, to redress the balance of power in Europe, had been obscured by the fact that it had assumed the character of a crusade. The background political thinking of May 1945, as set out in these working-level drafts, shows the extent to which rational political and emotional viewpoints were then, and still are now, pushed into the background and identical aims were, and still are, differently motivated.

Stellrecht then examines the possibilities of an Eastern orientation and the advantage which it could offer to Soviet Russia and Germany respectively. As a model agreement he cites the Tauroggen Convention of 1812 by which Prussia established satisfactory relations with Russia. This advantageous situation had been brought to an end by the spread of pan-Slavism, to which later was added the communist theme of 'world deliverance'. The intended analogy is clear – on one side pan-Slavism and communist ideology, on the other pan-Germanism and National-Socialist ideology.

Russia, he continues, had contrived to implement the concept of Slav unity, whereas in the West the 'ideological impulse' towards Germanic unity was still lacking. It was perfectly possible that Russia would avoid the error of trying to remove all National-Socialists. In addition she would try to win over the German soldiery, as Stalin was already trying to capture German nationalism. At the same time, however, the USSR would set up a communist organisation in Germany. In her zone she would succeed in turning the Germans eastwards and so the question arose whether the government would not be well advised to place itself at the head of such a movement. So far, of course, there was no indication that Russia intended to support the German Government. She might do so, however, since she wanted German officers and soldiers and they were bound by oath to the Grand Admiral. It might therefore be of advantage to Russia if Dönitz declared himself in favour of a European system under Russian leadership.

It is not clear what grounds Stellrecht had for his categorical statement that Russia 'wanted' German officers and soldiers. It must simply have been a widely-held view, as the incident in the torpedo-boat depot-ship shows was the case.

The great advantage for Germany Stellrecht considered to be 'that Russia might allow the Reich to retain its 1939 frontiers. This presupposes that America withdraws from Europe and that, particularly if Germany turns eastwards, England would be in no position to hold the European mainland.' A further advantage was that Russian power might not endure and might even be broken on the death of Stalin. Hitherto no Asiatic hegemony in Europe had been long-lasting and Germany would then automatically regain her position as a major power factor.

This section of the paper closes with a disquisition on the character and capabilities of the Slav race which is of pure pan-German origin and echoes Rosenberg and Hitler. It is full of clichés such as 'He likes to feel the master's hand' or 'he toes the line', etc. The only problem is said to be how long the 'Bolshevist ruling class with its Asiatic methods' can maintain itself. 'Slav blood cannot produce with a flick of the fingers a leadership class or master race capable of maintaining itself.' The possible transient nature of the Soviet state was compared to the stability of the British governmental structure.

The main disadvantages of an eastern orientation Stellrecht regarded as the absence of a Germanic partnership and of the 'balance of power'. Whereas the Western Powers had need of Germany in order to hold down Russia, once she had achieved her aims Russia would not require Germany any more. He also foresaw serious 'biological damage' since, following National-Socialist practice, he assumed that the entire ruling class would be eliminated.

Russia, he maintained, would not be over-hasty in pushing to the Atlantic; she could well afford to wait until the Americans withdrew from Europe. England and America, however, might well wish to see matters develop more quickly but it was already too late for anything to happen this year.

As further disadvantages should Germany turn eastward Stellrecht feared the collectivisation of agriculture and the elimination of the entrepreneur, whereas with the West the present economic structure would largely be maintained. In the latter case, however, he forecast that the lot of the farming community would be as bad as in the pre-1933 days.

He thought that the Russians would remove industrial installations but that the West would use other methods to ensure Germany's economic dependence.

Dependence on the East would drive Germany into intellectual and cultural isolation; in association with the West, however, she would have an opportunity to participate in a world-wide system. A Germany under Russian influence would lose her personality; this she might be able to retain in the West – provided she did not become ideologically perverted!

There was, nevertheless, a whole series of unknown factors to be taken into account, Stellrecht says; should Germany have a choice between East and West, however, the eastern solution appeared the more disadvantageous.

After a final reference to the necessity for a realistic appreciation free of any ideological considerations, Stellrecht ended his thesis with a recommendation for co-operation with the West. How this was to come about, however, only circumstances could decide.

Before he had even read this recommendation Dönitz had already made a move in this direction. On 17 May he was summoned to an interview in the *Patria* with General Rooks and Robert Murphy, Eisenhower's political adviser, and on this occasion he seems to have laid his cards on the table. Murphy first asked for proof of his authority and for copies of the radio messages from Berlin. Dönitz then gave his views on the situation, mentioning his efforts to withdraw troops from the East behind the western demarcation line and the steps he had taken to save the ablest German scientists from the Russians so that they might be available to the West in case of need. His warning against the possible Bolshevisation of Europe was couched in such urgent terms that Rooks and Murphy must have concluded that he was proposing a combined move by the Germans and the West to forestall eventual Russian hegemony in Europe. Though he made no direct offer (no record of this conversation has been found) both the Americans took his statement as an invitation to an anti-Bolshevist crusade – which basically was Dönitz' intention.[9] When his warnings did not produce the desired effect, Dönitz felt that he must take further steps. That same afternoon he gave an interview to Edward Ward, the BBC correspondent, and referred to the growing danger of communism in Germany.[10] Then he invited Rooks and Foord to a further talk in his office. A record of this meeting is available.[11] It shows that Dönitz thought that he must put more 'steam' behind the matter. It also shows that German views on the working level were in line with those at the top. Nevertheless in this conversation Dönitz did not call for combined military action:

'I told you yesterday that in the last months of the war and right up to the day of capitulation a vast stream of refugees had flowed from East to West out of fear of the Russians. In general the German people were anti-Russian. They thought: if once there is peace with the West, then we will straight away go on fighting against the Russians with all our might.

'Today the attitude of the German people in the area occupied by you is quite different. In all walks of life the view is gaining ground: Why don't we go along with the Bolshevists? A large section of the working class is already thinking this way. Many red flags are already out in Hamburg. Trucks and motor cycles with red flags are driving through the city. This tendency to go over to the Russian side has already invaded the middle class and all nationalist circles. Even in the Wehrmacht the view is gaining ground that co-operation with Russia is the right solution. The protagonists of this idea are the younger officers who come to me and to their senior officers and say so quite openly. They ask me, for instance: "Would it not have been better if, before capitulation, you had ordered all ships and U-boats to Kronstadt?"

'Western Germany, occupied by you, is therefore now tending, spontaneously and of its own volition, to go over to the Russians. This trend is very marked and developing very rapidly. The reasons are:

'1. The highly adroit behaviour of the Russians and on the other hand   2. your own fundamentally mistaken attitude to the German people.'

Dönitz then quoted examples to illustrate his two points. On the first he pointed out that Stalin had declared that he had no wish to dismember Germany or annihilate the German people and he was acting accordingly. Reports of rapid reconstruction in the Russian Zone were piling up. In Berlin the Underground was already running again and out in the country the railways were working. German workmen were allowed to speak to Russians,

German music was played, people were kindly treated, being offered cigarettes and sweets. The population in the West was hearing of all this and pro-Russian sentiment was 'snowballing'.

Treatment in the West was in complete contrast. There it was apparently assumed 'that the German people consisted entirely of criminals'. People wanted to remove from German mothers responsibility for bringing up their children. The statement that all German youth had been bad was an insult to every woman whose son had been killed. The newspapers were full of reports about the concentration camps; the German people knew that these stories were 'largely exaggerated and were propaganda'; in any case the people were not to blame since they had known nothing about them. People talked about war criminals when everyone knew that this was untrue. Compared to the rapid reconstruction in the East, everything was still at a standstill. Instead of allowing the railway organisation to get on with its job, it was bombarded with demands for data and statistics.

'The railwaymen are saying that, even after the worst air attacks, they had had traffic running again in a very short time'; traffic had never before been stopped for so long. 'The same goes for all other industries and public concerns. All you are interested in is the destruction of National-Socialism root and branch. Though the practice differs in different areas, members of the Party and of State agencies are being arrested down to the simple air raid warden. As a result everything is being paralysed since these men are not replaced: moreover it violates the nation's sense of fair play since everybody knows that the majority of those arrested are not wild Nazis but peaceful, decent respectable citizens. All you are doing is to destroy the only counter-weight to advancing communism. . . .

'All sections of the German people and the Wehrmacht, even those hitherto strongly Anglophile, are now rapidly turning away from you and towards Russia. The primary reason is this mistaken, ideologically inspired, determination to destroy National-Socialism root and branch. In my view this is a time of decision for the political future of West Germany. If you continue to treat the German people as you have done so far, they will turn to Russia and Stalin will undoubtedly seize his chance.'

Finally Dönitz pointed out that he himself was continuously being attacked in the Anglo-Saxon press, something which had never happened throughout the war. He and the U-boat war had always been fairly reported, as was only right in a fierce but fair battle. 'Power is yours; what you do with me is your affair. But you must be clear that in that case my influence with the Wehrmacht will vanish.'

Lüdde-Neurath says that the two Generals were visibly impressed – though presumably not in the way Dönitz intended.

Though less aggressively outspoken, the memorandum found on Speer's desk was equally unequivocal. On a whole series of points it cross-checks with Stellrecht's two papers and with the memorandum already discussed, the origin of which is obscure. It also includes a number of new thoughts.

The paper first examines the various peoples of Europe and their differing political systems, emphasising that 'in the final analysis one aspect of a European people's freedom must be liberty to chose their own way of life within their own political system'. Germany had been through an internal and external collapse, Allied propaganda was daily proclaiming as false the ideas of the previous system and the representatives of the previous order of things were being dubbed as criminals.

'Occupation has divided Germany into two halves, an eastern and a western. With the utmost interest the German people are now watching the representatives of the victor powers in order to see whether they represent a political system, a moral outlook and a way of life superior to those under which the Germans have so far lived. After such a war, fought with such bitterness and attended by such sacrifice, the vanquished naturally yearn for some better form of human existence to compensate for, and in a sense justify, the sacrifices made in spite of defeat. If victory could not be won to provide the German people with a better and more secure existence, if despite all their self-sacrifice fate decided otherwise, the immeasurable sacrifices of this war could still be justified if some system producing a superior form of human existence took the place of the old. So the German people look to the victors with burning interest and ask whether fate accorded them the victory because they were the representatives of higher human principles.'

The phraseology points to Speer as the author, since he was one of the few to consider the moral aspects of the debate. In a recent interview, however, he denied knowledge or authorship

of the document. The paper then repeats the well-known arguments about the Germans' natural inclination towards the West,
their disillusionment with the Western Powers and their superior
treatment by the Russians. 'Many Germans are therefore reaching
the conclusion that the home of true humanity is to be found in
the system represented by the Russian way of life.'

In this paper too the view is expressed that, as far as the youth
were concerned, there could be no return to the bourgeois way
of life: also that the younger officers and men saw greater prospects in the East than in the West.

'The desire of the German Government must be that both the
occupied halves of the country will emerge from their tribulations
at the same rate and that the German people will not feel that its
dignity has been affronted. The German Government cannot wish
for developments which, by driving people to extremes, would
turn Germany into a source of unrest. The German Government
cannot but imagine that this desire of theirs will be met with
sympathy on the part of the Allied Governments.' In addition,
he went on, the German Government could not possibly wish
to see the German people divided and living under different
systems. 'Nor, however, could it wish to see one or other system
take the place of the middle-of-the-road role which geography has
assigned to Germany. Its basic assumption is that every people
must work out its own political and ideological system according
to its own lights. . . .

'This principle of freedom of choice would seem to be violated
if a single political viewpoint and a single way of life become
mandatory for all Europe. In that case neither the peoples of
Europe in general nor the German people in particular would be
able to furnish their due contribution to the new order of freedom.

'The German Government feels that this would also apply if a
single political system was the possessor of overwhelming military
might. For centuries the object of British policy has been to
maintain the individuality of the European peoples, to ensure that
they would not tolerate any marked predominance by any one
nation.

'Should it appear, however, whether intentionally or uninten-
tionally, that this principle was not being followed in the case
of the future European order, then the German Government
would consider it better for the German people to take its rightful

place in that political system which seems destined by political developments to be the governing factor in the European order....

'If, however, the Allied Governments have made up their minds about the process already under way among the German people, the German Government is ready to co-operate within the framework of a European order in any way which will serve their people. It would be grateful if the possibility of so doing were no longer denied it.

'With its specialised knowledge of the German mentality it is in a position to make a special contribution to the construction of a long-term European order based on real knowledge of European conditions and requirements.'

This is at least clear. It approximates to a threat that, if the conditions to which it objected in the Western Zone were to continue, the German Government could and would opt for the East. The reference to a 'middle-of-the-road position' implied that Germany should retain the form of internal organisation considered necessary to her – in other words National-Socialism. The only meaning of freedom is apparently the right to set up any internal form of government one likes; there is no word about freedom of the individual.

In general, however, people realised that in the immediate future Germany had little hope of constituting an independent entity. This is clear from a Ministry of Economics office minute which says in so many words that the choice must be made; with the West there was a possibility 'that the area west of the Elbe might develop some semi-independence as a satellite; with the East Germany as a whole might achieve cultural and perhaps biological autonomy . . . Only if we decide for one of these two possibilities, can there be any freedom of action and this presupposes that use can still be made of the authority of Grand Admiral Dönitz and the energies of the younger generation.' This comes from Dr. Erhard Mäding, who had been a senior civil servant [Oberregierungsrat] in the Ministry of the Interior and was seconded to the RSHA in February 1944 as expert adviser to Desk III A 3 – 'Internal Administration of Reich Territory'. Ohlendorf, the Head of the Branch, had despatched him to Goerdeler, then under sentence of death, with a long questionnaire on the technicalities of reconstruction, including the part to be played by State and local agencies, detailed planning questions, etc. This Goerdeler was to work on in prison and the object may well have been to postpone his execution. Mäding had moved to Flensburg with Ohlendorf. Since the paper represented Mäding's personal views, it is questionable whether it can be taken as indicating pro-Eastern sympathies on the part of Ohlendorf; it does, however, show that members of the government were considering the possibility. Ohlendorf himself did no more than draw the Control Party's attention to the German people's increasing susceptibility to clever Soviet propaganda and to Dönitz' efforts in face of this threatening development.

Taking all these papers together it is striking that they envisage only an affiliation either to East or West; there is no thought of a major central European economic union or of some general European settlement on the lines of the United Europe movement. It is also significant that France is nowhere mentioned as a major power.

In a letter to Goebbels von Krosigk had complained that Germany had put forward no concrete plans for a new order.[12] No more did he himself when in May 1945 he became Head of the Government and the Foreign Affairs Office. He contented himself with a number of flowery phrases about immediate problems and the urgency of measures of assistance. More distant political aims 'for the good of the German people as members of a more peaceful mankind'[13] were only to be considered after the present emergency had been dealt with.

The only document of this period to give some indication of German ideas on the new order was drafted, not in Flensburg, but in Fuschl by a member of the Foreign Affairs Office; it is dated 1 May and was brought to Flensburg when the members of the Office were summoned north. It was a draft 'proclamation' by Dönitz to be published on conclusion of an armistice. With a little amendment it was turned into a 'Declaration by the German government on unconditional surrender' but it was apparently never published and was probably intended as an *aide-mémoire* for German missions abroad.[14] Both drafts take the nation-state, formed by history and kinship, as the foundation for the coexistence of peoples; no secret is made of the fact, however, that this called in question the continued existence of the German Reich. A further section dealt with the right of all states freely to determine their own internal structure. It was admitted, however, that this right was circumscribed 'when the interests of the community of states in general were violated or a threat appeared to the way of life of other peoples'.

The original draft accepted such limitations in the case of Germany, though with the proviso that there must be reciprocity; the 'declaration, however, said: "After its bitter experiences of this war the German people of its own free will recognises such a limitation". Here at least is some indication of common sense and self-criticism.'

Even some limitation of national sovereignty was said to be acceptable 'in the anticipation that the international organisation to be created will take account of Germany's requirements for existence'.

The rest of the paper deals with the necessity for improving the catastrophic situation in Germany, 'the core of the European continent'; otherwise 'the rest of the world would have to bury all hope of economic advance and political stabilisation'. The original draft contained a proposal for a German contribution to the rapid repair of war damage, but in the Flensburg version this was dropped.

There is nothing to show what limitations to her sovereignty Germany was prepared to accept, so that one suspects that lip-service was merely being paid to the Atlantic Charter. Moreover in his speech of 2 May von Krosigk had said that one could not find 'in San Francisco the fulfilment of that for which fearful humanity yearns' since no order could be based 'on turning the red fire-raiser into a keeper of the peace'.

In conclusion one cannot avoid the impression that both the internal and external political programmes of the Acting Government differed in no important respect from those of the ex-Reich Foreign Minister, von Ribbentrop; his letter, already quoted several times, included this: 'Externally, concentration of all Germans in their European homeland, no subjugation of foreign peoples: instead, freedom of all nations in Europe and close co-operation both with them and with the world powers for the maintenance of peace; internally, evolution in the sphere of ideology, particularly in cases where dogmatic insistence on ideological principles is liable to impair co-operation with other nations or where, in our enemies' view, such dogmatism will automatically lead to war.' Ribbentrop had added that, in these matters, there was much room for tactical manœuvre. This last piece of advice had evidently fallen upon willing ears.

Evolution but no fundamental internal reorganisation; externally, a return to the pre-war status; no offer of assistance in the repair of war damage; no concrete proposals for future co-operation, apart from a vague reference in an unpublished declaration to readiness to accept some limitation of sovereignty without specifying in what fields – such was the future political programme of the Acting Government and new Head of State.

Part Four

END OF THE ROAD

CHAPTER TWELVE

The Government Arrested

Oꜰ 2 May the *New York Times* described Dönitz as no more trustworthy than Himmler; he was clearly the German armed forces' nominee for peace negotiations. On the following days the paper referred to him on several occasions as 'the new Führer' or, mistakenly, as 'Reichsführer'. After the 8 May surrender, it pointed out, neither the Allies nor Sweden, Spain or Switzerland would take Dönitz' pretensions seriously.

The Allies were obviously determined to have surrender proclaimed by a man whom Hitler himself had chosen and not by some 'nondescript civilian'. The agreement of Dönitz was to set the seal on the defeat of the National-Socialist state and prevent the emergence of a new stab-in-the-back legend.[1] Initially there seemed to be no firm decision on the future treatment of the Grand Admiral. As a member of the Nazi élite, was he to be classified as a war criminal or was he merely to be regarded as the defeated Commander-in-Chief of a fighting service?

In the Allied countries the call for an unequivocal breach with the past grew daily louder; behind it could be detected anxiety that, though the Nazi Party had indeed been smashed, the General Staff and the Generals still had the confidence of the people and there were no signs of any new democratic movement. Dönitz' team was referred to in turn as a 'so-called government', a 'government' (in inverted commas), a 'stopgap regime', the 'surrender regime', the 'Flensburg group' or 'Flensburg circle'. The first unqualified reference to a German 'government' was in the announcement of its arrest.[2]

Ambassador Murphy says in his memoirs that Dönitz and his cabinet were surprised and 'stunned' by their arrest.[3] In fact the Intelligence Service had kept the Grand Admiral fully informed of the reports in the foreign press and from mid-May he was counting upon his arrest at any time. An announcement had already been drafted for the occasion:

'The enemy press has recently contained frequent references to and demands for my internment. The possibility must therefore be reckoned with that, as a further measure in the implementation of the surrender, the occupying powers will proceed to arrest me. In this event I expect the troops to maintain the strictest discipline and to refuse the temptation to use force. Any outburst will be answered by the occupying powers with new measures of oppression against the German Wehrmacht and the German people; this can only make more difficult the task laid upon me and all of us – to ensure that, in spite of its defeat, the German people continues to exist.'

As far as the Flensburg government was concerned, the first in the series of hostile statements in the enemy press was a comment in the London *Times*, forwarded by the Information Service on 12 May. This said that co-operation between Dönitz and the Allies could no longer be tolerated. Instead the Grand Admiral should figure on the list of war criminals. At the moment there was no leading personality with whom the Allies could negotiate and whom they could trust.

As an Annex to the 'Daily Report' on 12 May the Information Service attached an analysis of 'The Allies and the Reich Government'. It pointed out that Churchill's reference to Dönitz as the 'designated' Head of State[4] might constitute formal recognition but also implied considerable reservations. No other leading statesman had made any specific pronouncement. Their attitude could be inferred from the fact that they were allowing the Reich Government to continue in office. No one, however, had yet referred to it as 'a satisfactory successor to the previous German government'. On the contrary both press and radio had recently indulged in increasing polemics and criticism against the government. 'This gives the impression either of a publicity build-up preparatory to an imminent withdrawal of recognition; alternatively public opinion is determined to express its discontent with even the limited short-term recognition accorded the Reich Government.

'At the time of Adolf Hitler's death Germany's overall military situation was so unfavourable that the Allies could count with certainty on total victory in a foreseeable time. Purely from the viewpoint of Allied war strategy and the declared aim of Germany's complete defeat, at the time of the Grand Admiral's nomination there was no necessity for the Allies to recognise any new central political authority as successor to the late government or to take any stock of it; still less was this so since the manner of the Head of State's nomination is disputable under constitutional law.'

The appreciation then points out that initially unconditional surrender was considered to be a purely military matter, achievable as far as the Allies were concerned by a simple declaration from OKW. A government was not necessary for this purpose.

From this argument the conclusion was drawn that there must be other reasons for the government being allowed to continue in office. These lay in the lack of unanimity among the Allies on the question of who should play the leading political role in Germany in the future. British and Soviet interests were naturally conflicting. It must be assumed that both sides were holding ready a more or less complete government; the team proposed by Britain would probably enjoy the moral support of the United States, 'with the inclusion, however, of émigrés resident in the US'. The Reich Government was therefore regarded as a sort of makeshift, to be kept in being so long as differences on a possible solution remained unresolved. This might, but should not be allowed to, last a long time since 'the Allies are by no means faced with the alternative: either the Dönitz government or estrangement. If they wish, they can push the Reich government aside and embark upon a more or less unlimited transitional period during which they would assume complete sovereignty each in their own zone of occupation. There would then be no supreme political authority in the Reich and the powers involved in the overthrow of Germany would each fortify and consolidate their position in their own zone – all to the detriment of the German people and above all to the concept of a unified Reich. During this period there would be an underground struggle, each side striving to create a Reich authority of their own pattern and under their own guidance.'

This is a remarkable analysis. In fact, within the Allied coalition there were serious differences of view about the direction affairs should take, as had already been shown through the various national planning groups for military government. In addition there were internal rivalries, between SHAEF and the American Group for the Control Council, for instance.[5] There were also difficulties about spheres of authority in Great Britain. Reuter reported that confusion in regard to the Dönitz Government in Flensburg was becoming ever greater. There seemed to be no one authorised agency in London able to clear up the situation.[6]

On 14 May the Information Service produced a similar expression of opinion from *The Times*. It was quite essential, the paper said, to remove the existing confusion about the position of Grand Admiral Dönitz. He was acting as if he was a recognised Head of State. The position was not only anomalous but dangerous. This manifestation of ill-will in the British press had been sparked off by Field Marshal Busch's radio proclamation about his powers of command in the Schleswig-Holstein area.[7] A Reuter report in *The Times* stated that neither Busch nor Dönitz were sufficiently trustworthy to form a government with which the Allies could negotiate. Both should be put in their place. Moreover the incident showed the absolute necessity of announcing future Allied policy in Germany and installing a central Control Commission.

The extent to which Field Marshal Busch's order had drawn attention to the problem of the existence of a German government in Flensburg is shown by an article in the *New York Times* of 13 May written by John MacCormack and overlooked by the Information Bureau. It said: 'Recognition of Busch's authority would confirm Dönitz' leadership, upon which it is dependent. This would imply that the German Reich was still in existence and Dönitz was its Head of State. One would expect to see German regional governments staffed by German officials working under the Allied Military Government.'

Anthony Eden too seems to have been alarmed by Busch's announcement and wrote to Churchill who replied on 14 May: 'It is of high importance that the surrender of the German people should be completed through agencies which have authority over them. I neither know nor care about Dönitz. . . . The question for us is, has he any power to get the Germans to lay down their arms? . . . The orders [Busch's] seem to be to get the Germans to do exactly what we want them to do. We will never be able to rule Germany apart from the Germans. . . . Sometimes there are great advantages in letting things slide for a while. . . . It must of course be remembered that, if Dönitz is a useful tool to us, that will have to be written off against his war atrocities for being in command of submarines. Do you want to have a handle with which to manipulate this conquered people, or just to have to thrust your hands into an agitated ant-heap?'[8]

The Information Service quoted further indignant press comment about the Flensburg broadcasts. The *Daily Mail* had referred to a 'mysterious station'; the *Daily Express* had bemoaned the fact that a member of the military hierarchy, which the Allies had sworn to destroy, had been given 'renewed prestige and authority as Hitler's successor'; on 16 May the Exchange Telegraph press agency reported that *The Times* had again joined in the chorus of discontent about the Allied attitude to the 'Flensburg Germans'. After conducting a ruthless U-boat war, the report said, Dönitz was no fit partner either for implementation of the armistice terms or as Head of State. In many places the question was being asked whether he should not be treated as a prisoner of war. The confusion would only end with the formation of the Allied Control Commission and this would take some weeks. Till then Eisenhower was burdened with a great responsibility. His present visit to London, together with that of Montgomery, was connected with these problems. Possibly Churchill would make a statement in the Commons on the Allied attitude to Dönitz and the 'Flensburg Government'.

In Flensburg it was learnt that the American press was also taking a lively interest in the fate of the German government. A discussion was held on the leading article in the New York *Herald Tribune* of 16 May which said that the Allies could maintain order and administer Germany without the assistance of the Grand Admiral and a few Generals. The paper referred to a 'grotesque comedy', to a fake 'government', and asked why Dönitz and his men had not long since been incarcerated as war criminals. The *New York Times* leader of the same day, on the other hand, concentrated on the delay in the formation of the Allied Control Commission, from which the Dönitz Government would receive its orders direct, instead of from individual Allied commanders. The paper opined that German administrative problems were far too urgent to be postponed any longer. If central direction was too long in coming, one day a concerted political line would become impossible.

The German leaders awaited Churchill's statement with considerable suspense. At 10.0 p.m. on 16 May Hamburg Radio announced that to a question that afternoon about the Dönitz Government he had replied as follows: 'I am not sure whether any machinery of government, whether central or regional, can be said to exist at present in Germany and in any case I should prefer to speak of administrations rather than governments. . . . In general the Germans must run their country themselves. We have no wish to burden ourselves with it.'[9]

To the members of the Acting Government this was highly ambiguous. They had so far made no pretence to do more than administer. On the very next day, however, hopes of a favourable turn of events fell further. Field Marshal Busch reported that co-operation with Montgomery was becoming increasingly difficult and on several occasions he had been subjected to humiliating treatment.

On 17 May the *Daily Sketch* reported a press conference by General Clay in which he said that one of the first tasks was the condemnation of war criminals. Dönitz, Göring, von Rundstedt and Kesselring, together with other prominent National-Socialists, would be removed from their present locations and imprisoned pending a decision on their sentences as war criminals.

Also on 17 May the *Daily Express* published a statement by Robert Murphy to the effect that a German government had not been recognised and Dönitz was regarded as the representative of the German High Command. The task of the latter was the disarmament and demobilisation of the German forces. When this was complete, the High Command would be disbanded. Murphy also said that Dönitz was looked upon as a prisoner.

On this same 17 May, however, the meeting between Dönitz and Murphy took place. Whether the Grand Admiral had read Murphy's statement beforehand is not certain. What is certain is that at the conclusion of this meeting Rooks and Murphy reported to Eisenhower recommending the removal of Dönitz and the government.[10] Rooks had already reached this conclusion as a result of Dönitz' activities; he considered that the existence of a German government severely hampered Allied plans.[11] After their very first meeting Rooks had reported to SHAEF Dönitz' reference to the necessity of a central German authority in Germany. Before, however, deciding to recommend removal of the government, he wished to have Murphy's advice; they had known each other for more than two years, working together in Allied Force Headquarters, London and later in Casablanca, Oran and Algiers. Rooks had accordingly asked Bedell Smith whether Murphy might come to Flensburg. When, therefore, Dönitz developed his ideas on the threatened Bolshevisation of Europe, both Rooks and Murphy agreed that the moment had now arrived to put an end to the activities of the Flensburg Group. Rooks was particularly suspicious of the fact that Himmler was still at large. He suspected that Dönitz and the government were covering up for the Reichsführer.[12] Collaboration with them would therefore remove all credibility from and jeopardise Allied plans for the punishment of war criminals and the de-Nazification of Germany.

The behaviour of Dönitz himself, therefore, seems to have been the factor which led to and accelerated his arrest and that of the government. He had not managed to divorce himself sufficiently from the leading Nazi figures such as Himmler and his insistence on the necessity for a showdown with Bolshevism seemed to the Americans mere repetition of Nazi slogans. Sooner or later he would undoubtedly have been arrested owing to pressure of public opinion. At the time, however, Eisenhower apparently still wished to make use of OKW for the rapid disarmament and demobilisation of the Wehrmacht. On receipt of the Control Party's report he told Rooks on 18 May that such a step would have to be discussed with the Russians; at the same time, however, all measures were to be taken preparatory to the arrest of Dönitz and his staff. On 19 May he instructed British 21st Army Group to liaise with the Control Party concerning the arrest of members of the government and OKW.[13]

The decision to proceed to the arrest was therefore clearly not the result of Russian pressure or, as Dönitz put it, 'in the interests of friendship with Russia',[14] or, in von Krosigk's words, 'a sacrifice on the altar of Anglo-Russian friendship'. The Russian Control Party only arrived on the evening of the day on which Rooks despatched his recommendation. The Russian attitude may have been a contributory factor, as was pressure of public opinion in the Allied countries. In fact the general atmosphere forced the decision.

Concentrated Soviet press attacks on Dönitz and his government began with an announcement from Radio Moscow on 17 May and reached their peak on 20 May. It may be inferred that

Eisenhower's intentions had meanwhile become known in Moscow and had met with approval. In chorus *Pravda*, *Isvestia* and *Krasnaya Svesda* published articles on the subject on 20 May. In *Pravda* 'Observer' wrote that the Allies were capable of maintaining order in Germany without the assistance of Dönitz, von Krosigk and defeated generals. The Hitler leaders seemed to be suffering from the delusion that they could remain 'on the surface'. An end must be put to this state of affairs. Leaving disarmament to the German Wehrmacht was equivalent to 'turning the poacher into the gamekeeper'. *Isvestia* declared that the case of Dönitz was developing into a dangerous political game causing anxiety in all countries; *Krasnaya Svesda* asked whether people wanted to create chaos in Europe and in the case of those who allowed Dönitz and his shadow government to continue, answered the question in the affirmative.

Neither does the government's arrest apparently stem, as is often supposed, from the famous Joint Chiefs of Staff directive JCS 1067.[15] This directive set out the first phase of US policy for Germany and formally remained in force until 1947. Though complete by 14 May, according to Clay it was only made available to leading American personalities on 21 May and then under a ban of the strictest secrecy.[16] In Section 3 of Part I a central German administration was not wholly excluded and in certain circumstances some form of central control was envisaged over:

   (a) Vital public services such as railways, communications and power.
   (b) Finance and external affairs.
   (c) Production and distribution of vital commodities.

Section 6, however, laid down that 'all those who have actively supported Nazism or militarism and all other persons who have shown hostility to Allied aims should be removed and excluded from all public offices and important positions'.

Even supposing that Eisenhower had received the directive before 21 May, it can only have reinforced him in his decision. It was certainly not the real reason for the Flensburg arrests.

In Flensburg government circles people were aware of the increasingly hostile press reaction; they observed that the occupation authorities were acting with growing severity. They did not, however, realise that the measures they feared were being precipitated by their own behaviour.

OKW had few illusions. At the conclusion of a situation report dated 18 May General Winter of OKW South announced that since 16 May his southern detachment had ostentatiously been treated as prisoners of war and were being accommodated accordingly.

After Kesselring's arrest command in the Southern Zone was taken over by the next most senior commander present, Colonel-General (Air Force) Otto Dessloch. He was fully occupied with the demobilisation of the Luftwaffe and therefore nominated General Siegfried Westphal, Kesselring's Chief of Staff, to act for him as C-in-C West. This arrangement was approved by US Seventh Army and Sixth Army Group, with which the negotiations on demobilisation took place. It did not accord with the ideas of General Winter, however, since for all practical purposes he was now excluded from the chain of command. On 19 May the Americans put an end to the confusion. They appointed Westphal C-in-C South and placed under him all German Army and Air Force units in the area, thus excluding from the chain of command OKW South, Army Group G and the High Command of the Luftwaffe. Negotiations were henceforth carried on direct between Westphal and US Seventh Army.[17]

Westphal reported the decision to Jodl. On 20 May he received the following radio reply: 'You will have to make the best of this appointment too. Like the rest of us, you must lay a few eggs before becoming a boiling fowl.'[18]

This was a crude way of expressing what the Allied press had said on many occasions: Dönitz and his men should be used as long as circumstances required and, once they had done their job, be got rid of.

OKW drafted a letter to the Control Commission saying that the Head of OKW South reported that he and his staff were being treated as prisoners of war. As a result Article 5 of the Prisoners of War Convention of 27 July 1929 was in force and the members of this staff would henceforth give no information other than their name, rank and number. OKW was therefore no longer in a position to assemble data concerning the Southern Zone. The letter was probably never sent.

On 22 May Jodl deleted the heading 'Confidential' on a letter from Wagner, the officer responsible for the Labour Service in the North, commenting: 'Today nothing is confidential any more.' That afternoon Dönitz was summoned to appear in the

Patria next morning with Jodl and von Friedeburg. His comment on hearing the news was: 'Pack your bags.'

On 23 May his reception on board the *Patria* confirmed his suspicions. No one was waiting for the Germans at the gangway, no officer was present, no sentry presented arms. There was nothing but a large crowd of press reporters. The scene had obviously been well prepared by SHAEF. The previous day Reuter and American United Press had carried reports on the Control Party and had indicated that some action would take place in Flensburg in the next few days. UP reported that a group of SHAEF correspondents had left Paris for some definite destination. It could only be Flensburg.

Dönitz, Jodl and von Friedeburg entered the ship's bar which had been turned into a conference room. There they found General Rooks together with Brigadier Foord, General Truskov and one or two interpreters. Rooks said that he had summoned them on instructions from General Eisenhower. In agreement with the Soviet High Command the Supreme Commander had decided that the Acting German Government and OKW with their respective staffs should be arrested as prisoners of war. As a result the Acting German Government was dissolved. Its members, together with those of OKW, would be taken into custody by British 21st Army Group. From this moment each of them must regard himself as a prisoner of war. On leaving the room they would be accompanied to their quarters by an Allied officer. There they might pack, take with them as much luggage as they needed and take lunch. They would then be escorted to an aircraft and leave at 1.30.[19] Rooks asked Dönitz whether he had any statement to make and received the reply. 'Any word would be superfluous.'[20] Jodl handed over information demanded – three file covers containing personal memoirs and military files.[21]

This official procedure for arrest had been carried out decorously. The sequel was a degrading, though obviously well engineered, spectacle.

As usual, members of the government and certain officers had gathered at 10.0 a.m. for the Foreign Minister's daily conference. Hardly had the conference begun, when fully armed British soldiers burst into the room shouting 'Hands up'. All the Germans were forced to strip completely and minutely searched for weapons and secret papers; in other rooms officers and female secretaries together had to submit to similar treatment.[22]

When Schwerin von Krosigk showed fight against a particularly undignified examination, a senior German officer next to him calmed him down with the words 'Keep smiling'.[23]

The only man to contrive to retain his trousers was the Deputy Chief of the OKW Operations Staff – his boots were so tight that the British soldiers could not pull them off. Thereupon the Captain in command tore off his Knights Cross and stamped on it. Even watches and rings were taken and disappeared into British soldiers' pockets. Murphy merely comments that 'in the manner of soldiers from time immemorial, they . . . "liberated" some souvenirs'.[24]

The prisoners were then marched, hands above their heads, into the courtyard where they were formed up in a row and in this posture photographed, filmed and sketched by some sixty to eighty reporters. This scenario lasted some three-quarters of an hour and they were then led off to fetch their baggage. Their rooms had meanwhile been searched and looted.

In Flensburg Police Headquarters Dönitz and his aide were forced to submit to a similar unpleasant search. Dönitz' marshal's baton was removed and certain private possessions stolen from his luggage. The 'enclave' was cordoned off by two infantry battalions, an armoured regiment drove in and a further infantry battalion was held in reserve.[25]

The arrest was obviously intended as a 'big show' designed to make the German leaders look ridiculous and deprive them of all dignity. In the *New York Times* of 24 May Drew Middleton wrote: 'The Third Reich died today' and he implied that all had been as simple as the dismissal of an unwanted servant or the removal of an obnoxious insect. Murphy revealed the true purpose of the action. He says: 'After the arrest of Grand Admiral Dönitz and his associates, not even a remnant remained of any German government. The conquerors of the Nazis were in complete control and the administration of Germany was their responsibility.'[26]

With their declaration of 5 June 1945 the Allies officially assumed supreme governmental authority in Germany. The 'transitional period' foreseen as a possibility on 12 May by an agency of the Acting Reich Government had begun. The 'underground struggle' between the partners in the wartime coalition intensified and the division of Germany became its outward and visible sign. Both are still with us today.

Epilogue

THIS short period of German history, which I prefer to call that of the 'Twenty-three-day Government' rather than the usual 'Dönitz Government', is characterised by three great decisions: Hitler's decision to nominate Dönitz Head of State and Supreme Commander of the Wehrmacht, Dönitz' decision to bring the war to an end as soon as possible and Eisenhower's order for the removal of Dönitz and his associates.

Hitler's last will and testament showed that the Führer principle pure and simple had been abandoned by the Third Reich's creator himself. Power was transferred to a collegiate, in which, deliberately, the non-political Dönitz was to be flanked by two of the party archangels, Goebbels and Bormann. Almost automatically the highest offices of state fell to Dönitz owing to the disappearance of Göring and Himmler and the necessity to lend some form of credibility to the Dictator's final charge to fight on. Dönitz was the only Service Commander-in-Chief with any prospect of holding the loyalty of the mass of the soldiery. In the event of the reversal of alliances for which he hoped, Dönitz was the sole personality, Hitler must have thought, with any chance of acceptance by the Anglo-Saxon ex-enemies. The war at sea had, after all, been conducted as a much fairer fight than that on land.

In view of the military and economic situation Dönitz' decision to bring the war to an end as soon as possible and on the best terms obtainable by Germany was also dictated by circumstances; it was based upon a realistic appreciation of the situation. At the time even Himmler had become convinced that the war in the West must be ended, though he wished to continue to fight against the East for a time. His motives, however, were different from those of Dönitz. Dönitz was intent on his programme, initiated months before, of rescuing soldiers and refugees from the East; Himmler – like Hitler before him – was trying to gain time pending the possibility of an alliance with the West. Dönitz gave way to such wishful thinking only after capitulation, influenced by his associates and by the looming disagreements between the former allies.

Eisenhower's order for the removal of the 'Flensburg Group' was based on a recommendation from his local representative and his political adviser. The real impulse apparently came neither from the leaders in Washington, nor from the Chiefs of Staff, nor even from his Russian ally. It was a locally-inspired move. The decision was in accord with the wishes of the general public; political leaders in the Allied countries, on the other hand, had so far adopted a wait-and-see attitude and some – particularly Churchill – had regarded support for some central German authority as desirable, at any rate for a time. The unexpected existence of Dönitz and his government undoubtedly embarrassed the Allies. With their arrest the proclamation, prepared since end April, assuming supreme governmental authority in Germany could be solemnly issued. By the government's removal, however, the Allies deprived themselves of the possibility, as originally intended, of implementing Germany's unconditional surrender with the full backing of the law.

All the leading figures in this interregnum following Hitler's death had already played a part in the Third Reich. Dönitz, von Krosigk and Jodl belonged to two interlocking power groups on which the German monarchy had been based and from which Hindenburg had drawn his support in the Weimar Republic days – the officer corps and the aristocracy. All three men had been brought up in the Prussian tradition of devotion to duty, obedience and an authoritarian state. Each of them may be regarded as an outstanding expert in his field, exhibiting at the same time the shortcomings frequently associated with specialisation – overconcentration on their own domain and consequential narrowness of outlook. In their case this was translated into a fateful alienation from politics.

All of them gave proof of an exaggerated nationalism, born of the shock of the 1918 defeat, which had produced among the German people a 'trauma of national consciousness' (Eugen Lemberg's description). They were also representatives of that 'integral nationalism' (Maurice Barrès's words) which allots to the nation absolute pride of place in the scale of values. The behaviour of Dönitz, the Grand Admiral, Jodl, the General Staff officer, and von Krosigk, the finance expert, is only to be explained by this deification of the nation, which turned wrong into right and even admitted crime if done in the name of this ideal. 'There is something terrifying about love of country; it is so exclusive that it will sacrifice everything to the public interest, without pity, without fear, without respect for humanity' – and these are no twentieth-century words; they came from Saint-Just during the French Revolution.

Another important component in these men's characters was a basic attitude of militancy springing from their experiences in the trenches of the First World War. The central motive for their actions and for their sympathy with National-Socialism, however, was still a hyper-developed sense of nationalism. This is clear if the uniformity of their reactions be compared with those of Speer, who played a leading role in the early part of the period under consideration. This uniformity stemmed, not from membership of the same class of society or from the influence of a similar education; partially, but only partially, it stemmed from the fact that they were qualified experts who thought that, being absorbed in technical problems, they were absolved from political responsibility. But the real background to the attitude of them all was an excess of love for Germany.

Hitler had been adept in raising this love of country to the status of an ideology, a religion. In the eyes of many Germans he thus acquired mythical stature and became identified with the notion of 'Super-Germany'. Jodl was the man most prone to these romanticised and irrational ideas but even Dönitz was not totally immune to them. Speer's ambivalent attitude during the final months of the war illustrated the damage which the 'People and Führer unity' concept had suffered as a result of the recklessness of Hitler's decisions, and his obviously growing incapacity to appreciate a situation realistically.

Many students of the human sciences have examined nationalism as a historical phenomenon, but there are still differences of view over the classification to be applied to National-Socialism. Some see in it the 'germ of a disease' present in German history ever since Martin Luther – a notion propounded by Edmond Vermeil and current in the Allied camp after the war; others regard it rather as a perverted form of the German virtues; finally it has been classed as a copy-book example of 'integral nationalism', the seed of which was sown in the post-World

War I period. This turns it into a European problem rather than a specifically German one. Wilhelm Röpke, a German writer of distinction, says: 'Germany suffered a particularly severe attack of the disease because in her case national characteristics, international infection and exceptional temporary circumstances combined to produce a specially dangerous situation.' The root cause of this fatal development in Germany lay not merely in the typical German attributes, not merely in her economic and social difficulties, not merely in some general European crisis of liberalism and democracy or even in the personality of Hitler but in a combination and concatenation of these and other factors, in their 'cumulative effect', as Jacques Freymond puts it.

This book, which has been concerned with the fate of individual personalities, cannot deal exhaustively with the origins and details of these complex developments; much more research is required in the realms of political science and sociology. It is interesting, however, to note the extent to which the behaviour of these individuals conformed to the political and intellectual currents of the time and how typically they reacted to a given historical situation. The vital question here is that of personal guilt as opposed to the irresistible pressure of their environment.

Dönitz' attitude on assuming the offices of Head of State and Commander-in-Chief of the Wehrmacht deserves respect. During this short period he did not, of course, rise to 'heroic heights'; he did, however, have the courage to eat his own words about fighting to the bitter end and to act as the requirements of the situation and his conscience dictated. He cannot have found it easy to renounce his traditional military ideas; in his turbulent three weeks of office in Flensburg, however, he did not succeed in divorcing himself from National-Socialist concepts of government. The measure of self-restraint imposed upon him is shown by the fact that he felt it necessary to justify himself even in the case of measures which today we regard as perfectly proper. Nowadays he is commended for actions which were by no means ordinary judged by the standards of the world in which he had so far lived, and which earned him the distrust and ill-will of men who had lately been his associates.

It is to Dönitz' credit that he hearkened to the voice of reason and humanity. Surrender brought his task to an end: he himself would have preferred to go. The appeals of his military and civilian advisers – with the exception of Speer – not to jeopardise the future existence of the Reich by a premature withdrawal caused him to remain and to become involved in political activity for which he was not qualified and which, in fact, precipitated his own arrest and that of his associates.

His claim that his authority stemmed from Hitler has been described as 'crazy'. In view, however, of Himmler's attitude, the distribution of the actual sources of power and the general expectation that the Reichsführer-SS would take over, this can hardly be described as a superfluous challenge. Dönitz did indeed possess authority and was generally respected; he was no charismatic personality, however, and above all he was no second 'Führer'. In addition it would never have entered his head to seize power. He could therefore do little else than base his claim upon his nomination by Hitler.

He paid with ten years in Spandau for his part in Hitler's war, a part dictated by a sense of military discipline, misguided idealism, exaggerated nationalism, political ineptitude and sheer ambition.

Many of his ex-enemies have long since forgiven him and paid tribute to his professional achievements. To him Germany owes the fact that the destruction of the country was not even greater and that it was not involved in a final senseless battle. He saved many soldiers from years of Soviet captivity. These services should be recognised; his errors, committed in a past now behind us, when martial virtues and political failings were inextricably intermingled, should stand as a warning.

As for Generals Keitel and Jodl, in May 1945, when all central direction had ceased, they looked for an end to the war in a final 'honourable' battle. Their proposals took as little account of their overall responsibility as of reality.

Jodl believed that, even after surrender, play could be made with Germany as a factor in the power politics game and that the German Wehrmacht still had work to do. He suffered from illusions which gave one to think that, like Hitler, he was prone to wishful thinking and was a believer in impractical possibilities. He was no mere colourless executive without will or spirit of his own; he was more than a compliant tool. In Hitler he saw the man who could fulfil his own national ambitions and in pursuance of this idea he felt that he must accept, and indeed lend his name to, much that was criminal. The true proportions of

Hitler's criminality he only realised in Nuremberg. He was continuously exposed to the influence of the Dictator; he was worked to the limit that man could endure; and so he never cleared his own mind on the position in which he was putting himself. He was a craftsman of war lacking any real comprehension of the wider historical implications.

In Flensburg the spell of Hitler gradually faded and Jodl's judgement became sounder, though he was still subject to violently alternating moods. Nevertheless a real change in his thinking seems to have begun. A few days before his arrest he said: 'When it is said that the human race as a whole rather than the community of a people is the overriding factor, then I must say: Every war is a crime against the concept of Europe and the community of peoples and mankind.' The Allied court decreed that he should pay with his life for his actions as one of Hitler's most senior General Staff officers.

The best illustration of the extent to which moral values and norms had been swept away by the deification of the nation is provided by Schwerin von Krosigk, Hitler's ex-Finance Minister. The judgement of the American Military Tribunal betrays an undercurrent of mystification that a man like Krosigk could participate in the Third Reich's discriminatory legislation. Coming from ex-enemies, the judgement pays a remarkable tribute to his character, but then goes on to say that 'neither the attempt to show himself useful, nor the desire to help individuals, nor even the dictates of patriotism' can be valid as justification or excuse. Lutz von Krosigk did not plan any illegalities, but he accepted them and participated in them when they seemed to promote what he regarded as the good of the nation. A century earlier Cavour had succinctly described this double standard of behaviour: 'If we were to do for ourselves what we do for our country, what rascals we should be.'

As Chief Minister of the Acting Government in Flensburg von Krosigk stood for peace and moderation. His reason was not solely a belated sense of humanity and morality but political calculation. He wished to recover Germany's damaged prestige and make the Reich a desirable ally once more.

Albert Speer was another who exerted a moderating influence, particularly in saving men and material. To him we owe the fact that all orders for destruction and paralysation were quickly

cancelled. The *New York Times* of 4 May remarked that his order
of the 3rd might equally well have come from General Eisenhower, so similar was it to the latter's directives. Speer was the
only man with the courage openly to oppose Hitler's frenzy for
destruction. Both as a member of the last Reich Government and
in the dock at Nuremberg he stood unequivocally by what he
had done and accepted full personal responsibility.

In May 1945 the Twenty-three Day Government initiated among
the German people a process of self-examination which is still
continuing today. In the case of Dönitz and his associates their
ties to the Third Reich were still too strong. Nevertheless, partly
voluntarily and partly compulsorily, they took the first steps
towards liquidation of the war and the legacy of National-
Socialism. Their programme for the rescue of the maximum
possible number of men shows that they had already divorced
themselves from the Nazi leviathan and Hitler's blind thirst for
destruction, his determination to pull everything down with him
in his fall. Surrender marked an even clearer dividing line.
Hitler's Germany went down, but thanks to Dönitz it did so in a
comparatively orderly manner, making subsequent reconstruction
possible. After unconditional surrender the hallmark of the
Acting Government's actions and those of oĸw was 'as if' – in
the words of a contemporary observer. They acted as if the
Wehrmacht still had a role to play, as if a German government,
with the momentum of yesterday, could still guide Germany
into a new future. The activity both of the government and oĸw
after capitulation is of only minor importance. Dönitz described
himself as 'a Head of State without a country – with a government
without authority'.

Is it therefore fruitless to concern ourselves with this period?
I think not, for reasons which lie in the answers to two questions:

In retrospect is it true to say that the arrest of the Flensburg
government necessarily marks the beginning of the course of
treatment prescribed by the Allies, that of compulsory intro-
spection and self-examination?

In answer to this: the ideas and proposals of Dönitz and his
government, the fact that only the most prominent Nazis were
eliminated and the indications even before the war was over that

this would be the case point to the conclusion that Nazis would have been tolerated in leading positions and that the result would have been a Nazi regime 2nd edition, a watered-down Führer state still with inadequate parliamentary control. This would have made the German people's self-examination even more difficult.

Acceptance of the OKW representatives and of certain members of the government might, indeed, have aggravated the situation and increased the danger of a third world war.

In the light of these considerations the removal both of the government and OKW was right – though the manner in which it was done was not.

The second question is this: Had Dönitz been more circumspect over his political views about the threat of communism in Europe and had he introduced some element of democracy, could he have ensured the continued existence of some central German authority and so prevented the partition of the Reich? This has been held up against Dönitz and his associates.

Any such action lay outside the political comprehension of those involved. Suppose, however, that a central German authority had continued to exist either in the form of the Acting Government or in a government broadened by the inclusion of democratic representatives. Even so it could hardly have been an effective instrument, for it would have been the subject of a tug-of-war for influence over it; Germany would thus not only have become the stake in the cold war but would inevitably have been branded as the instigator of it. Torn this way and that between East and West, any German authority would have had to decide for one party or the other. The opposing side would have set up a counter-regime and things would have developed much as they did in practice with each side clinging to its own sector and installing therein the personalities and system of government which it liked.

Perhaps, therefore, a hypothesis may be deduced from the experience of the Dönitz interregnum: even the Federal Republic and the political regime established in the ex-Soviet zone of occupation may be only transient phenomena; for the creation of a new Germany perhaps new forces, springing from this latest period, are required to rebuild Germany's lost unity. If we are to attain this national goal, however, never again must we give way to such a paroxysm of nationalist sentiment, never again must the principles of humanity, liberty and the rule of law be sacrificed, never again must crimes against humanity be committed or war be let loose upon the world.

Notes

(The very comprehensive annotation in the original German has been reduced by omitting references to sources not available in English)

Prologue

1. *International Military Tribunal, Nuremberg* (hereafter referred to as *IMT*), Vol. XL, p. 421. Underlining as in orginal.

2. By the end of the war the total of civilian casualties including 'racial Germans' had reached 3,640,000.

3. See Anne Armstrong: *Unconditional Surrender. The Impact of the Casablanca Conference upon World War II*, pp. 109–67.

4. Kesselring: *Memoirs*, p. 282.

5. This must have been one of the last reports, probably an isolated one, from Otto Ohlendorf's Section [Amt] III of the RSHA; the series 'SD Reports on Internal Questions' had been stopped in July 1944, primarily at Bormann's instigation. Some of the last reports on the break-up of the leadership may well have reached Hitler.

6. See Manvell and Fraenkel: *Goebbels*, p. 273.

7. A far more effective organisation under General Gehlen known as 'Foreign Armies East' was formed independently of Schellenberg.

8. See Trevor-Roper: *The Last Days of Hitler*, p. 117 and Schellenberg: *Memoirs*, p. 441.

9. See Manvell and Fraenkel: *Heinrich Himmler*, pp. 157 et seq.

10. See Bernadotte: *The Fall of the Curtain*, pp. 50–9; Schellenberg, *op. cit.*, pp. 353–7; Kersten: *The Kersten Memoirs*, pp. 14 et seq., 273–4 (Kersten also tells of the last-minute efforts to save the Jews); Manvell and Fraenkel, *op. cit.*, p. 234; Trevor-Roper, *op. cit.*, p. 149; Pogue: *The United States Army in World War II; The Supreme Command*, pp. 476–7.

11. Truman: *Memoirs*, Vol. I, pp. 92–103; Churchill: *The Second World War*, Vol. VI; 'Triumph and Tragedy', pp. 465–8.

12. De Gaulle: *Memoirs*, Vol. III; 'Salvation', pp. 44–6.

13. See Schmidt: *Hitler's Interpreter*, p. 270; Pogue, *op. cit.*, p. 475.

14. It was sent to Dönitz by Ribbentrop on 2 May.

15. Bernadotte (*op. cit.*, p. 16) refers to Ribbentrop as a supporter of a separate peace with Russia.

16. It must have originated either from the entourage of Bormann and General Krebs or from SS circles opposed to Himmler and Schellenberg.

17. In the margin of this passage is the pencilled comment 'Nonsense'.

18. Privately Goebbels was far more pessimistic and appeared no longer to believe in an accommodation with the West.

19. See Trevor-Roper, *op. cit.,* p. 109; also Bullock: *Hitler, A Study in Tyranny,* p. 371.

20. For the first passage about Vlassov's army see Dallin: *German Rule in Russia,* p. 650.

21. Goebbels thought the study so remarkable that he wished to show it to Hitler and have it printed as a special annexe to the *Situation Report.* The memorandum has not so far been found.

22. See Trevor-Roper, *op. cit.,* p. 115 and Kersten, *op. cit.,* pp. 11, 226–32, 286–90.

23. Together with all other Cabinet Ministers von Krosigk had been a signatory of the law of 1 August 1934, under which the offices of Chancellor and President were combined in the person of Hitler.

24. For a comprehensive account see Armstrong, *op. cit.,* p. 95; also Pogue, *op. cit.,* p. 477, Kesselring, *op. cit.,* pp. 289–90, Dulles and Gaevernitz: *The Secret Surrender,* and p. 151 below.

25. Between 15 July and 18 August 1944.

26. See *IMT,* Vol. XVI, p. 491. For Speer's numerous attempts to point out the hopelessness of the situation see *Nazi Conspiracy and Aggression,* US Printing Office, Washington D.C. 1948, pp. 945–58, also pp. 83–6.

27. The best description of the atmosphere in the Führer's bunker is still that in Trevor-Roper, *op. cit.*; see also Bullock, *op. cit.,* pp. 784–99 and Shirer: *The Rise and Fall of the Third Reich,* pp. 1112–34.

28. Chief of Staff of the Army from 21 July 1944 to 23 March 1945.

29. *IMT,* Vol. XVI, p. 492; see also Trevor-Roper, *op. cit.,* p. 93.

30. Wolff had tried out the ground with Hitler in February 1945 and on 18 April was given authority to negotiate – but not to capitulate.

31. See Gilbert: *Nuremberg Diary,* p. 129.

32. Pogue, *op. cit.,* p. 469.

33. Kesselring, *op. cit.,* p. 275.

34. See Hubatsch: *Hitler's War Directives,* p. 207.

35. Bormann's order for destruction and evacuation; see also *IMT* Vol. XVI, pp. 499–500.

36. See Hubatsch: *Hitler's War Directives,* pp. 212–13.

37. Kesselring had relieved Field Marshal von Rundstedt on 22 March.

38. See Warlimont: *Inside Hitler's Headquarters,* p. 513.

39. See *Nazi Conspiracy and Aggression, op. cit.*; Keitel: *Hitler's Last Days in Berlin,* pp. 1275–6.

40. See 'Führer Conferences on Naval Affairs', *Brassey's Naval Annual 1948*, p. 482.

41. See Hubatsch: *Hitler's War Directives*, pp. 210–11.

42. *Ibid.*, pp. 211–12.

43. Winter had succeeded General Warlimont in November 1944.

44. Gerhard Herrgesell, one of Hitler's shorthand typists, gave Percival Knauth, the correspondent of *Time*, a detailed account of the scene some fourteen days after it happened; see also Trevor-Roper, *op. cit.*, pp. 131–2.

45. Pogue, *op. cit.*, p. 471.

46. *IMT*, Vol. IX, p. 441.

47. *Ibid.*, pp. 9–10 (Bodenschatz' statement).

48. Note by Jodl dated 22 May 1945 to the Head of the Russian Control Commission attached to OKW, General Trussov (sic).

49. At the time of the German-Russian Pact Krebs was Military Attaché in Moscow and was regarded as a Russophile. His nomination as Chief of Staff gave rise to all sorts of rumours about a possible understanding with Russia.

50. Speer, who was present, said explicitly that Bormann showed Hitler the telegram addressed to Ribbentrop, *IMT*, Vol. XVI, p. 531.

51. Robert von Greim had won the 'Pour le Mérite' (the German V.C.) in the First World War. In 1920 he had flown Hitler to Berlin at the time of the Kapp *putsch*, when he was proposing to join the new national government. For a detailed description of Greim's period in the Führer's bunker see Trevor-Roper, *op. cit.*, pp. 165–72.

52. Trevor-Roper, *op. cit.*, p. 156.

53. Pogue, *op. cit.*, p. 472.

54. Truman: *Memoirs*, Vol. 1, p. 67.

55. In the last resort only 94,000 men were available for the defence of Berlin. They included 60,000 Volkssturm (Home Guard) and Hitler Youth to which were added at the last moment LVI Panzer Corps, 20 Panzergrenadier Division, 9 Parachute Division, 28 SS-Grenadier Division ('Charlemagne'), 11 SS-Grenadier Division ('Nordland') and a few non-German formations – all much under strength.

56. Captain (Navy) Assmann issued the first order on this subject at midnight on 24 April. The necessary air transport was not available, however, and would not be ready until the next night. The extent to which reserves had already been squandered is illustrated by the following: one battalion of 463 men in Stralsund was alerted for movement from the Naval Air Station Pütnitz and one battalion of 472 men was to be flown from Rostock to Berlin. In addition 1,000 men from Fehmarn were to be moved by air to Wismar to join Rerik's Air Corps and a further 800 by land to Pasewalk for Army Group Vistula.

On the afternoon of 25 April arrived a further telegram from Hitler to Dönitz with an urgent request to provide naval troops. Dönitz thereupon ordered the Kiel Fortress Regiment (3,500 men) and the Sylt Fortress Battalion (2,500 men) to be ready to move. Further forces totalling 3,100 men were to be equipped with personal weapons only.

By 27 April it was clear that air transport of troops to Berlin was impracticable. The remaining landing area was too small and the few transport aircraft still available were urgently required for the movement of ammunition.

57. During the night 26/27 April one hastily constituted battalion landed at Gatow airfield and was used by Hitler to defend the Reich Chancellery.

58. It is not clear whether this news arrived on the 27th or 28th. Bernadotte *op. cit.,* p. 52) says that he heard it over the radio on the evening of 28th. Trevor-Roper (*op. cit.,* p. 181) gives the time as 9.0 p.m. on 28th. Other accounts indicate the 27th.

59. On 2 December 1944 Himmler had been given command of a sector in the West as Commander-in-Chief Upper Rhine. At the end of January he was appointed C-in-C Army Group Vistula but on 23 March had been abruptly relieved by Colonel-General Heinrici.

60. Von Puttkamer, Hitler's Naval Aide who was in the Southern Zone, did not forward this message to Dönitz until 11.07 p.m. on the 29th; it was received at 3.05 a.m. on the 30th. Von Puttkamer added: 'Situation in Berlin very serious'; the C-in-C of the Luftwaffe was in the Reich Chancellery wounded, the military in comparative security, but 'in view of the Berlin situation, Party and State leaders will shortly be in danger. General Winter and I consider intervention by you is indicated.'

61. Trevor-Roper, *op. cit.,* p. 189.

62. *Ibid.,* p. 218.

63. Dönitz himself thought it possible that Speer's suggestion was decisive—see Dönitz: *Memoirs,* p. 442.

64. See Warlimont, *op. cit.,* pp. 301–2.

65. Trevor-Roper, *op. cit.,* p. 205.

66. Keitel: *Hitler's Last Days in Berlin, op. cit.,* p. 1282.

67. A certain Wolfgang Klemusch apparently flew Flying-boat No. BV-138 from Copenhagen to Berlin to fetch Major Johannmeier. As the latter could not prove his identity he was ordered off the flying-boat and Klemusch flew back, his mission a failure. In the Foreword to his 3rd edition Trevor-Roper mentions a statement by Dönitz that he had despatched an aircraft to fetch the courier but Dönitz can no longer remember this. See also Trevor-Roper's introduction for the discovery of the three copies of the testament.

68. The supposition that Hitler poisoned himself or that Eva Braun shot him is probably based on a tendentious Soviet account. It is, however, possible that he both took poison and shot himself. See Introduction to Trevor-Roper, *op. cit.*

69. As the result of an error on the part of the duty officer in the transmitting room this radio message was published carrying Goebbels' signature only.

Chapter 1

1. Dönitz: *Memoirs*, p. 300.

2. *Ibid.*, p. 5.

3. *Ibid.*, pp. 2–4.

4. Douglas M. Kelley: *22 Cells in Nuremberg*, p. 106; Leonhard Seagren: 'The Last Führer', *U.S. Naval Institute Proceedings*, Vol. 80, No. 5, May 1954, p. 524.

5. Friedrich Ruge: 'Dönitz the Last Führer', *ibid.*, Vol. 80, No. 10, October 1954, p. 1157.

6. Raeder: *Struggle for the Sea*, p. 94.

7. Dönitz, *op. cit.*, p. 303.

8. Lieutenant-Commander (as he then was) Heye urged Raeder, the C-in-C of the Navy, to make representations to Hitler but nothing happened.

9. Dönitz, *op. cit.*, p. 304.

10. As a further comparison it should be mentioned that the French submarine fleet of the period was almost double that allowed to Germany under the Naval Agreement – see Raeder, *op. cit.*, Vol. II, p. 60.

11. For details see Dönitz, *op. cit.*, p. 12.

12. In November 1936 Germany adhered to the London Submarine Agreement under which submarines were bound to obey the rules laid down for commerce raiders.

13. Dönitz, *op. cit.*, pp. 13–15.

14. *Ibid.*, pp. 18–20.

15. F. L. Carsten: 'Germany, From Scharnhorst to Schleicher: the Prussian Officer Corps in politics, 1806–1933' in *Soldiers and Government* edited by Michael Howard, p. 76.

16. Hannah Arendt: *Eichmann in Jerusalem*, p. 23 (not in English version).

17. *IMT*, Vol. XIII, pp. 297–8.

18. *Ibid.*, p. 299.

19. Dönitz in Nuremberg while under cross-examination on the employment of foreign labour – *IMT*, Vol. XIII, pp. 323, 364.

20. Lit. 'Plate Glass Night' – 9 November 1938 when an officially inspired anti-Jewish pogrom took place, the windows of numerous Jewish businesses being broken.

21. Dönitz, *op. cit.*, pp. 305–6.

22. Arendt, *op. cit.*, p. 122.

23. *IMT*, Vol. XIII, p. 392.

24. See pp. 242–4 below.

25. Kelley, *op. cit.*, p. 106.

26. On 20 March 1946 Captain (Navy) Pfeiffer said at Nuremberg of the problem of employing 12,000 concentration camp labourers in the shipyards: 'Conditions in the concentration camps were not generally known in Navy Headquarters; I did not know myself, nor do I think that the C-in-C knew'; see also Dönitz' statements – *IMT*, Vol. XIII, pp. 342–3, 403.

27. Conversation with Captain (Retd) Günter Hessler.

28. Schellenberg, *op. cit.*, p. 116.

29. Dönitz, *op. cit.*, p. 41.

30. *Ibid.*

31. *Ibid.*, p. 42.

32. *Ibid.*, pp. 42–3.

33. *Ibid.*, pp. 44, 47.

34. *Ibid.*, p. 307. Dönitz supports this view with a somewhat inaccurate quotation from Fuller's book, *The Second World War*; the statement is quoted out of context and therefore distorts Fuller's thinking.

35. Michael Balfour: *Four-Power Control in Germany and Austria, 1945-46*, p. 54.

36. *Ibid.*, p. 55.

37. *IMT*, Vol. XIII, pp. 300–1.

38. Intelligence tests carried out in Nuremberg showed that almost all the accused were of above-average intelligence. Schacht scored the highest marks, followed by Seyss-Inquart, Göring and Dönitz in that order – see Gilbert: *Nuremberg Diary*, p. 19; Kelley describes Dönitz as 'highly intelligent'.

39. Raeder, *op. cit.*, p. 230.

40. Statement by Raeder while in prison in Moscow. See also *IMT*, Vol. XXXIX, p. 526, where Raeder describes Dönitz as a 'Hitler boy'. This greatly incensed Dönitz and he referred to Raeder as 'a jealous old man' – see Gilbert, *op. cit.*, pp. 207, 211. In his memoirs Raeder revised his earlier statements and praised Dönitz' capabilities as a naval officer: 'It was not until the days of joint defence at the Nuremberg trials and the subsequent long years at Spandau that I fully learnt to appreciate his character as a man' – Raeder, *op. cit.*, p. 219.

41. Kelly, *op. cit.*, p. 219.

42. Manstein: *Lost Victories*, pp. 274–5; Raeder, *op. cit.*, p. 96.

43. See also *IMT*, Vol. XL., pp. 103–8.

44. *IMT*, Vol. XIII, p. 398.

45. Statement by Admiral Wagner, *IMT*, Vol. XIII, pp. 467–8.

46. *Führer Conferences on Naval Affairs*, pp. 427–9, 438, 484; see also Prologue Note 56 above.

47. *IMT*, Vol. XIII, p. 321.

48. Quoted from Puttkamer's book *Die Unheimlicher See*; see also Anthony Martienssen: *Hitler and His Admirals*, p. 228.

49. Keitel at Nuremberg, *IMT*, Vol. X, p. 484; Dönitz expressed himself similarly with the proviso that Hitler only accepted his advice on matters affecting the Navy and naval strategy, *IMT*, Vol. XIII, pp. 300, 303.

50. *IMT*, Vol. V, p. 202; Vol. XIII, p. 297.

51. See Chester Wilmot: *The Struggle for Europe*, pp. 617–20.

52. *IMT*, Vol. XIII, p. 307.

53. Dönitz, *op. cit.*, p. 309.

54. *IMT*, Vol. XIII, pp. 249–50, 309.

55. *Ibid.*, p. 327.

56. See pp. 247-8 below.

57. *IMT*, Vol. XIII, pp. 442–3.

58. Dönitz, *op. cit.*, pp. 431–2.

59. See pp. 175-6 below.

60. *IMT*, Vol. XIII, p. 301.

61. *Ibid.*, pp. 303–4.

62. The 'Night and Fog' order and the 'Commissar' order were apparently not applicable to the Navy and Dönitz told Hitler that the Navy was unaffected by them.

63. Gilbert, *op. cit.*, p. 337.

64. *IMT*, Vol. V, p. 204. Closing address by Dönitz at a conference of naval commanders held in Weimar on 17 December 1943.

65. *Ibid.*, p. 392.

66. *IMT*, Vol. V, p. 205; see also his complaint against the Army mentioned by Wheeler Bennett in *Nemesis of Power*, p. 645.

67. See Dönitz, *op. cit.*, pp. 401–5.

68. The captured copy was dated January 1945 and bore the signature of General de Guingand, Montgomery's Chief of Staff.

69. On Wegener see pp. 127 below.

70. For Stuckart see pp. 123 below. On 27 April Stuckart informed Dönitz that he had detailed Jacobi, a senior civil servant (Ministerialdirigent) as liaison officer to him and to Gauleiter Wegener.

71. See p. 25 above.

72. Unpublished (typed) manuscript written by Dönitz in Nuremberg.

73. *Ibid.*; see also Dönitz, *op. cit.*, p. 439 where he gives the date erroneously as 28 April.

74. What follows is based on an interview with Günter Hessler. His main conversation with Dönitz probably took place on the morning of 28 April.

75. Dönitz (*op. cit.*, p. 454) gives the date of this meeting as 2 May. Possibly there were two different interviews.

76. Information from Dönitz to the author 15 August 1965. The ships to be taken over by the Admiral were discussed in detail with Bertram, Chairman of Norddeutscher Lloyd, and set out in an OKW directive.

77. Trevor-Roper, *op. cit.*, p. 51.

78. On Ohlendorf see pp. 122–3 below.

Chapter 2

1. Lüdde-Neurath in his book mentions a conversation on the subject in the Führer's bunker in early April and a telegram from Puttkamer on 29 April had given a hint.

2. From the daily report of 8 May written by Dönitz' aide.

3. *IMT*, Vol. XIII, p. 306.

4. Admiral Godt entered the Navy as a midshipman on 1 July 1918. In January 1938 he was appointed Senior Staff Officer to Admiral Submarines; shortly before the outbreak of war he was made Head of the Naval Operations Section; see *IMT*, Vol. XIII, p. 523.

5. From summer 1933 to summer 1935, first as Lieutenant-Commander and then as Commander, Wagner had been a Desk Officer in the Operations Section of the Navy; from April 1939 to June 1941 he was Head of the Operations Group, initially Senior Operations Desk Officer, in the Operations Section of Naval Headquarters. In March 1956 he was promoted Rear-Admiral and accepted into the Federal Navy as Deputy Head of the Naval Section in the Federal Defence Ministry. In June 1961 he became Commander NATO Naval Forces North Centre and Chairman of the North Centre Planning Group, taking over from the British Rear-Admiral S. M. Townsend in Kiel-Holtenau. In 1962 he was appointed Commander, Allied Naval Forces, Baltic Approaches.

6. The appointment took effect on 1 May 1945.

7. From a conversation with Admiral Wagner.

8. Lüdde-Neurath entered the Navy in spring 1933 and was commissioned in 1936. He spent his entire service in destroyers and torpedo boats. His final rank was Lieutenant-Commander.

9. Trevor-Roper, *op. cit.*, pp. 87 and 265; see also Chester Wilmot, *op. cit.*, p. 90; Kelley (*op. cit.*, p. 160) says: 'He toadied to Hitler much in the same fashion as da Vinci buttered up Ludovico Sforza.'

10. See *IMT*, Vol. XVI, p. 430.

11. *Ibid.*

12. Speer's statement (*IMT*, Vol. XL, pp. 394–5) that his staff consisted almost exclusively of non-Party experts is not altogether accurate. A check on his staff list shows that the majority of them belonged to the NSDAP.

For this information I am indebted to Peter Becker of the Department of History, University of South Carolina, who was preparing a dissertation on Speer as Minister of Armaments.

13. Dönitz handed over responsibility for naval equipment to Speer in summer 1943. In March 1944 the so-called 'Fighter Staff' was formed, giving Speer partial responsibility for production of aircraft (fighters). He was not made responsible for all aircraft until July 1944.

14. *IMT,* Vol. XVI, p. 484.

15. *Ibid,* p. 485.

16. *Ibid.,* pp. 487–8.

17. *IMT.,* Vol. XL, pp. 417–19.

18. *IMT.,* Vol. XVI, p. 497.

19. *Mein Kampf* (James Murphy's translation, Hurst & Blackett, London 1939), p. 283.

20. See Hubatsch: *Hitler's War Directives,* pp. 206–7.

21. Speer's statement in *IMT,* Vol. XVI, pp. 501–2.

22. *Ibid.,* p. 502.

23. *IMT,* Vol. XLI, pp. 438–42.

Chapter 3

1. On 1 May, as a logical consequence of this reorganisation, an Operational Division (Army) was formed in the OKW Operations Staff from parts of the previous staff and the General Staff of the Army. It consisted of three sections: Operations Section (Army), Organisation Section (Army) and Section Ic (Intelligence) formed from parts of the General Staff Sections 'Foreign Armies East' and 'Foreign Armies West' together with parts of Section Ic of the OKW Operations Staff.

2. On 2 September 1943 Himmler had written to Dönitz: 'I need hardly assure you that we shall be very good friends.' Their relationship was never particularly close, however; Lüdde-Neurath describes it as 'correct and polite'.

3. The meeting is described in Dönitz, *op. cit.,* pp. 443–4.

4. *Ibid.,* p. 447.

5. Field Marshal von Blomberg so described him to Hitler and Keitel also described himself the same way; see Gilbert, *op. cit.*

6. He was forced to retire for marrying an ex-prostitute.

7. G. M. Gilbert: *The Psychology of Dictatorship,* p. 218.

8. The best known and most notorious were the 'Commissar Order' of 6 June 1941, the 'Communist Decree' of 16 September 1941, the 'Night and Fog' Order of 7 December 1941 and the 'Commando Decree' of 18 October 1942.

9. Gilbert: *Nuremberg Diary,* p. 110.

10. See Bormann's telegram quoted on p. 28 above.

11. See Pogue, *op. cit.,* p. 443.

12. Throughout his book *Inside Hitler's Headquarters* Warlimont gives many sidelights on Jodl.

13. Gilbert, *op. cit.,* p. 38.

14. In Nuremberg (*IMT,* Vol. XV, p. 301), Jodl claimed that this jump in rank was accidental.

15. See Kelley, *op. cit.,* p. 121.

16. On the controversies between the Army General Staff and OKW on the so-called higher organisation see Warlimont, *op. cit.,* pp. 6-29 and elsewhere.

17. As early as 1938 Naval Headquarters refused to admit that overall strategy should be dealt with by OKW.

18. Kesselring (*op. cit.,* p. 265) says: 'He had an extremely difficult position, as Hitler was by no means easy to influence and the unanimity of any suggestion jointly put to him was frustrated by the disharmony between OKH and OKW. Those who presume to judge Jodl do not know what his diplomacy prevented and achieved. His critics should first show that under the circumstances they would have done better.'

19. See Warlimont, *op. cit., passim.*

20. Warlimont, who was Deputy Head of the OKW Operations Staff from the outbreak of war until autumn 1944, gives numerous examples of the problems on which Jodl manifested interest or lack of it.

21. See Gilbert, *op. cit.,* pp. 220-1.

22. At the age of 23 Jodl married Irma Gräfin von Bullion, daughter of his then regimental commander. She died in Königsberg on 18 April 1944. On 7 March 1945 he married Luise Katharina von Benda, receptionist to Generals Adam, Beck and Halder, who had been a friend of the Jodl family for years.

23. While inspecting the western defences Hitler had said: 'Anyone who does not hold this position is a cur.'

24. Warlimont, *op. cit.,* p. 16.

25. *Ibid.,* p. 17.

26. *Ibid.,* p. 44.

27. *Ibid.,* pp. 185-6, 247, 334, 379-80, also *IMT,* Vol. XV, p. 297.

28. *Ibid.,* pp. 256-7.

29. *Ibid.,* p. 619; Note 34.

30. *IMT,* Vol. XV, p. 300.

31. This is partially confirmed by Warlimont (*op. cit.,* p. 430). Referring to a discussion between Dönitz, Keitel and Jodl, of which he only learnt after the war and during which Jodl voiced his anxieties, Warlimont comments: 'Jodl never spoke . . . in this vein . . . to his own staff.'

32. *Ibid.,* p. 463.

33. *IMT,* Vol. XV, p. 295. See also pp. 333–4: 'I can only say that, even if I had heard of these things, I would not have believed them until I had seen them with my own eyes.'

34. Gilbert, *op. cit.,* p. 28.

35. *IMT,* Vol. XV, p. 295.

36. Discussion with General Anderson 19 May 1945. Anderson apparently ended the interview with the words: 'I entirely understand the German point of view that negotiations are impossible and I assure you once more of my comprehension.'

37. *IMT,* Vol. XV, p. 429.

Chapter 4

1. Dönitz, *op. cit.,* p. 446.

2. The proposal to inform von Steengracht probably emanated from Speer.

3. Dönitz, *op. cit.,* p. 446.

4. Schellenberg, *op. cit.,* pp. 441, 455.

5. Much of the detail in this chapter is taken from von Krosigk's Memoirs and Diary. Neither being available in English, references are not given. [Translator]

6. Prior to the First World War Rhodes scholarships were in the gift of the Kaiser. He selected candidates either from his acquaintances or on the advice of the Ministry of Culture which maintained a list of pupils from such schools as Schulpforta and Rossleben. This was how Schwerin von Krosigk was chosen. After the First World War a selection committee was formed consisting of three ex-Rhodes scholars and four public figures. They were the trustees of the German scholarship endowment. Schwerin von Krosigk was a member of the committee up to the outbreak of World War II.

7. He voted in turn for the German Nationalists, the Popular Conservatives and finally for the DVP [Deutsche Volkspartei – German People's Party].

8. Armaments expenditure was phased as follows: (in marks) 1934, 4·1 billion; 1935, 5·5 billion; 1936, 10·5 billion; 1937, 11·0 billion; 1938, 17·2 billion; 1939, 11·9 billion. The big jump between 1937 and 1938 was caused first by the construction of the Siegfried Line (2 billion) and secondly by payment for the previous year's deliveries. In his book *76 Jahre meines Lebens* Schacht quotes figures given by Keitel in Nuremberg: 1935/36, 5 billion; 1936/37, 7 billion; 1937/38, 9 billion; 1938/39, 11 billion; 1939/40, 20·5 billion.

9. *IMT,* Vol. XXXVII, pp. 492–8.

10. Previously, under a law of 30 August 1924, the Bank had been authorised to advance up to 100 billion for a period of three months; at the end of each

financial year, however, the Reich was obliged to clear all its debts to the Bank.

11. The subject had been under discussion even before Hitler's seizure of power.

12. On 4 November 1941 an urgent letter, signed by von Schlüter, was despatched by the Finance Ministry prescribing the dismissal of Jews not employed in economically important occupations and confiscation of their possessions apart from 100 marks and 110 lbs of baggage. Von Krosigk does not think that he saw this instruction beforehand but that von Schlüter merely discussed with him the technicalities concerning Jewish property abandoned on evacuation.

13. See Gerald Reitlinger: *The Final Solution,* p. 16.

14. Hannah Arendt: *Eichmann in Jerusalem,* p. 47.

15. Trevor-Roper, *op. cit.,* pp. 84, 102.

16. *Ibid.,* pp. 109, 257.

17. Shirer: *The Rise and Fall of the Third Reich,* p. 1315.

18. See *IMT,* Vol. XVI, p. 4.

19. For these three personalities see pp. 124–6 below.

20. In his memoirs von Krosigk says that the word used in Kritzinger's memorandum was 'desired'. He took little account of the wording but says that he protested to Kritzinger because it seemed equivocal and asked why 'ordered' had not simply been used.

21. In his diary (entry of 24 April) von Krosigk says that on the morning of 21 April Kritzinger had a violent disagreement with Goebbels, who protested against the move of the senior authorities from Berlin, saying that this seriously compromised the defence of the city (Goebbels was now by directing the Berlin Defence Commissariat). Kritzinger does not mention this argument but, together with Hitler's decision to remain in Berlin, it was undoubtedly the background to his memorandum.

22. Von Krosigk's diary shows clearly that he had placed his money on Himmler. In an article written in 1955, however, he says that he and Stuckart had reckoned Dönitz' chances high.

23. Dönitz, *op. cit.,* pp. 446–7.

Chapter 5

1. See p. 32 above.

2. Dönitz, *op. cit.,* p. 452.

3. Jodl's initial draft read as follows: 'Do not depart from the Führer's decision and leave the Reich Marshal in the accommodation assigned.' The final text of the message read: 'No change in treatment of Reich Marshal. Previous instructions apply.'

4. See Ewan Butler and Gordon Young: *Marshal without Glory,* p. 259; also Manvell and Fraenkel: *Hermann Göring,* pp. 310–11.

5. See pp. 146–50 below.

6. See Manvell and Fraenkel: *Heinrich Himmler,* pp. 244 et seq.

7. From 23 April when Professor Grawitz committed suicide in Berlin.

8. Letter of 18 May from Jodl to the Head of the Control Commission mentioning this fact and forwarding Rosenberg's and Thierack's letters.

9. See Kersten: *The Kersten Memoirs,* p. 220.

10. After the war Stuckart was sentenced to three years' imprisonment by an Allied tribunal. This did not prevent him becoming Chairman of the 'League of Refugees and Dispossessed' in 1951. His new career was cut short by a fatal motor car accident in 1953.

11. He committed suicide in prison in Nuremberg on 6 April 1947.

12. Statement by Milch, *IMT,* Vol. IX, p. 65.

13. Riecke was not in the dock at Nuremberg. Taken prisoner by the Americans, he was exchanged for Darré.

14. See pp. 220–3 below.

15. pp. 6–7 above.

16. Seldte died in Fürth Hospital in 1947.

17. Letter of 15 May from von Krosigk to General Rooks.

18. At the Wilhelmstrasse trial in April 1949 von Steengracht was sentenced to seven years' imprisonment but was released in February 1950; see Reitlinger: *The Final Solution,* p. 515.

19. See p. 63 above and Chapter 2, Note 5.
20. See pp. 250–60 below.

Chapter 6

1. The Swedish historian Sjöstedt, for instance, takes the view that Dönitz was originally determined to fight on in accordance with Hitler's ideas and only decided to bring the war to an end on 1 May after receipt of definitive news of Hitler's death.

2. See Bullock, *op. cit.,* p. 786.

3. Dönitz, *op. cit.,* p. 445.

4. Interview with the author, 10 August 1965.

5. Dönitz, *op. cit.,* p. 445.

6. Keitel says that he suggested this formula.

7. The best-known instance is that of General Blumentritt who on his own initiative took steps towards capitulation.

8. See the appreciation dictated by Dönitz to his aide while in prison; Dönitz, *op. cit.,* pp. 447–9; Kesselring, *op. cit.,* p. 283; Eisenhower: *Report by*

the Supreme Commander to the C.C.S., p. 144.

9. A note dated 19 May, giving the situation as at 9 May, mentions only 100,000.

10. Estimated strengths in the North-West and Denmark (including Navy, Luftwaffe and ancillaries) 400,000, in Norway, 380,000.

11. In his *Kriegswirtschaft und Rüstungsindustrie* (p. 282), however, Hans Kehrl says: 'In December 1944 there were still more than 900 serviceable jet aircraft and they had fuel for three months, Why they were never used will always be a mystery.'

12. Strang: *Home and Abroad,* pp. 221 et seq.

13. See John L. Snell: *Dilemma over Germany,* p. 173; also Pogue, *op. cit.,* p. 468; in his *Memoirs* Field Marshal Montgomery says (p. 332): 'My object was to get there in time to be able to offer a firm front to the Russian endeavours to get up into Denmark, and thus control the entrance to the Baltic.'

14. See de Guingand: *Operation Victory,* pp. 451–3.

15. De Guingand (*op. cit.,* p. 458) gives the number of German forces to be evacuated from Denmark in mid-May as 160,000.

16. See pp. 228–30 below.

17. Sentences of death were still being carried out on 4 May. Cases were reported in the press in the summer of 1966.

18. Montgomery: *Memoirs,* p. 334; de Guingand, *op. cit.,* p. 453. Later both Montgomery and Eisenhower stated erroneously that Field Marshal Busch and General Lindemann had made offers of capitulation; see Montgomery: *From Alamein to the Sangro,* p. 220 and Eisenhower: *Crusade in Europe,* p. 463.

19. Pogue, *op. cit.,* p. 480; Eisenhower, *op. cit.,* p. 463; Butcher: *Three Years with Eisenhower,* p. 680.

20. Churchill: *The Second World War,* Vol. VI, 'Triumph and Tragedy', p. 468.

21. In his *Memoirs* (p. 335), Montgomery states that von Friedeburg offered only the surrender of Army Group Vistula, Ninth and Twelfth Armies. This story is repeated by de Guingand (*op. cit.,* p. 453), and Eisenhower (*Report to C.C.S.,* p. 144). After all that has been said, it seems both incredible and senseless that Dönitz should have wished to continue to fight in Schleswig-Holstein and have offered *solely* the surrender of the Eastern armies.

22. Montgomery, *op. cit.,* p. 336; also Introduction to *Germany surrenders unconditionally,* National Archives Publication No. 64–4, Washington D.C. 1945, p.1.

23. Montgomery, *op. cit.,* p. 337.

24. Dönitz, *op. cit.,* pp. 457–9.

25. Radio messages were sent to C-in-C Denmark, Navy Headquarters, Naval Headquarters East, Luftwaffe Headquarters and General Christian. They specified that fighting against the Soviets was to continue with all possible resources.

26. In his *Memoirs* (pp. 339–40) Montgomery gives a text differing slightly from that handed over to the German authorities. The original, written on ordinary paper, was kept by Montgomery and only photostat copies sent to headquarters. Reproduced on p. 7 of *Germany surrenders unconditionally, op. cit.*

27. See Pogue, *op. cit.*, p. 481.

28. In another telegram dated 29 April he had reported on the formation of guerilla bands and described the popular mood in Bavaria as 'apathetic to hostile'.

29. See pp. 153–4 below.

30. Pogue, *op. cit.*, pp. 469, 503 et seq.; Truman, *op. cit.*, pp. 132–6.

31. See p. 16 above.

32. Dönitz, *op. cit.*, pp. 449, 455.

Chapter 7

1. A similarly foolhardy operation had already been carried out on 9 March.

2. Manuscript note by Jodl on a manuscript draft of a radio announcement by the Naval Press Service. After two further messages it emerged that these announcements were being issued over the Wilhelmshaven radio by a Party member opposed to the armistice and calling for revolt.

3. Truman, *op. cit.*, p. 122.

4. See Eisenhower, *op. cit.*, p. 461.

5. Butcher, *op. cit.*, p. 672.

6. Bedell Smith: *Eisenhower's Six Great Decisions*, pp. 204–5.

7. Dönitz, *op. cit.*, p. 462.

8. Churchill reported the visit of a delegation under the Czech Minister Hruby.

9. De Guingand, *op. cit.*, p. 455.

10. As a result of this message the first orders issued gave the timing as 1 a.m.; but see Dönitz, *op. cit.*, p. 463, where the time is given as midnight 8/9 May; also given in the *War Diary*.

11. Dönitz, *op. cit.*, pp. 461–2.

12. See Chester Wilmot, *op. cit.*, p. 771.

13. For graphic descriptions see Butcher, *op. cit.*, p. 682 and Drew Middleton in the *New York Times* of 9 May 1945.

14. Pogue, *op. cit.*, pp. 487–8.

15. Bedell Smith, *op. cit.*, p. 210.

16. From a manuscript note by Jodl dated 29 April 1945, made available by Frau Jodl. See also Pogue, *op. cit.*, p. 488 and Butcher, *op. cit.*, p. 692.

17. Eisenhower, *op. cit.*, p. 465.

18. Pogue, *op. cit.*, p. 490; Butcher, *op. cit.*, p. 693.

19. There are two German versions of the capitulation instrument. The first received at 0740 on 7 May, is the more categorical.

20. Strang (*op. cit.*, pp. 221–3) records the drafting of a new preamble to the Commission's proposal, but not the controversy about its wording.

21. Robert Murphy: *Diplomat among Warriors*, pp. 296–7; Bedell Smith: *Moscow Mission*, p. 8.

22. Text in *Foreign Relations of the United States, Diplomatic Papers. Conferences at Malta and Yalta 1945*, Department of State Publication No. 6199, pp. 113–18. Article 12 provided for the assumption of supreme governmental authority in Germany by the Three Powers. Unconditional surrender was to apply not only to the military but also to the political sphere. The US agreed the text on 9 August 1944, Great Britain on 21 September and the USSR on 14 February 1945.

23. Pogue, *op. cit.*, p. 485.

24. See Philip Mosley: 'Dismemberment of Germany: Allied Negotiations from Yalta to Potsdam' in *Foreign Affairs* No. 3 of April 1950, pp. 487–98.

25. Bedell Smith: *Moscow Mission*, p. 8.

26. Murphy, *op. cit.*, p. 296.

27. Pogue, *op. cit.*, p. 486.

28. *Ibid.*, p. 490.

29. *Ibid.* Pogue does not quote the whole letter however.

30. See p. 154 above.

31. A graphic account of this journey was written by McFee Kerr, the Reuter correspondent.

32. Schörner himself did leave his troops in the lurch and fled in a Fieseler-Storch. He was taken prisoner by the Americans and handed over to the Russians. He remained in prison in Russia until his return to East Berlin in 1955. Thence he went to Munich where he was sentenced to four and a half years' imprisonment.

33. Pogue, *op. cit.*, pp. 490–1; Kay Summersby: *Eisenhower was my Boss*, p. 242.

34. See *Germany surrenders unconditionally*, *op. cit.*, p. 31.

35. Pogue, *op. cit.*, pp. 491–2.

36. See *Germany surrenders unconditionally*, *op. cit.*, p. 39. The German text as given in the Official Journal of the Allied Control Commission Germany of 30 April 1946 differs from the original in paras 1 and 4.

37. Truman, *op. cit.*, p. 122; Pogue, *op. cit.*, pp. 493–4; Butcher, *op. cit.*, p. 694.

38. See pp. 179–81 below.

39. See pp. 116–17 above.

40. In one version the penultimate sentence reads: 'My motives are neither

lust for power nor ambition, but only my love of Germany and my sense of
duty. . . .'

41. In his book General Rendulic says that by 9 May more than 600,000 men
of Army Group South had been taken prisoner by the Americans and that
some 200,000 must have escaped capture altogether.

42. The latest estimates put the casualties of all three services at 4,200,000.

43. An estimate by Headquarters Southern Zone dated 22 May even referred
to total losses of 9,730,000 including wounded and missing.

44. In *Bilanz des Zweiten Weltkrieges* Helmut Arntz gives a round figure of
20 million for Russian war losses, military and civilian losses for Europe less
the USSR he puts at 17,910,000 and those of the US at 229,000 military only.

Chapter 8

1. Pogue, *op. cit.*, p. 496.

2. This order actually refers to a 'cease-fire', not 'surrender'.

3. This order is signed by Jodl with 'Approved by Grand Admiral Dönitz'
in the margin.

4. Pogue, *op. cit.*, p. 509.

5. *Ibid.*, p. 508.

6. See p. 144 above.

7. *Mutatis mutandis* a similar message was sent to C-in-C North-West for
Holland.

8. Pogue, *op. cit.*, p. 508.

9. *Ibid.*, p. 509.

10. *Ibid.*, p. 510.

11. See pp. 229–30 below.

12. Pogue, *op. cit.*, p. 510.

13. *Ibid.*, pp. 510–11.

14. See pp. 200–79 below.

15. Montgomery: *Memoirs*, p. 367.

16. Balfour, *op. cit.*, p. 53.

17. Keitel's version of this conversation is that the Russians were trying to
keep him in Berlin, so that he himself might issue orders for surrender on
the Eastern Front.

18. See p. 57 above.

19. See p. 137 above.

20. On 4 May the *New York Times* reported that Dönitz had moved to
Copenhagen with his shadow government; the next day it said that he had
gone to Oslo with his 'portable capital'.

21. This letter is mentioned in Trevor-Roper, *op. cit.,* p. 245.

22. Though he signed the record of this conversation, in the so-called 'Wilhelmstrasse Trial' Admiral Bürkner made no mention of it to the American Military Tribunal, merely saying that he was in Berlin as a sort of 'Head of Protocol'.

23. When OKW was reorganised Colonel Meyer-Detring was appointed Section Head in the 'Army' Branch. He was responsible for two Groups, No. V dealing with problems in the various Army theatres of war, and No. I under Lieutenant-Colonel de Maizière for special tasks such as liaison with the Reich authorities.

24. Pogue, *op. cit.,* pp. 497–8.

25. See pp. 273 *et seq.* below.

26. In a letter of 30 November 1965 General Rooks confirmed to the author that the message came from Eisenhower's headquarters.

27. Pogue, *op. cit.,* p. 497.

28. Warlimont, *op. cit.,* p. 643 (Note 38). Warlimont adds that this was Jodl's personal opinion and bore no relation to reality.

29. General Fangohr, the Head of the Liaison Staff, was told on arrival that he was to regard himself as a prisoner of war.

30. In his diary Jodl mentions a conversation on 11 May about Plan Eclipse with a Lieutenant-Colonel from Montgomery's staff. He makes no mention of this in his note on his conversation with Rooks, which is very short.

31. See p. 220 below.

32. These names may not be spelt correctly; one report refers to the General as Truscov and in many he is Trussov.

33. See p. 223 below.

34. *IMT,* Vol. V, p. 205.

35. His decision had been taken on the previous day.

36. General Rooks' reply was in line with the official American viewpoint.

37. See pp. 261–2 below.

38. John Snell: *Dilemma over Germany,* p. 182.

Chapter 9

1. Speer's underlinings.

2. See pp. 171–3 above.

3. As late as 21 May he applied to the Control Party for men to be released or given leave from the Wehrmacht.

4. Dönitz, *op. cit.,* pp. 470–1.

5. See Balfour, *op. cit.,* p. 9.

6. On 15 May, for instance, the 'Labour Service North' demanded urgent payment of three million marks.

7. The Western Allies had made preparations to assume administrative responsibility in Germany; the structure and duties of the German ministries had been studied by experts and parallel Control Sections formed. In autumn 1944 separate national planning groups were set up; the American was headed by Brigadier-General Cornelius Wickersham, the British by General Stanley Woodburn Kirby and the French by General Louis-Marie Koeltz; see Clay, *op. cit.,* pp. 8–9 and Pogue, *op. cit.,* pp. 346 et seq.

8. See Reitlinger: *The Final Solution,* p. 347.

9. In August 1946 Best was sentenced to death in Copenhagen. As a result of fresh evidence, however, in 1949 the sentence was commuted to one of five years' imprisonment. He was released in August 1951.

10. See Schellenberg: *Memoirs,* pp. 454 et seq. In general, apart from a few differences of dates and the usual exaggerations, these check with Bernadotte's account in *The Fall of the Curtain,* pp. 55–6.

11. See Schellenberg, *op. cit.,* p. 456. The draft has not been found but Dr. Giselher Wirsing, who tidied it up, remembers its existence. It was apparently a sort of proclamation of surrender. Schwerin von Krosigk has no recollection of receiving such a draft.

12. Information to the author from Schwerin von Krosigk.

13. Bernadotte, *op. cit.,* p. 55.

14. Schellenberg, *op. cit.,* pp. 460–1. Schellenberg erroneously gives the date of his telephone conversation with Böhme as 8 May. That there was a telephone conversation is proved by a manuscript note by von Steengracht on the telegram to Thomsen.

15. See Brassey's *Annual, op. cit.,* pp. 488 et seq.; Martienssen, *op. cit.,* p. 241.

16. The Swiss Ambassador himself described the case as unprecedented in diplomatic history. Since, however, Germany had no government and in effect no longer existed, he said, there was no cause for Switzerland to continue to function as Protecting Power. After the First World War, when the German Government was recognised, German property had been returned to Germany; see *New York Times,* 16 May 1945, p. 7.

Chapter 10

1. Information from Dönitz to the author.

2. Information from Dönitz to the author.

3. See pp. 5–6 above.

4. Wheeler-Bennett, *op. cit.,* p. 699 (footnote).

5. See p. 207 above.

6. Wheeler-Bennett, *op. cit.,* p. 699.

7. In his *aide-mémoire* of January 1945 he had characterised any idea that

the German people would accept such a government as utopian; see p. 9 above.

8. *Summary of News of the War and German Surrender,* p. 1.

9. See p. 116–17 above.

10. Arendt, *op. cit.,* p. 23 (not in English version).

11. SHAEF Control Party at OKW, Serial No. 6: 'To Colonel-General Jodl, 17 May 1945.' On the German translation is noted in green ink: 'To Jodl: Rooks told me the opposite today.'

12. See p. 218 *et seq.* above.

13. See p. 112 above.

Chapter 11

1. Eade, *op. cit.,* p. 126.

2. A note, dated 21 May, on the interrogation of Lieutenant-Colonel Boehm-Tettelbach by a Russian Lieutenant-Colonel records that Air Fleet Reich had been ordered by the British occupation authorities to give no information to the Russians but to refer them to the British and make clear that they were British prisoners of war.

3. This comes from a remark by von Krosigk in his diary but there is no other evidence.

4. Unfortunately his present whereabouts could not be established and so this supposition could not be confirmed.

5. See pp. 120–1 above.

6. *Mein Kampf* (James Murphy's translation), pp. 509, 541.

7. Published under the title *Hitler's Secret Book,* introduction by Telford Taylor, translated by Salvator Attanasio, Grove Press, New York, 1962.

8. In separate interviews and without knowledge of the passage in Stellrecht's memorandum.

9. Letter from General Rooks to the author 30 November 1965; Robert Murphy: *Diplomat among Warriors,* pp. 298–9.

10. The interview was never broadcast and so far the exact text is unknown.

11. The heading (in pencil) reads: 'Talk with General Rooks and Foord, 10.0 a.m. 20 May.' It is not clear who drafted the record. In an interview Dönitz stated that, though the contents were correct, the wording was not his.

12. See p. 14 above.

13. From the interview with Edward Ward.

14. According to Andor Hencke and Schwerin von Krosigk.

Chapter 12

1. See *New York Times* leaders of 9 and 16 May.

2. *Ibid.*, 15, 16, 20, 23 and 24 May.

3. Murphy, *op. cit.*, p. 299.

4. See p. 248 above.

5. See 'American Organisational Plans for Military Government in Germany' in *Documents on American Foreign Relations* 1944–45, Norwood Press, Princeton 1947, Vol. VII, July 1944–July 1945, pp. 211–17.

6. *New York Times,* 15 May 1945.

7. See p. 192 above.

8. Churchill: *The Second World War,* Vol. VI, 'Triumph and Tragedy', p. 646.

9. *Hansard* 16 May, p. 2465. Churchill had expressed himself similarly to Truman saying that there was no intention of assuming full responsibility. The Germans should solve their problems themselves; Truman, *op. cit.,* p. 224.

10. Pogue, *op. cit.,* p. 499; Murphy, *op. cit.,* p. 299.

11. Letter from General Rooks to the author 30 November 1965.

12. On 20 May the *New York Times,* reporting the arrest of Rosenberg, voiced the suspicion that Himmler was still in Flensburg and called for a 'housecleaning'.

13. Pogue, *op. cit.,* p. 499.

14. Dönitz, *op. cit.,* p. 473.

15. Full text in *Documents on American Foreign Relations, op. cit.,* Vol. VII, pp. 193–211 and *Documents on Germany under Occupation,* edited by B. van Oppen (Royal Institute of International Affairs, Oxford University Press, London 1955, pp. 13–27); for the origins and an analysis of the directive see Snell, *op. cit.,* pp. 176–82; a not altogether accurate summary is given in Balfour, *op. cit.,* pp. 39–40.

16. Clay, *op. cit.,* pp. 16–17.

17. Pogue, *op. cit.,* p. 500.

18. Pencilled note by Jodl on Westphal's radio message.

19. The English text of Rooks' communication is given in *Yank,* Continental edition of 3 June 1945; see also *New York Times,* 24 May 1945, p. 9.

20. *New York Times,* 24 May 1945, p. 9.

21. *Ibid.*

22. Dönitz' secretary took her own life after this. Admiral von Friedeburg escaped this undignified treatment by suicide. His corpse was rifled.

23. Information from Schwerin von Krosigk.

24. Murphy, *op. cit.,* p. 300.

25. According to the *New York Times* of 24 May (p. 9), the two battalions were the Cheshire Regiment and the Shropshire Light Infantry and the reserve battalion the Herefordshire Regiment. The entire action was directed by Brigadier Churcher.

26. Murphy, *op. cit.,* p. 300.

Bibliography

(Note: In principle this bibliography has been confined to works written in or translated into English. A small number of the more important German works not available in English have, however, been included)

ARENDT, HANNAH: *Eichmann in Jerusalem – A report on the banality of evil,* Faber & Faber, London 1963.

ARMSTRONG, ANNE: *Unconditional Surrender,* Rutgers University Press, New Brunswick 1961.

BALFOUR, MICHAEL: *Four-Power Control in Germany and Austria,* Oxford University Press, London, New York and Toronto 1956.

BERNADOTTE, COUNT FOLKE : *The Fall of the Curtain,* Cassell & Co., London, Toronto, Melbourne and Sydney 1945.

BORMANN, MARTIN : *The Bormann Letters,* introduction by Prof. Trevor-Roper, Weidenfeld & Nicolson, London 1954.

BULLOCK, ALAN : *Hitler, A Study in Tyranny,* Odhams Press, London 1964.

BUTCHER, HARRY C. : *Three Years with Eisenhower,* Heinemann, London 1946.

BUTLER, EWAN & YOUNG, GORDON : *Marshal without Glory,* Hodder & Stoughton, London 1951.

CARSTEN, F. L. : 'Germany from Scharnhorst to Schleicher' in *Soldiers and Governments,* edited by Michael Howard, Eyre & Spottiswoode, London 1957.

CHURCHILL, WINSTON S. : *The Second World War,* Vol. VI, Cassell & Co., London 1954.

CLAY, LUCIUS D. : *Decision in Germany,* Harvard University Press, Oxford University Press, New York and London 1950.

DALLIN, ALEXANDER : *German Rule in Russia,* Macmillan, London and New York 1957.

DAVIDSON, EUGEN : *The death and life of Germany,* Alfred A. Knopf, New York 1959.

DICKS, HENRY V. : 'German personality traits and national-socialist ideology' in *Propaganda in War and Crisis* by Daniel Lerner, George W. Stewart, New York 1951.

DÖNITZ, KARL : *Memoirs,* translated R. H. Stevens, Weidenfeld & Nicholson, London 1959 (*Zehn Jahre und Zwanzig Tage,* Athenäum Verlag, Bonn, 3rd edition 1963).

DULLES, ALLEN & GAEVERNITZ, GERO : *The Secret Surrender,* Weidenfeld & Nicolson, London 1946

EADE, CHARLES (compiler) : *War Speeches,* by the Rt. Hon. Winston S. Churchill, Cassell & Co., London, Toronto, Melbourne and Sydney 1946.

EISENHOWER, DWIGHT D. : *Crusade in Europe,* Doubleday, New York 1948, Heinemann, London 1949.

Report by the Supreme Commander to the Combined Chiefs of Staff, HMSO 1945.

FRANÇOIS-PONCET, ANDRÉ : *The Fateful Years,* translated by Jacques le Clerq, Victor Gollancz, London 1948.

GAULLE, CHARLES DE : *Memoirs; –* Vol. III, 'Salvation', translated by Richard Howard, Weidenfeld & Nicolson, London 1960.

GILBERT, G. M. : *Nuremberg Diary,* New American Library, New York, 1947.

GILBERT, G. M. : *The Psychology of Dictatorship,* Ronald Press Co., New York 1950.

GÖRLITZ, WALTER : *Keitel,* *Verbrecher oder Offizier,* Musterschmidt Verlag, Göttingen, Berlin, Frankfurt 1961.

GÖRLITZ, WALTER : *Der Zweite Weltkrieg,* Steingrüben-Verlag, Stuttgart 1952.

GÖRLITZ, WALTER : *The German General Staff,* translated by Brian Battershaw, Hollis & Carter, London 1953 (*Der Deutsche Generalstab,* Verlag der Frankfurter Hefte, Frankfurt 1953).

GUINGAND, FRANCIS DE : *Operation Victory,* Hodder & Stoughton, London 1947.

HITLER, ADOLF : *Mein Kampf,* translated by James Murphy, Hurst & Blackett, London 1939.

HOLBORN, LOUISE W. (editor) : *War and Peace of the United Nations,* World Peace Foundation, Boston 1943–8.

HUBATSCH, WALTER : *Hitler's War Directives,* edited and with an introduction by Prof. Trevor-Roper, Sidgwick & Jackson, London 1964.

INTERNATIONAL MILITARY TRIBUNAL, NUREMBERG : *The Nuremberg Trial,* English version, HMSO 1947–9.

JACOBSEN, H–A. : *Der Zweite Weltkrieg in Chronik und Documenten,* Wehr und Wissen Verlag, Darmstadt 1961.

KELLEY, D. M. : *22 Cells in Nuremberg,* W. H. Allen, London 1947.

KERSTEN, FELIX : *The Kersten Memoirs,* introduction by Prof. Trevor-Roper, translated by Constantine Fitzgerald and James Oliver, Hutchinson, London 1956.

KESSELRING, A. : *Memoirs,* translated by Lynton Hudson, William Kimber, London 1953 (*Soldat bis zum letzten Tag,* Athenäum Verlag, Bonn 1953).

KOLLER, KARL : *Der letzte Monat,* Norbert Wohlgemuth Verlag, Mannheim 1949.

KROSIGK, LUTZ GRAF SCHWERIN VON : Tagebuch, unpublished manuscript, part with Institut für Zeitgeschichte, Munich.

KROSIGK, LUTZ GRAF SCHWERIN VON : Memoiren, unpublished manuscript.

LÜDDE-NEURATH, WALTER : *Regierung Dönitz,* Musterschmidt Verlag, Göttingen 1964.

MANSTEIN, ERICH VON : *Lost Victories,* translated by A. G. Powell, Methuen, London 1958 (*Verlorene Siege,* Athenäum Verlag, Bonn 1955).

MANVELL, ROGER & FRAENKEL, HEINRICH : *Heinrich Himmler,* Wm. Heinemann, London, Melbourne, Toronto, Cape Town, Auckland 1965.

MANVELL, ROGER & FRAENKEL, HEINRICH : *Doctor Goebbels,* Wm. Heinemann, London 1960.

MANVELL, ROGER & FRAENKEL, HEINRICH : *Hermann Göring,* Wm. Heinemann, London 1962.

MARTIENSSEN, ANTHONY : *Hitler and his Admirals,* Secker & Warburg, London 1948.

MONTGOMERY, FIELD MARSHAL THE VISCOUNT OF ALAMEIN : *Memoirs,* Hutchinson, London 1947.

MONTGOMERY, FIELD MARSHAL THE VISCOUNT OF ALAMEIN : *From Normandy to the Baltic,* Hutchinson, London; Houghton Mifflin, Boston 1947.

MORGENTHAU, HANS J. : *Germany and the Future of Europe,* University of Chicago Press, Chicago 1951.

MURPHY, ROBERT : *Diplomat among Warriors,* Collins, London 1964.

PAPEN, FRANZ VON : *Memoirs,* translated by Brian Connell, André Deutsch, London 1952 (*Der Wahrheit eine Gasse,* Paul List Verlag, Munich 1952).

POGUE, FORREST C. : *United States Army in World War II – European Theatre of Operations,* Vol. IV.: *The Supreme Command,* Office of the Chief of Military History, Department of the Army, Washington D.C. 1954.

RAEDER, ERICH : *Struggle for the Sea,* Wm. Kimber, London 1959 (*Mein Leben,* Schlichtenmayer Verlag, Tübingen 1956–7).

REITLINGER, GERALD : *The Final Solution,* Valentine Mitchell, London 1953.

REITLINGER, GERALD : *The SS – Alibi of a Nation,* Wm. Heinemann, London, Melbourne, Toronto 1956.

SCHELLENBERG, WALTER : *The Schellenberg Memoirs,* introduction by Alan Bullock, translated by Louis Hagen, André Deutsch, London 1961 (*Memoiren,* Verlag für Politik und Wirtschaft, Köln 1956).

SCHMIDT, PAUL : *Hitler's Interpreter,* edited by R. H. C. Steed, Wm. Heinemann, London, Melbourne, Toronto 1951 (*Statist auf diplomatische Bühne 1923–45,* Athenäum Verlag, Bonn 1949).

SCHRAMM, PERCY ERNST (editor) : *Kriegstagebuch des Oberkommandos der Wehrmacht – Das Ende des Krieges,* Bernard & Graefe Verlag für Wehrwesen, Frankfurt/Main 1961.

SEABURY, PAUL : *The Wilhelmstrasse,* University of California Press, Berkeley and Los Angeles 1954.

SEAGREN, LEONHARD : 'The last Führer', in *US Naval Institute Proceedings,* Vol. 80, May 1954.

SHIRER, W. L. : *The Rise and Fall of the Third Reich,* Secker & Warburg, London 1961.

SHULMAN, MILTON : *The German Defeat in the West,* Secker & Warburg, London; E. P. Dutton, New York 1954.

SMITH, WALTER BEDELL : *Moscow Mission,* Wm. Heineman, London, Melbourne, Toronto 1950.

SMITH, WALTER BEDELL : *Eisenhower's Six Great Decisions,* Longmans, Green & Co., New York, Toronto 1956.

SNELL, JOHN L. : *Dilemma over Germany,* The Hauser Press, New Orleans 1959.

STRANG, LORD : *Home and Abroad,* André Deutsch, London 1956.

SUMMERSBY, KAY : *Eisenhower was my Boss,* edited by Michael Kearns, Dell Publishing Co., New York 1948.

TREVOR-ROPER, PROF. HUGH : *The Last Days of Hitler,* Macmillan & Co., London and New York, 3rd edition 1956.

TRUMAN, HARRY S. : *Memoirs* – 'Year of Decisions', Hodder & Stoughton, London 1955.

United States official publications: *Documents on American Foreign Relations 1944–5,* Vol. VII, Norwood Press, Princeton 1947; *Documents on Germany under Occupation,* edited by Ruhm van Oppen, Institute of International Affairs, Oxford University Press, London 1955; *Malta and Yalta 1945,* Department of State publication 6199, Washington D.C. 1955; *Führer Conferences on Naval Affairs,* Macmillan, New York 1949; *Nazi Conspiracy and Aggression,* Supplement B, US Printing Office, Washington D.C. 1948.

WARLIMONT, WALTER : *Inside Hitler's Headquarters,* translated by R. H. Barry, Weidenfeld & Nicolson, London 1964 (*Im Hauptquartier der deutschen Wehrmacht,* Bernard & Graefe Verlag, Frankfurt 1962).

WHEELER-BENNETT, SIR JOHN W. : *The Nemesis of Power,* Macmillan, London, St. Martin's Press, New York 1953.

WILMOT, CHESTER : *The Struggle for Europe,* Collins, London; Harper Bros., New York 1952.

ZINK, HAROLD : *The United States in Germany 1944–45,* Van Nostrand, Princeton 1957.

Index

317